Towards a Film Theory from Below

thinking|media

series editors:
bernd herzogenrath
patricia pisters

Towards a Film Theory from Below

Archival Film and the Aesthetics of the Crack-Up

Jiří Anger

BLOOMSBURY ACADEMIC
NEW YORK • LONDON • OXFORD • NEW DELHI • SYDNEY

BLOOMSBURY ACADEMIC
Bloomsbury Publishing Inc, 1359 Broadway, New York, NY 10018, USA
Bloomsbury Publishing Plc, 50 Bedford Square, London, WC1B 3DP, UK
Bloomsbury Publishing Ireland, 29 Earlsfort Terrace, Dublin 2, D02 AY28, Ireland

BLOOMSBURY, BLOOMSBURY ACADEMIC and the Diana logo are trademarks
of Bloomsbury Publishing Plc

First published in the United States of America 2024
Paperback edition published 2026

Copyright © Jiří Anger 2024

Tahnia Ahmed has asserted her right under the Copyright,
Designs and Patents Act, 1988, to be identified as Author of this work.

For legal purposes the Acknowledgments on p. viii constitute an extension
of this copyright page.

Cover design: Daniel Benneworth-Gray
Cover image © Paolo Sanfilippo

All rights reserved. No part of this publication may be: i) reproduced or transmitted in any form, electronic or mechanical, including photocopying, recording or by means of any information storage or retrieval system without prior permission in writing from the publishers; or ii) used or reproduced in any way for the training, development or operation of artificial intelligence (AI) technologies, including generative AI technologies. The rights holders expressly reserve this publication from the text and data mining exception as per Article 4(3) of the Digital Single Market Directive (EU) 2019/790.

Bloomsbury Publishing Inc does not have any control over, or responsibility for, any third-party websites referred to or in this book. All internet addresses given in this book were correct at the time of going to press. The author and publisher regret any inconvenience caused if addresses have changed or sites have ceased to exist but can accept no responsibility for any such changes.

Library of Congress Cataloging-in-Publication Data

Names: Anger, Jiří, 1990- author.
Title: Towards a film theory from below : archival film and the aesthetics of the crack-up / Jiří Anger.
Description: New York : Bloomsbury Academic, 2024. | Series: Thinking media ; vol 21 | Includes bibliographical references and index.
Identifiers: LCCN 2023049233 (print) | LCCN 2023049234 (ebook) | ISBN 9798765107263 (hardback) | ISBN 9798765107270 (paperback) | ISBN 9798765107287 (ebook) | ISBN 9798765107294 (pdf)
Subjects: LCSH: Kříženecký, Jan, 1868-1921–Criticism and interpretation. | Motion pictures–Aesthetics. | Motion pictures–Digitization.
Classification: LCC PN1998.3.K759 A85 2024 (print) | LCC PN1998.3.K759 (ebook) | DDC 791.4301–dc23/eng/20231206
LC record available at https://lccn.loc.gov/2023049233
LC ebook record available at https://lccn.loc.gov/2023049234

ISBN: HB: 979-8-7651-0726-3
PB: 979-8-7651-0727-0
ePDF: 979-8-7651-0729-4
eBook: 979-8-7651-0728-7

Typeset by Deanta Global Publishing Services, Chennai, India

For product safety related questions contact productsafety@bloomsbury.com.

To find out more about our authors and books visit www.bloomsbury.com
and sign up for our newsletters.

Contents

List of Figures	vii
Acknowledgments	viii

	Introduction: What Is Film Theory from Below?	1
	Four Theoretical Pillars	5
	Starting from a Detail	10
	Operating Between Materiality and Figuration	15
	Thinking Through the Crack-Up	22
	The Life Cycle of the Crack-Up	26
1	Keep That Image Burning: The Color Veil and the Cinema That Never Stops Ending	31
	The Mummy Complex and the Death Drive of Cinema	36
	Slow Decay versus Vibrant Creation	42
	Decasia and the Horror of Hybrid Matter	46
	Seeing the World-Without-Us Frame by Frame	51
	Coda: The Death of Cinema Extended into Eternity	56
2	Do Archivists Dream of Electric Horses? Static Electricity and the Quadruple Logic of Indexicality	59
	Cinematic Indexicality and Its Relation to Reality	63
	Between Trace and Deixis	66
	Pleasures and Threats of Static Electricity	71
	Horse Racers Struck by Lightning	74
	Coda: In Praise of Impure Reality	80
3	Trembling Meaning: Camera Instability and Transduction in Archival Moving Images	83
	Transduction as a Mechanism of Distribution and (Meta)Stability	88
	Image Instability—Technological Problem or Aesthetic Potentiality?	92
	The Black Wave (Dis)Appearing Between the Frames	96
	Coda: Towards a Transductive Film Scholarship	102

4	The Milestone That Never Happened: The Scratched Kiss and	
	the Failed Beginning of Czech Cinema	105
	The Archive Effect of Cinematic Firsts	110
	The Limits of Nostalgia	116
	The Powers of the False	121
	Scratch That Kiss	125
	Coda: Never Happening, Always Repeating	130
5	Touching the Film Object with Surgical Gloves: Frankensteinian	
	Frames and the Fragile Malleability of Cinematic Faces	131
	Approaching Films Haptically	135
	The (Im)Possibility of Videographic Touching	140
	The Cinematic Face as Frankenstein's Monster	145
	Coda: The Perks of Touching the Untouchable	152
6	Shaping the Unshapeable? Videographic Deformation and	
	the First Frames of Czech Cinema	155
	Breaking the Film Object	158
	Frames Caught Between Then and Now	163
	Coda: Towards Videographic Archival Editions?	170

Conclusion: *Digital Kříženecký* Off the Scale?   173

Bibliography   181
Filmography   203
Supplements   206
Index   207

Figures

All the digitized films of Jan Kříženecký, the videographic essay *The First Frames of Czech Cinema* (covered in Chapter 6), and other contextualizing materials can be accessed here: **krizenecky.nfa.cz**.
All of the figures were provided by the National Film Archive (Národní filmový archiv) in Prague.
© Národní filmový archiv

I1.1	*Grand Consecration of the Emperor Franz I Bridge* (Slavnostní vysvěcení mostu císaře Františka I.; Jan Kříženecký, 1901, source: nitrate print)	4
I1.2	*The First Day of the Spring Races of Prague* (První den jarních dostihů pražských; Jan Kříženecký, 1908, source: original negative [digitally inverted])	4
I1.3	*Opening Ceremony of the Čech Bridge* (Slavnost otevření nového Čechova mostu; Jan Kříženecký, 1908, source: original negative [digitally inverted])	4
I1.4	*An Assignation in the Mill* (Dostaveníčko ve mlýnici; Jan Kříženecký, 1898, source: nitrate print)	4
I1.5	*Laughter and Tears* (Smích a pláč; Jan Kříženecký, 1898, source: nitrate print)	4
1.1–1.11	*Grand Consecration of the Emperor Franz I Bridge* (Slavnostní vysvěcení mostu císaře Františka I.; Jan Kříženecký, 1901, source: nitrate print)	32, 53, 56
2.1–2.12	*The First Day of the Spring Races of Prague* (První den jarních dostihů pražských; 1908, source: original negative [digitally inverted])	60, 75, 78
3.1–3.8	*Opening Ceremony of the Čech Bridge* (Slavnost otevření nového Čechova mostu; 1908, source: original negative [digitally inverted])	84, 99
4.1–4.8	*An Assignation in the Mill* (Dostaveníčko ve mlýnici; Jan Kříženecký, 1898, source: nitrate print)	106, 127
5.1–5.13	*Laughter and Tears* (Smích a pláč; Jan Kříženecký, 1898, source: nitrate print)	132, 148, 150, 151
6.1	The first frames of all Kříženecký's films that were digitized from the original nitrate carriers (1898–1911, source: vintage prints and original negatives)	156
6.2–6.5	*The First Frames of Czech Cinema* (Jiří Anger and Adéla Kudlová, 2021)	167
6.6	*Cyclists* (Cyklisté; Jan Kříženecký, 1898, source: nitrate print)	170

Acknowledgments

The book you are holding or swiping through in your PDF/EPUB Reader results from more than six years of work, which were spent mostly between two institutions. The first one is the Department of Film Studies at Charles University in Prague, where I studied and then participated in the grant project KREAS (2020–22). The second one is the National Film Archive (Národní filmový archiv) in Prague, where I had the privilege to curate and study the so-called first Czech films, created by Jan Kříženecký between 1898 and 1911 and digitized by the National Film Archive in 2017. This experience at the intersection of the academic and archival worlds shaped not only the form and content of my book but also my coming-of-age as a researcher, for which I am eternally grateful.

From the Department of Film Studies, I wish to thank professors Lucie Česálková, Ivan Klimeš, Kateřina Svatoňová, and Petr Szczepanik, and doctoral students Tereza Frodlová, Jakub Jiřiště, Martin Mišúr, and Marek Šindelka for their piercing and incisive feedback on the project. As for the National Film Archive, I have greatly profited from cooperating closely with the restoration team led by Jeanne Pommeau and having the chance to examine the films in meticulous detail and without digital retouching. Other people who contributed to the digitization and subsequent research of Kříženecký's films include Michal Bregant, Jonáš Kucharský, Adéla Kudlová, Jan Křipač, Rémi Llorens, Jaroslav Lopour, Matěj Strnad, Jonáš Svatoš, Alena Šlingerová, Jan Trnka, and many others. My deepest gratitude goes to the members of our Research Support Department (Ladislav Cubr, Helena Černohorská, Lucie Česálková, Monika Duyen Vrtišková, Jan Kolář, Martina Nalevanková, Petra Nejezchlebová, Soňa Weigertová, Julie Wittlichová, and particularly Linda Šplíchalová), who provided an extremely helpful and friendly environment for the project and nourished my fascination for Kříženecký throughout the years.

Besides the university and the archive, another, less official "institution" inspired my project: the scene around videographic criticism. Ariel Avissar, Johannes Binotto, Katie Bird, John Gibbs, Catherine Grant, Liz Greene, Evelyn Kreutzer, Kevin B. Lee, Barbara Zecchi, and others made me think about archival film and found footage in ways that transcend the theory-practice divide and allow to reimagine what academic thinking and writing can be. Again, both the Department of Film Studies and the National Film Archive encouraged my activities on this front; the latter even provided grounds for creating a videographic essay, *The First Frames of Czech Cinema* (coauthored by Adéla Kudlová), which serves as a supplement to the final chapter of this book.

Overall, there are numerous people I would like to thank for discussing the book with me and/or reading parts of the manuscript at various stages of completion. Professor Bernd Herzogenrath proved to be a key inspiration in developing a *film theory from below* as a way of thinking *with* films as material objects. The spring semester of 2021 I spent at Goethe University Frankfurt under his tutelage, as well as many of our debates before and afterwards, contributed immensely to the book's current shape. Tomáš Jirsa dedicated nuanced attention to my project throughout all of its stages, from initial doubts to final revisions of the book manuscript. Byron Davies enriched the manuscript in its late stage with his insight into contemporary philosophy and experimental cinema.

Other people who deserve to be listed here for their comments and ideas (and have not been mentioned earlier) are Tomáš Bazika, Kateřina Krtilová, Terezie Límanová, Bori Máté, David Martin-Jones, Ewa Mazierska, Devin Orgeron, Eszter Polónyi, Čeněk Pýcha, David Sorfa, Michal Šimůnek, Josef Vojvodík (and anonymous reviewers of my articles). Online and offline conference feedback from scholars, archivists, and curators such as Ewa Ciszewska, Tobias Ebbrecht-Hartmann, Tone Føreland, Šárka Gmiterková, Tomáš Koblížek, Elif Rongen-Kaynakçi, Jacqueline Sheean, Mario Slugan, Malcolm Turvey, Christa van Raalte, and Mark Williams was also of immense help. Grammar and stylistic corrections were courtesy of Kevin Johnson; throughout the writing process, *Grammarly* and *DeepL* were invaluable companions.

Concerning the process of preparing the book manuscript, first I want to thank Bernd Herzogenrath and Patricia Pisters, editors of the Thinking Media series, for giving me the chance to publish. Revisions were facilitated by specific suggestions for improvement by both reviewers, and thanks to Katie Gallof, Alyssa Jordan, Stephanie Grace-Petinos, Amy Brownbridge, Akshaya Ravi Pemmasani, Pradheepa Balasubramanian, Nandhini Senthil Kumar, and others, the production process went smoothly. I am also grateful to the Czech Film Fund for providing the funds for printing in color and, again, to the National Film Archive (particularly to Petra Nejezchlebová and Linda Šplíchalová) for issuing an application to the Fund in the first place, because many distinctive qualities of the digitized films of Jan Kříženecký cannot be appreciated in black and white. Special mention goes to the endorsers of my book: Shane Denson and Katherine Groo.

However, the biggest thank you goes to my closest friends, relatives, and pets. Chiefly, Veronika Hanáková, my intimate partner in crime and a promising media scholar in her own right, went through all the project stages with me, offering precious feedback and emotional support.

Note

An early version of Chapter 1 was published as "Keep That Image Burning: Digital Kříženecký, Color Veil, and the Cinema That Never Stops Ending" in *The Moving Image: The Journal of the Association of Moving Image Archivists* 20, nos. 1–2 (2020): 123–55. Chapter 2 is a revised version of my article "Do Archivists Dream of Electric Horses? Digital Kříženecký, Static Electricity, and the Quadruple Logic of Indexicality" in *Studies in Eastern European Cinema* 13, no. 1 (2022): 90–111. Chapter 3 reuses material previously published as "Trembling Meaning: Camera Instability and Gilbert Simondon's Transduction in Czech Archival Film" in *Film-Philosophy* 25, no. 1 (2021): 18–41. Finally, Chapter 6 contains segments from a study "Shaping the Unshapeable? Videographic Curation of Early Czech Cinema" published in *Iluminace* 34, no. 1 (2022): 9–29.

Introduction

What Is Film Theory from Below?

"And then, ten years this side of forty-nine, I suddenly realized I had prematurely *cracked*."[1] With these melodramatic words, Francis Scott Fitzgerald closes the opening litany of his essay "The Crack-Up," published in the *Esquire* magazine in 1936. Here, and in the following two confessional texts,[2] he reflects on the life trajectory that led him from a young, self-confident, and successful novelist to a seemingly washed-up, middle-aged alcoholic who is no longer sure of his identity. The author found himself bereft of values, with "a feeling that [he] was standing at twilight on a deserted range, with an empty rifle in [his] hands and the targets down. No problem set—simply a silence with only the sound of [his] own breathing."[3] Despite being significantly younger and living my life nowhere near as dramatically as the iconic American writer, on the brink of starting to write the book you are reading right now, Fitzgerald's laments seemed oddly relatable.

At one point, sometime in 2019, I began to feel that the way I had been doing film theory and film-philosophy had run its course. As much as the ongoing research on affect, body genres, and experimental cinema meant to me,[4] I came to believe that it is still too invested in a "top-down" scheme of analysis. No matter how much the individual films and filmmakers fascinated me, I somehow felt the need to scrutinize them according to methodological frameworks (such as affect theory) and in the context of big categories (such as melodrama or experimental cinema). While I had always sought to discover ways in which idiosyncratic works of art (such as films by Rainer Werner Fassbinder, Kenneth Anger, Carmelo Bene, or Werner Schroeter) disturb these concepts and whereby they connect the concepts in

---

[1] Francis Scott Fitzgerald, "The Crack-Up," *Esquire*, 1936, accessed December 31, 2022, https://www.esquire.com/lifestyle/a4310/the-crack-up/.
[2] All the three essays—"The Crack-Up," "Pasting It Together," and "Handle with Care"—were later published in Fitzgerald's posthumous collection *The Crack-Up*. Francis Scott Fitzgerald, *The Crack-Up* (New York: New Directions, 1945).
[3] Francis Scott Fitzgerald, "Pasting It Together," *Esquire*, 1936, accessed December 31, 2022, https://www.esquire.com/lifestyle/a4310/the-crack-up/.
[4] Jiří Anger, "(Un)Frozen Expressions: Melodramatic Moment, Affective Interval, and the Transformative Powers of Experimental Cinema," *NECSUS European Journal of Media Studies* 8, no. 2 (2019): 25–47.

an unexpected way or even transform them, at the same time I struggled to account for what makes the films truly specific and speculatively generative. In this, I did not necessarily mean specific on the larger level of narration or diegesis, but within the tiniest units themselves—scenes, shots, frames— and between them. It is not that I had been ignoring these micro-levels, yet even the most minuscule details and micro-movements I discovered were still all too familiar, all too intentional, all too representational, and for these reasons, all too ready to be subsumed under grand theories and concepts.

Of course, this kind of analysis does not fit every audiovisual phenomenon and has its own pitfalls: it can come off as overly subjective, arbitrary, incomprehensible, particularist, or devoid of context. Nor does it make sense to dispense with established methodologies, concepts, and categories, as details negotiate their function and meaning in relation to bigger wholes. Nonetheless, an encounter with a unique corpus of film objects gradually persuaded me, maybe even forced me, to design an approach that would let their idiosyncratic qualities shine.

The body of work that fueled my desire for what I will call *film theory from below* was the collection of the "first Czech films," made by Jan Kříženecký in the former Austro-Hungarian Empire between 1898 and 1911. As a DVD/Blu-ray curator at the National Film Archive (*Národní filmový archiv*) in Prague, I had the opportunity to participate in the digitization of Kříženecký's films from their original nitrate materials, which had been virtually unseen for around a hundred years.[5] Those images differed from what I had previously associated with early cinema or what we would now call "archival film" or "archival footage."[6] They depict a localizable world of the past, show us glimpses of life in East-Central Europe at the turn of the nineteenth and twentieth centuries, as well as signs that the films covered a long distance in time, and yet seem uncanny, almost otherworldly. The images are riddled with physical deformations: vibrating colors, lightning bolts, blurry movements, scratched canvas, spliced frames, and so forth. Sometimes these deformations assemble into "weird shapes": a pedestrian swallowed by an amorphous color veil (Figure I1.1); a horse racer struck by a lightning bolt

---

[5] See the short report on the digitization project: Jeanne Pommeau and Jiří Anger, "The Digitization of Jan Kříženecký's Films," *Iluminace* 31, no. 1 (2019): 104–7.

[6] For the definitions and conceptualizations of archival film and archival footage, see Jaimie Baron, *The Archive Effect: Found Footage and the Audiovisual Experience of History* (London: Routledge, 2014); Giovanna Fossati, *From Grain to Pixel: The Archival Life of Film in Transition*, 3rd Revised ed. (Amsterdam: Amsterdam University Press, 2018); Catherine Russell, *Archiveology: Walter Benjamin and Archival Film Practices* (Durham: Duke University Press, 2018); Katherine Groo, *Bad Film Histories: Ethnography and the Early Archive* (Minneapolis: University of Minnesota Press, 2019); Sylvie Lindeperg and Ania Szczepanska, *Who Owns the Images?* (Lüneburg: Meson Press, 2021).

(Figure I1.2); esteemed gentlemen approaching the camera on a trembling bridge like a fuzzy black wave (Figure I1.3 GIF);[7] a kiss disappearing behind a scratched wall (Figure I.4); a face stitched together like Frankenstein's monster (Figure I1.5). Spectators unfamiliar with the dusty depths of film archives (as I was at the start) would probably take these phenomena as interventions by experimental filmmakers or visual artists, but here they are, without any known intention or predesigned agency. The enigma these weird shapes posed is precisely what provoked me to investigate the film artifacts further, both in their material, historical, and aesthetic concreteness and for the broader implications they can have on the theory of film medium.

In terms of form and content, the films of Jan Kříženecký look fairly similar to the earliest cinematic works by the Lumière Brothers and their operators around the world (after all, Kříženecký was inspired by the French pioneers and shot almost all of his films using the Lumière equipment). Most of Kříženecký's films are vignettes of everyday rush in the city of Prague, composed in a single static shot and lasting only a few tens of seconds. Nevertheless, the decidedly noninterventionist digitization process unveiled features of the image one would not have focused on or perceived as significant. The National Film Archive restorer Jeanne Pommeau decided not to refer to the project as "digital restoration." According to her, digital retouching would, especially in cases of significantly deteriorating film materials, inevitably lead to creating the films anew.[8] In other terms, how can we return the images to their original form and historical context if this is not allowed by the condition of the film stock and the lack of functional technological dispositif from the period in which they were made?

Therefore, while the newly accessible films boast high-definition picture quality, achieved by scanning the materials in 4K, and many new options for exhibition and manipulation, the digitization did not efface the deformations present in the material but rendered them all the more visible in the image. It preserved not only damages and instabilities caused by the ravages of time but also distortions inherent in the material properties of the original nitrate prints and negatives, as well as those resulting from the mechanical functioning of the Lumière camera (*Cinématographe-type*) that Kříženecký used. This strangely hybrid form enabled me to perceive weird shapes that one usually does not encounter among the rips, dots, and dust in stock archival

---

[7] The camera trembling in *Opening Ceremony* is better visible in GIF format (see Chapter 3). I originally uploaded the GIF on the *Gfycat* website on June 2, 2019; unfortunately, the site shut down in September 2023. You can access the GIF at krizenecky.nfa.cz or download it here: https://drive.google.com/file/d/1GWoVHgksDT01mnghFA2rFWMCZH_JwC_n/view?usp=sharing.

[8] Pommeau and Anger, "The Digitization of Jan Kříženecký's Films," 106.

Figures I1.1–I1.5 The Films of Jan Kříženecký: *Grand Consecration of the Emperor Franz I Bridge* (Slavnostní vysvěcení mostu císaře Františka I.; 1901, source: nitrate print); *The First Day of the Spring Races of Prague* (První den jarních dostihů pražských; 1908, source: original negative [digitally inverted]); *Opening Ceremony of the Čech Bridge* (Slavnost otevření nového Čechova mostu; 1908, source: inverted original negative [digitally inverted]); *An Assignation in the Mill* (Dostaveníčko ve mlýnici; 1898, source: nitrate print); *Laughter and Tears* (Smích a pláč; 1898, source: nitrate print) © Národní filmový archiv.

footage nor in crystal-clear digitally restored films. Material-technological elements—not only more traditional damages like splices or scratches but also intrinsic deformations such as a yellowish-orange color, marks of static electricity, or camera instability—impinge upon the form and content to such an extent that they endow the moving images with speculatively and aesthetically generative features. Showcasing what features these are and what they can do with our notions of film theory is the raison d'être of this book.

Four Theoretical Pillars

The proposal of *film theory from below* lies in an attempt to grasp the digitized corpus of early Czech film artifacts (what I will call *Digital Kříženecký*)[9] from the viewpoint of their accidental deformations, all the weird shapes that surface in the image and affect the films' aesthetic functions and effects while decentering, distorting, and transforming the existing conceptual and methodological frameworks associated with archival film and moving-image media in general. Why *from below*? The argument rests on four pillars.

1. Theory as Micro-Perspective

The term "theory from below" can evoke the phrase "history from below," which began gaining currency in the 1960s and which has been recently updated for the purpose of film-historical study by Efrén Cuevas.[10] This trend in academic historiography questioned the macrohistorical focus on major historical events and their protagonists and the quantitative approaches to the past. Besides the overarching aim of foregrounding the everyday lives of individuals and social groups, their experiences, actions, and habits in specific times and places,[11] the history from below marked a shift from macro-perspective to micro-perspective, to figures, events, and phenomena that are hidden, marginal, or unnoticed. The change in the scale of observation should not present an end in itself but serve to develop a different understanding of the object of study and its context. As Jacques Revel explains, "varying the

---

[9] The term is inspired by Metahaven's artistic project called *Digital Tarkovsky*: Metahaven, *Digital Tarkovsky* (Moscow: Strelka Institute, 2018).
[10] Efrén Cuevas, *Filming History from Below: Microhistorical Documentaries* (New York: Wallflower Press, 2022).
[11] John Brewer, "Microhistory and the Histories of Everyday Life," *Cultural and Social History* 7, no. 1 (2010): 92.

focal length of the lens is not simply about enlarging (or shrinking) the size of the object caught in the viewfinder, but about altering its form and structure . . . about transforming the content of what is being represented (in other words, the decision about what is actually representable)."[12]

In other words, the shift of scale is a productive analytical gesture with a potential to transform not only the way we see a certain object or phenomenon but also which aspects of it can become visible and meaningful in the bigger picture. In this respect, the history from below may inspire a theoretical endeavor as well. *Digital Kříženecký* constitutes a perfect object for micro-analysis, with its weird shapes that overwhelm the image content and inspire us to look at it from different angles. The question is whether such an analysis can be representative, and if yes, of what, considering that I do not aim to delve too broadly into the historical context of early cinema and visual culture in the Czech lands, Austro-Hungarian Empire, or East-Central Europe but rather to present theoretical arguments that would be relevant to the study of archival film, found footage, and (audio)visual media in general. As idiosyncratic as *Digital Kříženecký* is, its uncertain identity, divided between photochemical origin and computer transcoding, figurative and material aesthetics, archival history and uncanny presence, early-cinematic form and experimental film vibes, unravels a symptom of larger processes that happen to film and moving images in the digital (or, maybe more precisely, post-digital)[13] age. Hybridity, ambiguity, and undecidability are qualities that now resonate across the audiovisual spectrum, and specific attention to details that demonstrate seemingly contradictory properties at the same time contributes to our understanding of the (after)life of film objects in the online landscape.

2. Theory as Archival Experience

The phrase *film theory from below* also has more prosaic but no less important connotations with gaining knowledge from experience. In my

---

[12] Jacques Revel, "Micro-analyse et Construction du Social," in *Jeux d'échelles: La micro-analyse à la expérience*, ed. Jacques Revel (Paris: Seuil/Gallimard, 1996), 19.

[13] The term "post-digital" emphasizes that the digital is no longer new and the binaries such as virtual/real, online/offline, or digital/analog are no longer tenable. However, examining the nuances between the digital and the post-digital is beyond the scope of this book, which is why I opt to write the "post" prefix in brackets throughout the manuscript: "(post)digital." For more on the concept of the post-digital and its implications, see, for example, Ryan Bishop, Kristoffer Gansing, Jussi Parikka, and Elvia Wilk, "Introduction," in *Across & Beyond: A Transmediale Reader on Post-digital Practices, Concepts, and Institutions*, ed. Ryan Bishop, Kristoffer Gansing, Jussi Parikka, and Elvia Wilk (Berlin: Sternberg Press, 2017), 11–29.

case, learning the basics of archival work from scratch and getting to know *Digital Kříženecký* first-hand was priceless. What I have in mind is not necessarily the trope of touching the film material with my own hands but the entire experience of finding out the stakes of converting the oldest national cinematic artifacts into digital form that made me realize the extent to which much film-theoretical analysis is based on abstraction. With Kříženecký's films, standards for projection speed, aspect ratio, image stability, or perforations do not apply, and each technological mishap inscribes itself into the image and disturbs our viewing habits. Archival practice teaches us not to treat these material interventions as unwanted side effects and deviations from image content but to acknowledge, in the words of Jurij Meden, that the "history of cinema is a history of scratches, tears, burns, blurry images, delayed changeovers, missing frames, imperfect framings, [and] random speeds."[14]

Further, archival practice is about specificity, about how even a minuscule detail localizable within a single frame can make a difference. Whether we watch Kříženecký's films from a Lumière nitrate print or a later-generation acetate copy, whether the frame rate is 18 frames per second or 24 frames per second, whether we leave the deformed materials as is or retouch a few dots and scratches here and there, it alters their materiality and historicity as well as their content and, in a more or less serious manner, our spectatorial experience. Theory still tends to take for granted that no matter where, when, how, and in what physical form we are seeing a cinematic work, it is more or less the same theoretical object. Even media theorists and philosophers who reflect on the changes of cinematic *dispositif* in the digital age[15] do not usually find the need to analyze and compare two or more artifacts of the same film. This is a stance that may intuitively make more sense if you are talking about *Taxi Driver*, *Pulp Fiction*, or *Barbie* and not about early Czech cinema, but every archivist would tell you that material and technological differences have consequences in all cinematic works—all the more so in the (post)digital landscape, where the ways in which our viewing practices are becoming ever more dispersed and heterogeneous.

---

[14] Jurij Meden, *Scratches and Glitches: Observations on Preserving and Exhibiting Cinema in the Early 21st Century* (New York: Columbia University Press, 2021), 25–6.
[15] See, for example, Shane Denson and Julia Leyda, eds., *Post-Cinema: Theorizing 21st-Century Film* (Sussex: REFRAME Books, 2016) or Dominique Chateau and José Moure, eds., *Post-cinema: Cinema in the Post-art Era* (Amsterdam: Amsterdam University Press, 2020).

3. Theory as Theoria

If the approach *from below* owes so much to historiography and archival practice, why do I still choose *film theory* as the main framework? In an interview for the academic journal *Iluminace*, which I led along with Tomáš Jirsa, Eugenie Brinkema claimed that the main task of theory is to go back to the original meaning of *theoria*: "a way to see differently."[16] In other words, theoretical thinking is neither about abstraction nor about mechanically applying Concept A to Film XY; its goal is to look at and construe something in a new light. As Kyle Stevens follows, "theory is, in this sense, creative. It creates new ways of seeing things."[17] He also reminds us that film theory loves taking risks: "Scholars searching for the security of boundaries, of systems to affirm one's correctness, may be averse to the risks of thought that the doing of theory requires."[18] A film theory that seeks broader patterns and affirms speculative thinking, yet does so with respect for specific and distinguishable qualities of its ever-changing objects and with the ambition to invent novel ways of seeing (and also hearing, touching, and so on), would be prepared to stand up to film-philosophy, which in the last few decades became the privileged space for debating conceptual questions of the film medium.

This does not mean that the present book avoids addressing existing theoretical and philosophical concepts and traditions; on the contrary, it refers to many theoretical authorities, even to the usual suspects of philosophy like Gilles Deleuze or Gilbert Simondon. Throughout the chapters, a reader will encounter many well-known and well-worn tropes of film and media studies from the last thirty years or earlier, such as the death of cinema, indexicality, or haptic visuality. As theoretical thinking always exists in a continuum, and as *Digital Křiženecký* inevitably invokes many of these notions, the aim is not necessarily to discard previous concepts but to make them pass through transformative encounters with singular objects deemed unworthy of critical analysis. We have heard more than enough about affect, hapticity, and the close-up, yet what happens to these notions when confronted with, for instance, a few frames from Křiženecký's *Laughter and Tears* (1898), where haptic visuality manifests itself through a face sewn together by a splice (Figure I1.5)? In this sense, *film theory from below* also equates thinking the existing theory *from below*, dragging it through the mud of incidental,

---

[16] Jiří Anger and Tomáš Jirsa, "We Never Took Deconstruction Seriously Enough (On Affects, Formalism, and Film Theory): An Interview with Eugenie Brinkema," *Iluminace* 31, no. 1 (2019): 80.
[17] Kyle Stevens, "Introduction: The Very Thought of Theory," in *The Oxford Handbook of Film Theory*, ed. Kyle Stevens (New York: Oxford University Press, 2022), 2.
[18] Ibid., 6.

incomplete, disfigured, ephemeral, and altogether weird shapes that *Digital Kříženecký* offers.[19]

4. Theory as Videographic Practice

Finally, *film theory from below* takes inspiration from the increasingly relevant attempts at thinking *with* and *through* images and sounds, not *about* them (in the sense of imposing external concepts on them),[20] which we perceive in experimental film practices such as found footage, essay film, and, in a more scholarly framework, "videographic criticism."[21] This approach is based on performing research by means of the moving images and sounds themselves, instead of in a traditional written text, thereby opening up a new epistemology of studying cinema in the (post)digital age. Its singular gesture lies in a shift of perspective, zooming in on ambiguous film objects frame by frame in order to let them do the theoretical thinking on their own terms. All the ambiguous descriptions of videographic operations in the text argue for an analytical approach that does not impose any final meaning on the examined phenomena; instead, it gains more reward from speculating what could happen if we put weird shapes in the foreground and attempted to extend their impulses further. In other words, the project champions process over results.

Videographic scholarship is indeed of a more speculative kind and does not promise universally verifiable findings and conclusions about the chosen objects of study. What it brings to the table is precisely a reimagination of what a film object is and can be in the (post)digital landscape, from which angles we can see it and investigate it, and how it can employ audiovisual means to rethink and reinvent our notions of materiality, historicity, and aesthetics of the film medium. At the same time, the approach is not entirely arbitrary and speculative, as it inherently depends on the material qualities of the digitized objects, the traces and gestures embedded in the individual frames and between them. The archival spirit guiding the book ensures that

---

[19] In this sense, Katherine Groo's notion of "bad film histories" will resonate throughout this book. Groo, *Bad Film Histories*.

[20] See Bernd Herzogenrath's concept of "practical aesthetics." Bernd Herzogenrath, "Toward a Practical Aesthetics: Thinking With," in *Practical Aesthetics*, ed. Bernd Herzogenrath (London and New York: Bloomsbury Publishing, 2020), 1–24.

[21] Christian Keathley, Jason Mittell, and Catherine Grant, eds., *The Videographic Essay: Criticism in Sound and Image* (Montreal: caboose, 2019); Volker Pantenburg, "Videographic Film Studies," in *Handbuch Filmanalyse*, ed. Malte Hagener and Volker Pantenburg (Berlin: Springer, 2020), 485–502. Not to confuse with "videographic cinema": Jonathan Rozenkrantz, *Videographic Cinema: An Archaeology of Electronic Images and Imaginaries* (London and New York: Bloomsbury Academic, 2020).

even the most abstract speculation always returns "down to earth." Therefore, the analytical process is neither wholly arbitrary nor empirical but oscillates between those poles.

These are the basic outlines of *film theory from below* that ground the research developed through this book. Before we can proceed to the analyses, however, we need to circle around the weird shapes and the worlds they open to (or withdraw from) us. A realization of *film theory from below* begins with considering the weird shapes among the various details and accidents in film theory. Then, it switches focus to the two spheres of the image, the *figurative* one and the *material* one, which the shapes bring together. Finally, it arrives at a mechanism that creates, maintains, and extends the shapes, which I term the "crack-up" after the already-mentioned F. S. Fitzgerald.

Starting from a Detail

As the few film stills (and one GIF) at the beginning hopefully showcased (Figures I1.1–I1.5), *Digital Kříženecký* offers a plethora of weird shapes, sometimes comical, often horrifying, and even more frequently both. Some of them hit us on first viewing, and others require a trained eye and take time to be discovered frame by frame, but when considering our overall aesthetic experience from the films from today's perspective, they can hardly be ignored. Although these shapes arise from the incidental intrusion of material-technological "defects" into the image, be it through wear and tear accumulated over more than a hundred years or due to mechanical and chemical properties of the Lumière film stock and cinematographic apparatus, they interfere with the images so severely that retouching them would rid the images of significant aesthetic power as well as historical value. Even those shapes that could have been, albeit in a different way than we perceive them now, already visible to early film spectators, are almost impossible to attribute to any aesthetic intention. It is documented that the first moving images exposed both creators and audiences to significant effects of the materiality of the medium,[22] but exploiting such effects for artistic purposes that we see in experimental cinema or video art was not yet epistemologically plausible.[23] The first and foremost aim of cinematic pioneers like Jan Kříženecký was to document reality in a condensed, eloquent, and ideally entertaining way, not

---

[22] See, for example, Yuri Tsivian, *Early Cinema in Russia and Its Cultural Reception* (Chicago: The University of Chicago Press, 1994).

[23] Benoît Turquety, *Inventing Cinema: Machines, Gestures and Media History* (Amsterdam: Amsterdam University Press, 2019), 231–48.

to create art, and accidents that we mention were authorized or tolerated rather than designed.

The weird shapes in *Digital Křiženecký* present a vital contribution to the long history of details in film and related media. Throughout the history of film theory, there have been numerous attempts to turn "the particular, the singular, and the unpredictable—in short, the antisystematic"[24] into focal points of analysis. The earliest days of cinema already provided a powerful myth that inspired toward taking details seriously: the myth of "the wind in the trees." During exhibitions of the Lumière actuality *Le repas de bébé* (1895), the primal attraction for the audiences reportedly was not the intimate portrait of the family but the "distant tree leaves blowing in the wind."[25] This archetypical detail has served many film and media scholars to shift the scale and question what viewers are really looking for in the image, as well as what forces outside authorial intention and constructed diegesis determine what we see.[26] This kind of detail is inextricably linked to the notions of contingency and unpredictability—unlike details that are carefully orchestrated and motivated within a fictional world (such as Rosebud in *Citizen Kane*), the wind in the trees participates in the film's figurative processes and aesthetic effects in a much more chaotic and volatile manner, as if it came from another place.[27]

During the twentieth century, many concepts tried to capture the distinguishing qualities of details like the wind in the trees. For instance, Roland Barthes's notorious term "punctum" describes unintended and uncontrolled features of a photograph that carry no instantly recognizable symbolic or representational meaning but "pierce" the viewer with affective power.[28] Punctum is achieved due to its unique relevance to the viewer's emotions, memory, and imagination,[29] as well as photography's dependence

---

[24] Mary Ann Doane, "The Object of Theory," in *Rites of Realism: Essays on Corporeal Cinema*, ed. Ivone Margulies (Durham: Duke University Press, 2003), 82.

[25] Jordan Schonig, *The Shape of Motion: Cinema and the Aesthetics of Movement* (New York: Oxford University Press, 2021), 19–20.

[26] Nico Baumbach, "Nature Caught in the Act: On the Transformation of an Idea of Art in Early Cinema," in *Cinematicity in Media History*, ed. Jeffrey Geiger and Karin Littau (Edinburgh: Edinburgh University Press, 2013), 107–16.

[27] For more on the link between detail and accident, see Noa Merkin, "Little Patch of Yellow: On the Detail in Film" (PhD diss., University of Chicago, 2020), 117–58.

[28] Roland Barthes, *Camera Lucida: Reflections on Photography* (New York: Hill and Wang, 1982).

[29] In this sense, punctum resonates with the madeleine moment in Marcel Proust's *In Search of Lost Time*, where the detail appears as an involuntary event, driven by the viewer's unconscious. See, for instance, Walter Benjamin, "On the Image of Proust," in *Walter Benjamin: Selected Writings Volume 2* (Cambridge: Belknap Press, 2005), 237–47.

on automatic technological processes and natural decay.[30] Barthes's concept resonates with the celebration of details found in many poststructuralist texts, with their belief in contingency and affectivity as principles that promise to decenter and eventually overcome stable, recognizable forms, signs, and meanings toward more fluid and ephemeral aesthetic forces.[31] At the same time, it indicates that details shift the locus of meaning from authorial intention and diegetic representation to the autonomous agency of technology or nature on the one hand and to the idiosyncratic viewpoint of the receiving subject on the other.

This notion of detail has found a substantial following in film and media studies since the 1990s. It has particularly informed influential thinkers associated with a return to cinephilia (for instance, Paul Willemen, Christian Keathley, or Girish Shambu)[32] and the affective turn (for example, Laura U. Marks, Anne Rutherford, or Jennifer M. Barker).[33] These scholars searched for alternatives against film-theoretical approaches grounded in semiotics, Marxism, and/or psychoanalysis, which were oriented toward generalizing categories such as representation, narration, genre, or apparatus. Instead, they focused on elements that disrupt, resist, or unsettle these structures and affect the embodied spectator in unpredictable and uncontrollable ways. Although detail was not always the exact term these theorists used, affect theory and the "new" cinephilia have largely shaped the place of peripheral moments in contemporary theoretical writing.

Even with their undisputable relevance and impact, these approaches often struggle when they have to account for the distinctive forms and shapes of the detail, as well as for what makes one detail differ from another. In much scholarly writing indebted to affect theory or the new cinephilia, the importance of contingent and peripheral moments lies more in their "capacity for some kind of systemic excess" than in their individual traits,

---

[30] Barthes, *Camera Lucida*.
[31] See, for example, Jean-Francois Lyotard, "Acinema," in *Acinemas: Lyotard's Philosophy of Film*, ed. Graham Jones and Ashley Woodward (Edinburgh: Edinburgh University Press, 2017), 33–42; Gilles Deleuze, *Francis Bacon: The Logic of Sensation* (London: Continuum, 2003).
[32] Christian Keathley, *Cinephilia and History, or The Wind in the Trees* (Bloomington and Indianapolis: Indiana University Press, 2005). See also Paul Willemen, "Through the Glass Darkly: Cinephilia Reconsidered," in *Looks and Frictions: Essays in Cultural Studies and Film Theory* (Bloomington: Indiana University Press, 1994), 223–58; Girish Shambu, *The New Cinephilia*, Expanded 2nd ed. (Montreal: caboose, 2020).
[33] Laura U. Marks, *Touch: Sensuous Theory and Multisensory Media* (Minneapolis: University of Minnesota Press, 2002); Jennifer M. Barker, *The Tactile Eye: Touch and the Cinematic Experience* (Berkeley: University of California Press, 2009); Anne Rutherford, *What Makes a Film Tick? Cinematic Affect, Materiality and Mimetic Innervation* (Berlin: Peter Lang, 2011).

as Eugenie Brinkema claims.³⁴ In other words, a detail does not primarily gain value in itself but for how it provokes, disturbs, or escapes established categories of representation, narration, genre, artistic intention, and so forth. Similarly, some more subjective, anecdotic, and poetic ruminations on cinematic details tend to celebrate them as ends in themselves, as results of idiosyncratic viewing experiences that confirm the fact that films cannot be reduced to closed systems and categories. The appeal of the wind in the trees in early Lumière films would therefore not reside in the individual forms and movements this wind may acquire in different moving images,³⁵ but chiefly in how it moved the audience and displaced its attention toward the nonfictional, nondiegetic, and unarranged.

In this context, it is also helpful to note, with Noa Merkin, that detail is an element that "constantly refers to the whole."³⁶ It exposes the fact that "we cannot see everything at once. In our perception of whole and detail, one will have a tendency to overshadow the other, causing it to momentarily disappear; yet by the isolation of detail [. . .], we make the whole visible in a particular way."³⁷ Even an accidental, unintentional, external force such as the wind in the trees remains embedded in the image, so it necessarily communicates with the represented figures and objects within the totality of the frame. Even though the trembling persons on a bridge (Figure I1.3 GIF) or horses hit by lightning (Figure I1.2) may not have been desired by the maker, they are nevertheless there, fulfilling aesthetic functions and evoking aesthetic effects, as well as revealing a film, a scene, a shot, or indeed a single frame³⁸ as a battleground where different gestures, traces, temporalities, materialities, and figurations confront each other and participate in the film's meaning.

Thus, on a general level, detail is accidental yet meaningful, peripheral yet inherently related to a whole, fluid yet gaining discernible forms. When confronted with the weird shapes in *Digital Křiženecký*, we need to go further from the notion of detail as negativity, excess, or subjective sensation and ask serious questions concerning the details' distinguishing qualities, differences, and paradoxes as well as their origin and circulation. The color veil, the horse hit by lightning, the trembling black wave, the scratched kiss, and the

---

³⁴ Anger and Jirsa, "We Never Took Deconstruction Seriously Enough," 67–8. For Brinkema's earlier critique of the negativist tendency in cultural affect theory, see Eugenie Brinkema, *The Forms of the Affects* (London and Durham: Duke University Press, 2014).
³⁵ See Schonig, *The Shape of Motion*, 19–22.
³⁶ Merkin, "Little Patch of Yellow," 3.
³⁷ Ibid., 8.
³⁸ Hannah Frank, *Frame by Frame: A Materialist Aesthetics of Animated Cartoons* (Berkeley: University of California Press, 2019).

Frankensteinian face pose a momentous challenge to the existing theoretical frameworks of the detail in at least two respects. First, these weird shapes emerge from clashes between two spheres of the image. The *figurative* sphere involves the image's content: what is represented in the image and how it is formally composed. The *material* sphere covers the image's physical carrier and technological underpinnings (film stock, camera, editing tools, projector, screens, and so on) and processes by which they shape the film's content. In the case of *Digital Kříženecký*, unplanned intrusions of the material dimension into the figurative one, either through degradation, inherent properties of the Lumière equipment, or both, give birth to surprising aesthetic forms and effects. Previous accounts of filmic details generally made no differentiation between details that appear within the figurative content captured by the camera (such as the wind in the trees) and details that arise from physical intervention or deformation (such as scratches or splices that may disfigure the face of a hero in an aging film). In the latter case, there are indeed many passages in theoretical and essayistic articles that describe in minute detail how a certain physical element disrupts representation, but rarely do they analyze the specific figurative-material assemblage that unfolds as a result. The appeal of the "electrocuted" horse racer does not stem merely from the fact that a technological actor (static electricity) accidentally infiltrates figurative content (a horse race); what matters is their mutual entanglement. This book will therefore ask questions about the specific relationship between figuration and materiality that gives birth to the weird shapes. Under what conditions do the figurative and material dimensions begin to communicate and produce meaning? Is the clash between figuration and materiality necessarily staged by external actors (human or nonhuman), or is it rather a tension that is always already present within the films? When the figurative and material elements assemble into a shape, do their differences evaporate, or do they continue to coexist as distinct entities and maintain their specificities?

Second, conceptualizations that focus on material details rarely delve into their origin. The damages and distortions we encounter in archival footage and films that appropriate it are often treated as universal signifiers—of decay, ruin, historicity, indexicality, the passage of time, and other such concepts. Never mind whether they are large blobs or small dots, whether they interact with the figurative content or seem completely detached from it, whether they appear in anonymous stock footage or specifically designed experimental films, whether they surface on nitrate prints or their digital copies—the details always indicate the same larger-than-life phenomena. Of course, the weird shapes in *Digital Kříženecký* can (and should) be related to many of these big concepts; however, it would be preferable if this occurred in accordance with the terms determined by the peculiar qualities of each detail. Each physical intervention in figuration has a specific source, a specific genealogy, and specific manifestations that relate to the big philosophical questions in distinctive ways. Before a material sign is understood to signify anything about the film medium and the world in general, it ought to be subjected to questions such as: What kind of deformation is it? Did it originate in the film's production process, or is it a product of later chemical and mechanical interventions, either accidental or purposeful? How does it relate to the image's figurative content? Does it affect the film to the extent that it creates forms and figures in their own right?

Addressing these questions requires further delineating the terms figuration and materiality and the tension that arises between them. *Digital Křiženecký*, understood in the context of archival film and found footage practices, allows us to approach their entanglement *from below* as a trigger of accidental aesthetics.

Operating Between Materiality and Figuration

Due to its ambiguous existence between analog past and digital presence (and future), *Digital Křiženecký* immediately speaks to the issues of film materiality. It revives many long-term debates on the ontology of the photographic image, connections between photochemical film and indexicality, or the death of cinema as a metaphor for the inherent vulnerability and mortality of filmic matter. Křiženecký's films, often monstrously deformed and virtually unrestorable, demonstrate that the aesthetic and figurative function of the moving image is ontologically tied to the material world. How can we resurrect even a glimpse of the event shot by the camera in *Grand Consecration of the Emperor Franz I Bridge* (Figure I1.1) when it is buried deep beyond a color veil full of various distortions? Its digitized version testifies, in its own way, to the entire history of its nitrate carrier and of film prints in general. As Paolo Cherchi Usai reminds us, since its birth, the film print succumbs to natural and mechanical laws: not only does it gradually deteriorate and lose its contours, but it also heads closer to ruination simply by passing through the projecting machine, and this does not even take into account the intentional or unintentional interventions by human or nonhuman actors. Even when entering the digital space, the entropic tendency continues through processes of compression and decompression, glitches, lags, buffers, and so forth. Not for nothing does Cherchi Usai emphasize that "cinema is the art of moving image destruction."[39]

Digital Křiženecký does not attempt to escape this death drive but rather embraces it and distributes it among a multitude of material actors. The analog-digital dichotomy is no longer sufficient to account for the phenomena taking place on the surface of the films. We have to deal with severe physical deformations as well as subtle digital artifacts or dead pixels; distortions inherent to the Lumière technology as well as those caused by temporal degradation, external intervention, or inappropriate conversion; together with intrusions by both humans (either Jan Křiženecký or later archivists or lab workers) and nonhumans (bacteria, fungi, algorithms, and so forth) all on the same plane. Jihoon Kim's notion of "hybrid moving images," an "array of impure image forms characterized by the interrelation of the material, technical, and aesthetic components of existing moving image media,"[40] presents a useful framework for understanding the distributed materiality of Křiženecký's digitized films. Kim's conception also allows for a concrete "dialectic of medium specificity and hybridity"; as he states, "what makes a hybrid cannot be understood if the individual properties being combined cannot be distinguished."[41] Further, Katherine Groo's theorization of hybridity in digitized archival films—more specifically, the badly damaged fragments of early ethnographic cinema from the collections of the EYE Film Institute Netherlands—can help us situate the chaotic mixture of material elements in *Digital Křiženecký* from the perspective of archival fragments rather than experimental art. Still, much work remains to be done to explain how material phenomena such as yellowish-orange color, camera trembling, or static electricity construct or reconstruct this hybridity, as well as the impact of digitizing in 4K quality, which significantly lowers the level of compression. In this endeavor, the existing theoretical accounts of filmic ontology and materiality go hand in hand with archival research on film

---

[39] Paolo Cherchi Usai, *The Death of Cinema: History, Cultural Memory, and the Digital Dark Age* (London: BFI, 2001), 6. For more on the "death of cinema" discourse, see, for example, Mary Ann Doane, "The Indexical and the Concept of Medium Specificity," *Differences* 18, no. 1 (2007): 128–52; D. N. Rodowick, *The Virtual Life of Film* (Harvard: Harvard University Press, 2007); André Gaudreault and Philippe Marion, *The End of Cinema? A Medium in Crisis in the Digital Age* (New York: Columbia University Press, 2015); Bernd Herzogenrath, ed., *The Films of Bill Morrison: Aesthetics of the Archive* (Amsterdam: Amsterdam University Press, 2017); Richard Grusin and Jocelyn Szczepaniak-Gillese, eds., *Ends of Cinema* (Minneapolis: University of Minnesota Press, 2020). For the general methodology of materialist media theory, see Grant Bollmer, *Materialist Media Theory: An Introduction* (New York: Bloomsbury Academic, 2019).

[40] Jihoon Kim, *Between Film, Video, and the Digital: Hybrid Moving Images in the Post-Media Age* (New York: Bloomsbury Academic, 2018), 3.

[41] Ibid., 6–7.

technology (especially that which focuses on the issues of digital preservation and restoration).⁴²

The definition of figuration in the present context is somehow tricky, as the term evokes numerous, sometimes even contradictory, associations. When talking about the figurative sphere of the image, the meaning lies firmly within the bounds of what we understand by figurative art—art that is clearly derived from real object sources and is, by definition, representational.⁴³ In this sense, figuration equals figurative content: the events, people, and objects originally depicted in the footage and how they are formally organized in the respective scenes, shots, or frames. Nevertheless, I employ the word figuration also for its ability to capture action and transformation. Considering that the focus of my research is examining moments when discernible figures undergo deformation due to the activities of material agents, allusions to the paintings of Francis Bacon are hardly avoidable. It was perhaps Gilles Deleuze who expressed most poignantly what continues to fascinate us about Bacon's works: how figurative bodies are being disarticulated by invisible forces of uncertain origin, only to emerge as Figures (with capital F) when they are placed into new relations with other figures.⁴⁴ The face of actor Josef Šváb-Malostranský in Figure I1.5 undergoes similar pressure from external forces—in this case, manifested by a splice—and transfigures into a stitched, deranged head, half Šváb and half Frankenstein's monster. Therefore, the tension lies between the figurative content, its physical deformation, and the weird shape that emerges from their encounter. With these allusions in mind, I still try to circumvent the term "figural"—which is often used in regard to Bacon's paintings—to avoid confusion with the adjective "figurative"⁴⁵ and

---

⁴² See particularly: Leo Enticknap, *Film Restoration: The Culture and Science of Audiovisual Heritage* (New York: Palgrave Macmillan, 2013); Kerstin Parth, Oliver Hanley, and Thomas Ballhausen, eds., *Work/s in Progress: Digital Film Restoration Within Archives* (Vienna: SYNEMA - Gesellschaft für Film und Medien, 2013); Paolo Cherchi Usai, *Silent Cinema: A Guide to Study, Research and Curatorship* (London and New York: Bloomsbury Publishing, 2019); Fossati, *From Grain to Pixel*; Turquety, *Inventing Cinema*.

⁴³ Antonia Pocock, "Figurative," *The University of Chicago, Theories of Media Keywords Glossary*, accessed December 31, 2022, http://csmt.uchicago.edu/glossary2004/figurative.htm.

⁴⁴ Deleuze, *Francis Bacon*.

⁴⁵ Whereas "figurative" is tied to representation, "figural" aims toward the emblematic and ideal. See Pocock, "Figurative." Deleuze claims that Bacon escapes the figurative by extracting and isolating the Figure from narration and representation. Deleuze, *Francis Bacon*, 2. For more on the tradition of figural thinking, see, for example, Jean-Francois Lyotard, *Discourse, Figure* (Minneapolis: University of Minnesota Press, 2011); Roland Barthes, *A Lover's Discourse: Fragments* (London: Vintage, 2002); D. N. Rodowick, *Reading for the Figural, or, Philosophy after the New Media* (Durham and London: Duke University Press, 2001); Tomáš Jirsa, *Disformations: Affects, Media, Literature* (New York: Bloomsbury Academic, 2021).

chiefly not to distract from conceiving a mechanism that produces weird shapes and keeps them alive (which I will define as the "crack-up" in a short while).

To gain more specific insight into the role weird shapes play in figuration, it is crucial to study the conditions under which minor, fleeting, unfitting, or in-between elements can acquire distinctive forms and contours. One inspiration source for this endeavor is Eugenie Brinkema's affective formalism, which highlights the necessity of locating seemingly elusive phenomena such as affects at the level of textual structure and composition.[46] To quote Brinkema, we should appreciate "how the form itself is surprising and speculative, the form which might not be already there but is produced and unfolded through active close reading."[47] If she finds affectively charged forms in details such as Marion's tear in *Psycho* (Alfred Hitchcock, 1960) or a killer tire in Quentin Dupieux's *Rubber* (2010), why not seek forms in *Digital Křiženecký* with its myriads of blobs, blotches, and blurs that communicate with the figurative content (implicitly or explicitly)?

Further, the book draws on research undertaken in the last decade by a small circle of young US film scholars (Hannah Frank, Ryan Pierson, Alla Gadassik, Jordan Schonig, Noa Merkin, and others) that aimed specifically at studying figures and forms of peripheral, fleeting, and contingent phenomena in film (particularly animation).[48] For instance, Schonig's concept of "motion forms" announces the need for a specific "vocabulary for theorizing the movement of the moving image without resorting to the mere invocation or theorization of movement in general."[49] It demonstrates that even fleeting phenomena can gain specific forms and shapes. From his perspective, the proverbial wind in the trees is not just a contingent event revealed by the camera but a conversion of "formless motion into a spatiotemporally bound object by isolating a single point of view and inscribing the temporal flux of movement."[50] In a similar fashion, Pierson asks what would happen "if we looked not simply for movement or animacy as such but for figures—arrangements of units that seem to hold themselves together—and forces—

---

[46] Brinkema, *The Forms of the Affects*; Anger and Jirsa, "We Never Took Deconstruction Seriously Enough."
[47] Anger and Jirsa, "We Never Took Deconstruction Seriously Enough," 69.
[48] For a representative overview, see the recent *Journal of Cinema and Media Studies* dossier "Drawing on the Margins: Animation in Film and Media." Ryan Pierson, ed., "In Focus: Drawing on the Margins: Animation in Film and Media," *Journal of Cinema and Media Studies* 61, no. 1 (2021): 142–84.
[49] Schonig, *The Shape of Motion*, 2.
[50] Ibid., 26.

units of attraction or repulsion or direction that seem to hold the figures together [...]"[51]

Although the relationship between the figurative and material dimensions is natural to the film medium, throughout film history it has been anything but automatic. In very blunt terms, materiality and technology established themselves as separate from figuration, in the case of classical narrative cinema as something that must be effaced or in the case of modernist and avant-garde cinema as something that must be unmasked. However, one "genre" (or rather a filmmaking practice) that based much of its appeal on the relationship between the figurative and material dimensions is "found footage." This ambiguous term is generally understood as a creative method founded on recycling and reusing existing footage in a different context, usually to reveal hidden meanings or deconstruct the meanings that are conventionally accepted.[52] In its experimental variation—from its origins in the late 1960s and 1970s with pioneers such as Ken Jacobs, Ernie Gehr, or Al Razutis, through its second "golden age" during the 1990s and early 2000s with artists like Bill Morrison, Peggy Ahwesh, Matthias Müller, or Peter Tscherkassky, up to the contemporary period with works from Péter Lichter, Bori Máté, Michael Fleming, Guli Silberstein, and others—the accent is precisely on the tension between figurative content and its material-technological underpinnings. Material components of the film medium—photochemical, digital, or hybrid—are employed in order to deform the appropriated footage and "walk the line between figuration and abstraction."[53] Further, the deformations aim not only to showcase the distance between the current perception of the footage and how it was created and received in the past[54] but also to highlight it and extend it—either by numerous kinds of physical intervention (scratching, painting on the film, shaking the camera,

---

[51] Ryan Pierson, *Figure and Force in Animation Aesthetics* (New York: Oxford University Press, 2019), 2.

[52] For a general definition of found footage, see, for example, William Wees, *Recycled Images: The Art and Politics of Found Footage Films* (New York: Anthology Film Archives, 1993); Paul Arthur, "Bodies, Language, and the Impeachment of Vision," in Paul Arthur, *A Line of Sight: American Avant-garde Film Since 1965* (Minneapolis: University of Minnesota Press, 2005), 132–50; Christa Blümlinger, *Kino aus zweiter Hand: Zur Ästhetik materieller Aneignung im Film und in der Medienkunst* (Berlin: vorwerk 8, 2009); André Habib and Michel Marie, eds., *L'avenir de la mémoire. Patrimoine, restauration et réemploi cinématographiques* (Villeneuve d'Ascq: Presses Universitaires du Septentrion, 2013); Kim, *Between Film, Video, and the Digital*, 145–95.

[53] Alejandro Bachmann, "The Trace of Walk That Has Taken Place—A Conversation with Peter Tscherkassky," *Found Footage Magazine* 4, no. 4 (2018): 30.

[54] See Jaimie Baron's concept of the "archive effect" and the notions of "temporal" and "intentional" disparity (further elaborated in Chapter 4). Baron, *The Archive Effect*, 16–47.

burying the film under the ground, digital glitching, and others)[55] or by more subtle curatorial tactics that leave the archival footage mostly as is and rather select the fragments that fit the artist's intentions and find ways how to make certain elements more perceptible and resonant (slow motion, zoom, expressive music, and so forth).

In the last few decades, many reflections on the found footage phenomenon have been written (the "genre" even has its own journal, *Found Footage Magazine*, which provided valuable inspiration during the early stages of my research).[56] Theoretical accounts of found footage usually stress the destructive, distorting, or decompositional effects of physical intrusions or temporal decay on representational images and their wider cultural impact. For example, the articles on found footage in the influential edited volume *Carnal Knowledge: Towards a 'New Materialism' Through the Arts* (2013) place an emphasis on the disruptive quality of filmic matter in figurative images—on its potential to "undermine the grammar and syntax of the films" or reveal latent meanings and repressed traumas.[57] Such interpretations tend to emphasize the otherness of materiality in relation to traditional figuration—which is to an extent reasonable—but they often do so at the expense of underestimating the capacity of material deformations to communicate with the figures present in the appropriated footage. Furthermore, they forget that the appeal of many found footage films is born not only from decay but also from a certain persistence of the original figures, which refuse to simply disappear and instead enter into new configurations with and through the filmic matter. If we want to understand this complicated relationship in both its destructive and productive contours, we need to capture the minute interchanges between the two spheres and the forms and shapes they produce. It is necessary to dedicate more attention to moments such as the scene in Bill Morrison's film *Decasia: The State of Decay* (2002) where a boxer is seen fighting against an amorphous material blob

---

[55] Kim Knowles, *Experimental Film and Photochemical Practices* (Cham: Palgrave Macmillan, 2020).

[56] See, for instance, the special issues on Bill Morrison, Peter Tscherkassky, or Yervant Gianikian and Angela Ricci Lucchi. César Ustarroz, ed., "Special on Bill Morrison," *Found Footage Magazine*, no. 1 (2015); César Ustarroz, ed., "Special on Yervant Gianikian and Angela Ricci Lucchi," *Found Footage Magazine*, no. 3 (2017); and César Ustarroz, ed., "Special on Peter Tscherkassky," *Found Footage Magazine*, no. 4 (2018).

[57] Nicholas Chare and Liz Watkins, "The Matter of Film: Decasia and Lyrical Nitrate," in *Carnal Knowledge: Towards a 'New Materialism' Through the Arts*, ed. Estelle Barrett and Barbara Bolt (London and New York: I.B. Tauris, 2013), 75–87; Dirk de Bruyn, "Recovering the Hidden Through Found-Footage Films," in *Carnal Knowledge: Towards a "New Materialism" Through the Arts*, ed. Estelle Barrett and Barbara Bolt (London and New York: I.B. Tauris, 2013), 89–104.

(once presumably the image of a punching ball) that threatens to swallow him.[58] Here the figurative and material spheres, each in its own way and from a different place, unwittingly participate in producing a weird shape, neither of them giving up and leaving the other alone.

Throughout the book, I will argue that the weird shapes in *Digital Křiženecký* are something that brings the digitized early Czech films astonishingly close to found footage works. Despite fitting rather in the broader category of "archival film" or "archival footage," thanks to mass digitization, the number and accessibility of techniques by which even amateurs can deform images in a superficially similar fashion as the experimental auteurs have increased significantly.[59] Also, many born-analog artifacts circulating in the online space contain weird shapes due to improper conversion or defects of a digital kind, thus making the imagination of shapes hitherto visible in found footage films more widespread. Some of the weird shapes in *Digital Křiženecký*—such as the blobs stretching on the yellowish-orange image surface in *Grand Consecration* (Figure I1.1)—recall figures that filmmakers like Bill Morrison would choose for their symphonies of decay. Others—such as the trembling black wave in *Opening Ceremony of the Čech Bridge* (Figure I1.3 GIF)—look like intentionally orchestrated experiments with the limits of cinematic motion in the vein of Ken Jacobs. The films of Jan Křiženecký remind us that the place of the author in found footage filmmaking is much more unobtrusive than the existing scholarship, which typically champions selected filmmakers as grand auteurs, would have us believe. Jacobs's statement that "a lot of film is perfect left alone, perfectly revealing in its unconscious or semi-conscious form"[60] might be overstated—the appropriator is still the one who chooses and shapes the material. Nevertheless, *Digital Křiženecký* demonstrates that many aesthetic effects displayed in celebrated works by experimental artists can be accomplished through serendipity—accidents that stem as much from the predispositions of film technology as from its aging and circulation, from the film's photochemical origin as well as its digital simulation. Whether the tension between figuration and materiality is generated by artistic intervention, the ravages of time, or inherent technological properties, it comes down to a "difference in degree" rather than a "difference in kind," as Henri Bergson would have it.[61] If film theory and history focused less on

---

[58] Bernd Herzogenrath, "Decasia. The Matter | Image: Film is also a Thing," in *The Films of Bill Morrison: Aesthetics of the Archive*, ed. Bernd Herzogenrath (Amsterdam: Amsterdam University Press, 2017), 86.
[59] Lev Manovich, *The Language of New Media* (Cambridge: MIT Press, 2002).
[60] Ken Jacobs, "Perfect Film," *Light Cone*, accessed December 31, 2022, https://lightcone.org/en/film-4154-perfect-film.
[61] Henri Bergson, Matter and Memory (New York: Zone Books, 1990).

the achievements of individuals and universal themes such as the passing of time and more on the inherent creativity of idiosyncratic material traces and gestures, ideally in conjunction with specific figurative content, the examination of found footage could yield a significantly richer and more varied range of weird shapes.

Thinking Through the Crack-Up

Now that the basic stage for understanding figuration and materiality is set, the challenge lies in conceptualizing the mechanism that makes the production and maintenance of weird shapes possible. But how to name something that signifies rupture and connection at the same time? Where can we find a concept that brings and keeps the seemingly disparate spheres together while maintaining their differences? In what ways can it contain experimental found footage works as well as the accidental creativity of archival fragments? Returning to the opening anecdote, I propose to call this mechanism "the crack-up." Fitzgerald's narrative of a personal crisis also involves a broader reflection of the crack-up as something that has been present all along: "*Of course* all life is a process of breaking down."[62] Thirty years later, this sentence captured the interest of Gilles Deleuze, who developed it into a concept in two "series" of *The Logic of Sense* (1968): "Porcelain and Volcano" and "Zola and the Crack-Up."[63] In the crack-up (*fêlure* in French), Deleuze found a fitting term for describing an ontological void that prevents and simultaneously enables living existence and, by extension, any meaning that may come out of it. The silent operations of the crack-up continuously pursue their destroying activity without our knowledge, and when they burst onto the surface (when the "volcano replaces the porcelain"), it is already too late to halt them yet always too early to ascribe them meaning. Nevertheless, if we follow the Deleuzian rumination, a real sense can emerge only at the limit of what is sensible, through an encounter with the unthinkable or the non-sensible—in our case, an encounter with a material-technological accident within the figurative image. The crack-up, then, stands for what "runs through and alienates thought in order to be also the possibility of thought."[64]

---

[62] Fitzgerald, "The Crack-Up."
[63] Gilles Deleuze, "Porcelain and Volcano," in *The Logic of Sense* (London: The Athlone Press, 1990), 154–61; Gilles Deleuze, "Zola and the Crack-Up," in *The Logic of Sense* (London: The Athlone Press, 1990), 321–33.
[64] Deleuze, "Zola and the Crack-Up," 332.

Why choose the crack-up over other words and concepts? The language of modern theory and philosophy is full of cracks, ruptures, fissures, and holes, as well as gaps, intervals, or in-betweens; what makes the crack-up actually and potentially different? One may also object that the comical or disturbing assemblages depicted in Figures I1.1–I1.5 are quite far removed from the alcoholics, neurotics, and train wrecks from Zola's and Fitzgerald's novels, or that the concept is too vague to account for such specific formal and technological phenomena. At first glance, the dictionary meanings of the crack-up, albeit all relevant and somehow related to what Deleuze and Fitzgerald describe, do not seem to suggest anything that specific:

Crack-up *noun* (COLLAPSE)
(a) an occasion when something that was joined together or united breaks into separate parts;
(b) a period of mental illness when someone is so upset or worried that they cannot think clearly or cannot deal with normal life;
(c) someone or something that is very funny.[65]

Assuming the meanings (b) and (c) are secondary, why not stick with the much more frequently used "crack"? After all, even though Deleuze subscribes to Fitzgerald, the English translation of *The Logic of Sense* employs the words crack-up and crack interchangeably. Still, I argue that the crack-up presents a speculatively generative term for the schizophrenic relationship between figuration and materiality in *Digital Kříženeckỳ*, and found footage and archival film in general, and that it allows us to approach these phenomena *from below*. I propose three key reasons:

1. The Crack-Up as Persistence

The crack-up does not connote only a singular rupture or accident, a sudden event that pierces through a whole; instead, it describes something providential or fatal. Fitzgerald's *of course* demonstrates that there is nothing immediate or unnatural about his premature crack. The crack-up is always already there, almost as the course of nature and the cosmos[66] that does not lead to any final revelation or absolution but persists in the cycles of surfacing and disappearing. We can understand the weird shapes in *Digital Kříženeckỳ* as specific actualizations and manifestations of the crack-up as a fundamental

---

[65] "Crack-up," *Cambridge Dictionary*, accessed December 31, 2022, https://dictionary.cambridge.org/dictionary/english/crack-up.
[66] Ryan J. Johnson, *Deleuze, A Stoic* (Edinburgh: Edinburgh University Press, 2020), 268.

condition of the film medium. Its emergence owed a lot to the marriage between the figurative and material worlds, which, nevertheless, eventually conformed to the needs of spectators and the industry for transparency and recognizability and condemned the film's material-technological underpinnings to the role of a supporting actor, with the occasional returns to the original tension through certain forms of experimental cinema, video art, and multimedia installations. It may sound like another grand narrative, but the main inspiration to get from the providential meaning of the crack-up is that it gives all the weird details and accidents in *Digital Kříženecký* (as well as in other archival artifacts and experimental or vernacular works that appropriate them) a sense of temporality and duration. Although the weird shapes hold contours only for a brief moment, if we think about them as conjectures of processes that are taking place all along, we can conceive them as self-sustaining wholes, not as deviations, defects, or derivatives. When we perceive the trembling black wave of figures approaching the camera in *Opening Ceremony*, why not interpret it as a return to the fundamental trembling of the cinematographic apparatus and the genuinely *moving* image, a return that, however ephemeral it is, can be extended into eternity?

2. The Crack-Up as Paradox

According to Fitzgerald, the crack-up provides "the ability to hold two opposed ideas in the mind at the same time, and still retain the ability to function."[67] Following this line of thought, the crack-up encapsulates a constitutive void that, despite being based on a never-ceasing cycle of breakdowns, establishes a means of transmission between two discernible worlds (in our case, the figurative one and the material one). When the lightning streak hits the horses in *The First Day of the Spring Races of Prague*, the material does not overshadow the figurative (nor vice versa). What counts is their "interference and interfacing,"[68] the short-lived yet generative interaction of new and surprising figures and shapes beyond the figurative-material scission. The weird shapes obscure neither the figurative content nor the formal composition; instead, they make visible the (media-material) conditions of their presence, as in the case of the trembling Cinématographe in *Opening Ceremony*. And vice versa, the emergence of the shapes does not reduce the image to an abstract humming of filmic matter; rather, the figurative and material elements negotiate their individual differences. The charm of the crack-up resides in the capacity to contain negativity and

---

[67] Fitzgerald, "The Crack-Up."
[68] Deleuze, "Porcelain and Volcano," 155.

productivity, difference and simultaneity, contingency and fate, at the same time, even within the tiniest cinematic units.

3. The Crack-Up as Surface

By being explicitly linked to weird shapes unfolding within the filmic matter, the crack-up gains the chance to be inscribed right where it belongs—on the surface of things or, more specifically, into the depth of the surface where thoughts can spring literally *from below*. According to Deleuze, the crack-up is "neither internal nor external" but "rather at the frontier"—"imperceptible, incorporeal, and ideational."[69] When it explodes on the screen, we see technological elements deforming the image content and figurative elements pulling toward abstraction, but the crack-up itself remains virtual—operating at the edge of both dimensions and regulating their interaction to make way for weird shapes to unfold. Crucially, and this might be a general contribution to Deleuzian philosophy, the crack-up should not be reducible to the affirmative language of becoming, lines of flight, and the production of the new that is usually associated with Deleuze.[70] After all, the void that the crack-up opens entails an imminent risk of "the shattering and bursting of the end,"[71] of the figurative image falling into the depths of filmic matter. Facing (though not fetishizing) the potential horror of the crack-up presents us with a chance to find the darker, more "dangerous" Deleuze that certain philosophers have recently searched for.[72]

This is why the crack-up forms the conceptual groundwork for all the examinations of strange encounters between figuration and materiality to follow. Sometimes support is provided by related concepts that help define the specific contours and stages of the crack-up. For example, Chapter 1 utilizes Eugene Thacker's concept of "world-without-us" to account for the instance when the crowd is in danger of being swallowed by the inert filmic matter, and Chapter 3 employs Gilbert Simondon's notion of "transduction" to describe the moment of the trembling bridge when the figurative and material dimensions appear to respond to each other and reach an equilibrium of sorts. Ultimately, though, the crack-up pervades throughout the text as a

---

[69] Ibid.
[70] The criticism of this affirmative bias of Deleuzian philosophy is most poignantly formulated in Benjamin Noys, *The Persistence of the Negative: A Critique of Contemporary Continental Theory* (Edinburgh: Edinburgh University Press, 2010), 51–79, or in Andrew Culp, *Dark Deleuze* (Minneapolis: University of Minnesota Press, 2016).
[71] Deleuze, "Porcelain and Volcano," 155.
[72] See, for example, Eugene Thacker, *In the Dust of This Planet: Horror of Philosophy*, Vol. 1 (Winchester: Zero Books, 2011); Culp, *Dark Deleuze*.

"gift"[73] from philosophy: one that provides an overarching metaphor for the paradoxical encounters between figurative and material elements yet always gives way to describe and analyze what makes the weird shapes in *Digital Kříženecký*, found footage, and archival films genuinely unique.

The Life Cycle of the Crack-Up

This book's ambition is to do film theory *from below*, from the perspective of archival film artifacts (however damaged or deformed they may be) and the details hidden within them, or more specifically, from the weird shapes that emerge as actualizations of the crack-up between the figurative and material dimensions and bear capacity to actually *reshape* theory. This is why each chapter focuses on a single Kříženecký film, a single weird shape, a single material origin of that shape, and a single theoretical concept or tradition that may undergo transformation by that shape (see Table I.1). The book proceeds from the most indistinguishable weird shapes to the relatively discernible, from the physical gestures that derive from the properties of the Lumière film materials (yellowish-orange color and static marks) and their Cinématographe (camera instability) to later interventions caused by improper handling (vertical scratches) or attempts to sew the damaged film back together (spliced frames). The order of concepts follows a gradual movement from the ontology of film (death of cinema, indexicality) through philosophical interplay (transduction) to the more epistemological aspects of film experience (archive effect, haptic visuality). However, the opening chapters also include epistemological moments, and vice versa, the closing parts often return to ontological questions.

The overall structure of the first five chapters is illustrated in Table I.1:

Table I.1 Structure of the Chapters

	Film	Weird Shape	Origin	Concept
1	*Grand Consecration*	Color veil	Yellowish-orange color	Death of cinema
2	*Spring Races*	Electric horses	Static marks	Indexicality
3	*Opening Ceremony*	Black wave	Camera instability	Transduction
4	*Assignation*	Scratched kiss	Vertical scratches	Archive effect
5	*Laughter and Tears*	Stitched head	Spliced frames	Haptic visuality

[73] "If a philosophical reading returns to film or literary studies some fact or insight regarding the nature or history of the medium and its meanings and effects, it is in the form of a gift." D. N. Rodowick, *What Philosophy Wants from Images* (Chicago: University of Chicago Press, 2018), 45.

Chapter 1—"Keep That Image Burning: The Color Veil and the Cinema That Never Stops Ending"—deals with *Grand Consecration of the Emperor Franz I Bridge* (Slavnostní vysvěcení mostu císaře Františka I.; 1901), probably the most distorted film from the digitized oeuvre. Due to its deformations, the people walking on the bridge are covered by a rippling color veil, oscillating between yellow and orange, with some degraded spots descending to red. The yellowish-orange color, typical for early Lumière nitrate prints, is of uncertain origin and unclear intention, yet it cannot be scraped away. Where does the color veil stand regarding the inevitably transforming ontology of film and the often-presumed death of cinema? And how can the crack-up between figuration and materiality at its rawest make us rethink the death drive of cinema as an aesthetic potentiality? The analysis of the first seven frames affirms the death of cinema in the plural, with individual color motifs as elements, each of which has its own aesthetic function and its own manner of dying.

Chapter 2—"Do Archivists Dream of Electric Horses? Static Electricity and the Quadruple Logic of Indexicality"—takes aim at the film *The First Day of the Spring Races of Prague* (První den jarních dostihů pražských; 1908). Here, tiny white streaks of lightning inconspicuously intervene in the image, sometimes even hitting the horse racers. Unlike many more traditional material traces in old films and photographs (rips, dots, and dust), these static marks point back to the film's shooting and production process and their envelopment in the world where natural and technological electricity intertwine. The chapter reassesses the indexicality of film, generally understood as a causal connection between the object of reality and its photographic reproduction, and shows how the crack-up reveals and differentiates a quadruple logic of indexicality, torn between figuration and materiality, trace and deixis, thereby broadening the variety of things and processes to which film can point or index.

Chapter 3—"Trembling Meaning: Camera Instability and Transduction in Archival Moving Images"—covers the actuality *Opening Ceremony of the Čech Bridge* (Slavnost otevření nového Čechova mostu; 1908), significant for its curiously trembling image. At one point, the horizontal and vertical shaking of the Cinématographe translates into the shaking of the people approaching the apparatus with such perfect timing that the figurative and material spheres appear to cooperate toward a common meaning and aesthetic effect. This manifestation of the crack-up communicates with Gilbert Simondon's notion of transduction, accounting for the autonomous distribution of elements between heterogeneous spheres while maintaining a certain (meta)stability of this distribution within a system. The emerging weird shapes of a trembling "black wave" showcase that the crack-up is reconcilable with an equilibrium of sorts. The chapter outlines how the equilibrium can be foregrounded for aesthetic and media-reflexive purposes and looped into eternity through experimental found footage practices.

Chapter 4—"The Milestone That Never Happened: The Scratched Kiss and the Failed Beginning of Czech Cinema"—focuses on the pioneering film of Czech cinema, *An Assignation in the Mill* (Dostaveníčko ve mlýnici; 1898). Immediately after actor Josef Šváb-Malostranský unveils the "Czech Cinematograph" poster, there is a sudden shift to a story of a failed tryst. However, what binds these two events together is a glimpse of perceptual ambiguity—is it two characters in search of a kiss or the scratched canvas of an abstract painting? The crack-up in the form of a scratched first kiss of Czech cinema opens a window onto the question of what creates the "archive effect" (Jaimie Baron) of the pioneering mo(nu)ments of national cinemas. The vertical scratches that simultaneously connect and disconnect the film's two segments remind us to what extent even the most treasured cinematic firsts are always already riddled with the powers of the false and bring the Czech film into surprising contact with essayistic experiments with first cinematic kisses.

Chapter 5—"Touching the Film Object with Surgical Gloves: Frankensteinian Frames and the Fragile Malleability of Cinematic Faces"—delves into another iconic film involving Šváb-Malostranský, *Laughter and Tears* (Smích a pláč; 1898). This study of facial expressions in a close-up is meant to reveal the minutest details, yet Šváb's visage is almost never visible in itself but concealed under numerous types of decay and deformation—sometimes even stitched together from various parts like Frankenstein's monster. Approaching such a fragile entity demands a "haptic" perspective that questions not only the integrity of the specific film object but also the mastering gaze of the analyzing subject. By discerning the crack-up actualized between two distinct forms of the close-up—a figurative one (the facial shot) and a material one (the splice)—the chapter portrays the cinematic face as a landscape filled with diverse materialities and autonomous processes and highlights the potentialities stemming from combining the two facial modalities in extraordinary ways.

What further unites all the chapters is an emphasis on the broader context of found footage and archival film. Experimental found footage works such as Bill Morrison's *Decasia* (2002), Al Razutis's *Lumière's Train, Arriving at the Station* (1979), Sami van Ingen's *Flame* (2018), Siegfried A. Fruhauf's *La sortie* (1999), Thom Andersen's *Eadweard Muybridge, Zoopraxographer* (1975), or Michael Fleming's *Never Never Land* (2018) provide a comparative foundation for analyzing Kříženecký's films—not only for addressing similar theoretical issues or employing similar material traces and gestures but also for showing that polished and unpolished forms of the crack-up can be thought of together. Furthermore, films made by (and for) the Lumière Brothers and Edison, early Biograph films, and early ethnographic films from the Eye Institute serve to situate *Digital Kříženecký* within the problematic realm of archival fragments emerging in the digital landscape and undergoing various degrees of intervention.

Finally, there is the influence of videographic criticism. All the chapters involve videographic moments in which the weird shapes are examined frame by frame, stopped in an instant of a blur, slowed down almost to the point of freezing, repeated in a loop, or shown as sutured together from different image parts. These subtle operations undertaken with editing software enable us to showcase and bracket the weird shapes and underscore the uncertain and ambiguous character of *Digital Kříženecký*. The selective manipulations with the digitized artifacts undertaken on the part of the scholar (pausing, zooming, slow motion, looping, and others), which are described throughout the book, remind us that any kind of analysis of a digital audiovisual object also involves participation in its continuous creation. The crack-up is never static, and the weird shapes are not exhausted by our current perception of them within the context of the digitized films. Taking the perspective *from below* seriously also means affirming the modulability of digital film objects, the potentialities within the color veils and black waves, and translating them into a play with words.

Thus, the final chapter (Chapter 6)—"Shaping the Unshapeable? Videographic Deformation and the First Frames of Czech Cinema"—involves both a videographic essay and its written elaboration and contextualization. It proposes a practical exercise that discloses a specific form of the crack-up in all of the films together—the one that lies within their opening frames. The video essay titled *The First Frames of Czech Cinema* contains the single "first frame" of each piece of digitized original film material (nitrate prints and negatives) assembled into a compilation that shows them in detail as well as part of a larger mosaic. On the one hand, the essay exploits the possibilities of digital technology to dissect film objects into their basic building blocks and view them from multiple angles; on the other, it is also a reflection of an early screening practice, when projectionists started the presentation with a still image that gradually evolved into a continuous movement. The videographic essay and its written elaboration allow us to expose the first Czech film frames as malleable objects with photochemical as well as digital features.

1

Keep That Image Burning

The Color Veil and the Cinema That Never Stops Ending

June 14, 1901. Jan Kříženecký shoots the grand consecration of the Emperor Franz I Bridge. The camera stands on the left side of the bridge and captures the people passing by. Some ignore the apparatus, others try to draw attention to themselves, at least for an instant. This is what the filmmaker, and perhaps also the film's audience, wanted to see in the resulting film. Yet, when we are watching the film now, another element makes itself visible in its own way. The walking figures are covered by a rippling color veil, varying between yellow and orange, sometimes even descending to red. Amidst this entropy of two conflicting planes, is there room for aesthetic figures and shapes to emerge? (Figures 1.1–1.4)

The 46-seconds-long,[1] incompletely preserved[2] actuality *Grand Consecration of the Emperor Franz I Bridge* (Slavnostní vysvěcení mostu císaře Františka I.; 1901, source: nitrate print) presents one of the most distorted films from *Digital Kříženecký*. Despite (or because of) high-resolution digital video, the images still burst with cracks, holes, and burns; some of the frames are missing or incomplete; others hold together only because of splices. Additionally, the edges of the frame are unstable, slightly shifting horizontally and vertically, and the circular perforations follow suit.[3] However, the most distinctive element is the vibrant color "veil," which not

---

[1] This length applies for 24 fps projection speed and includes the newly added opening titles.
[2] According to Zdeněk Štábla, the film originally consisted of three parts. Zdeněk Štábla, *Český kinematograf Jana Kříženeckého* (Praha: Československý filmový ústav, 1973), 112.
[3] In this case, the fluctuation is partly an effect of the digitization process. The perforations at the edges of the film strips were used as reference points for digital stabilization of the image. However, since the software was incompatible with the circular perforations, and also with the numerous mechanical damages, each frame had to be moved manually in the scanner. Hence, maintaining a stable image was not entirely possible. Jeanne Pommeau and Jiří Anger, "The Digitization of Jan Kříženecký's Films," *Iluminace* 31, no. 1 (2019): 105, 107. This slight shifting should not be entirely confused with the manifestations of camera instability covered in Chapter 3.

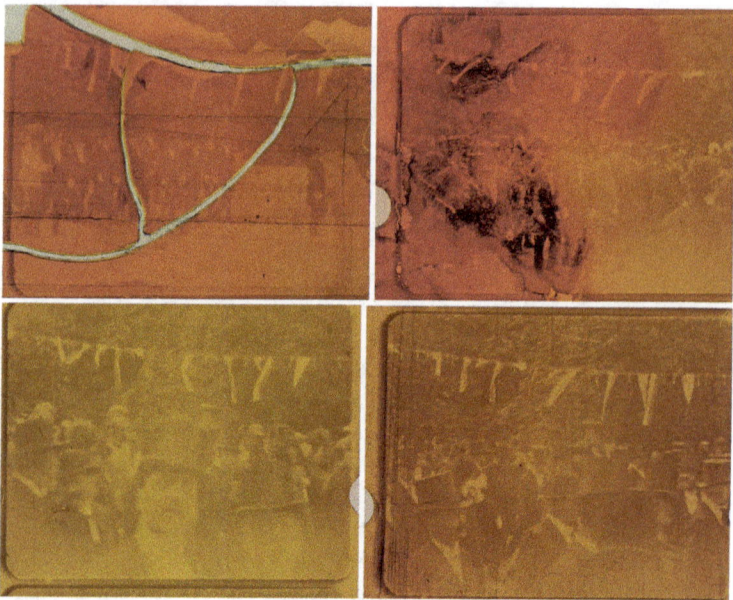

Figures 1.1–1.4 *Grand Consecration of the Emperor Franz I Bridge* (Slavnostní vysvěcení mostu císaře Františka I.; 1901, source: nitrate print) © Národní filmový archiv.

only surrounds and blurs the characters and objects represented in the film but also brings the punctured skin of the film to the foreground.

The origin of this yellow (or, more precisely, yellowish-orange) color remains unclear and is currently being investigated by Jeanne Pommeau. At first glance, it might seem reminiscent of tinting and toning practices for adding color to black-and-white films.[4] Nevertheless, the presence of the yellowish-orange color within all the surviving original nitrate

---

[4] Ibid., 106; see also Jeanne Pommeau, "The Digitisation of Kříženecký's Films" [videocommentary], in *Filmy Jana Kříženeckého/The Films of Jan Kříženecký*, ed. Jiří Anger, DVD/Blu-ray (Praha: Národní filmový archiv, 2019). For tinting, the positive print is immersed into a variety of dye baths, scene by scene. To this end, the print has to be cut into the corresponding fragments and reassembled after the dyeing process. In contrast to tinting, toning is not the simple immersion of a film into a dye bath but involves a chemical reaction converting the silver image. In this reaction, the neutral silver image in the emulsion of the positive film is replaced by one consisting of colored metal compounds. See Barbara Flueckiger, Eva Hielscher, and Nadine Wietlisbach, eds., *Color Mania: The Material of Color in Photography and Film* (Baden: Lars Müllers Publishing, 2019), and the related website Timeline of Historical Film Colors, accessed December 31, 2022, https://filmcolors.org/.

prints from Kříženecký's estate is remarkably consistent, especially given the diversity of colors that were used for tinting and toning during that period, often even within a single print. Furthermore, the shades and hues bear a striking resemblance to many existing (but mostly overlooked) color nitrate prints manufactured by Victor Planchon for the Lumière brothers, spread across film archives in various countries, and employed by various filmmakers and operators.[5] Nor can the color's presence be easily attributed to material degradation, at least not entirely.[6] Sure, the red stains and spots in many of the frames signify aging and decay, and the proportion between yellow and orange also varies, but the veil persists, always spreading over the entire surface of the print.[7] Even if we bear in mind the (still inevitable) shift between how the colors look on the original print and how they look in the digital file, the yellowish-orange in *Digital Kříženecký* does not exactly recall the sepia tone that we usually encounter in fading nitrate photographs.

Thus, the most valid hypothesis to this date is the one currently investigated by Pommeau—that the vintage prints from Kříženecký's estate already contained color prior to the printing process.[8] This hypothesis will have to be confirmed by chemical research—not only of the film prints from Kříženecký's estate but also of the Lumière prints in general, especially those from the same Lumière-Planchon series as the film strips used

---

[5] This fact is mentioned by Laurent Mannoni, who also speaks about the existence of red and blue prints besides the yellow-orange ones, but their existence has not been confirmed. He also criticizes the overlooking of such prints by the archival and scholarly community. Laurent Mannoni, "Les Appareils cinématographiques Lumière," *1895*, no. 82 (2017): 71.

[6] Eric Loné attributes the yellowish veil to "coloration," referring to "the natural impact on the medium's original colour of the way it was manufactured." Eric Loné, "Lumière," in Harold Brown, *Physical Characteristics of Early Films as Aids to Identification*, ed. Camille Blot-Wellens (Brussels: FIAF, 2020), 165.

[7] For a visual demonstration of various stages of nitrate deterioration, see, for example, Tania Passafiume et al., "Instructions: A Visual Glossary of Six Stages of Nitrate Film Base Deterioration," *Library and Archives Canada*, accessed December 31, 2022, https://www.bac-lac.gc.ca/eng/about-us/publications/electronic-books/Pages/visual-glossary-nitrate-deterioration.aspx.

[8] Jeanne Pommeau is currently working on a PhD dissertation on this topic. See, for example, Jeanne Pommeau, "Le mystère des couleurs des pellicules du Cinématographe Lumière," Conference paper presented at Domitor 2020, November 17, 2020, accessed December 31, 2022. https://domitor2020.org/en-ca/le-mystere-des-couleurs-des-pellicules-du-cinematographe-lumiere/. Jeanne Pommeau, "Studie ve žluté: Hypotézy o přítomnosti zapomenutých barev v lumièrovských filmových páscích," in *Digitální Kříženecký: Nový život prvních českých filmů*, ed. Jiří Anger (Praha: Národní filmový archiv, 2023), 76–107. Other than that, it is not known whether this particular issue has ever been seriously investigated.

by Kříženecký.⁹ If it were correct, that is, if the veil resulted from specific properties of the overlooked family of Lumière color prints, the weird shapes would be primarily attributed to intrinsic features of the film stock, not to external phenomena such as additive color processes or the ravages of time. Even if the hypothesis proved not entirely correct, *Grand Consecration* would, at the very least, demonstrate how much a film can owe its essence to the uncanny presence of a technological agent—a presence that is so consistent and so intrusive, and at the same time so diffused between different forms of materiality, that it cannot be erased or retouched without creating the film anew.

Nonetheless, the yellowish-orange color does not warrant our attention solely for its technical aspects. The main issue lies in its impact on the aesthetics of the moving image or, more specifically, in its influence on the relationship between the figurative content of the image and its material-technological dimension. The convoluted color veil that instantly arises and never disappears creates a membrane between the figures walking on the bridge and, paradoxically, also any other intrusions of the material world, be it the properties of the Lumière film stock or various traces of decay (including the decay of the color veil itself). This membrane constitutes a gap between the filmed event and us, shifting our attention to the interplay between technological elements of various origins on the surface while still maintaining our curiosity about what is going on "underneath." It may be described as a filter that determines what can or cannot be seen and recognized of the figurative space and the extent to which the intrusion of diverse material actors extends the range of figurative processes. In other words, the color veil highlights the dependence of figuration on the material carrier, and sometimes the discernible figures and technological components intertwine in such a manner that the emerging weird shape shows us how aesthetically and conceptually rich film destruction can be.

Through the color veil, the crack-up arises in its rawest, most abstract, most volatile form—it is impossible to determine whether the destructive impulses will not outweigh any struggle to represent. Owing to the seriousness of the deformations, any provisional balance between the figurative and material dimensions skews toward the material-technological ground. Throughout the film, we can see many frames that are either torn apart or covered by red stains

---

[9] The importance of conducting chemical research of Lumière nitrate prints is also highlighted by Benoît Turquety. Benoît Turquety, "Why Additive? Problems of Color and Epistemological Networks in Early (Film) Technology," in *The Colour Fantastic: Chromatic Worlds of Silent Cinema*, ed. Giovanna Fossati et al. (Amsterdam: Amsterdam University Press, 2018), 117–18. See also Benoît Turquety, "Not Corrected or Otherwise Manipulated: Digitizing the Films of Jan Kříženecký," *Iluminace* 32, no. 4 (2020): 124–30.

to such an extent that the figurative content (almost) disappears. However, the crack-up is not purely destructive—not only does the folding of the color veil stage a distinct form of figuration on its own, but it also draws attention to the mutual entanglement of actors that become involved in the figurative processes. The aesthetic effect of the film depends equally on traces of its photochemical history and its digital conversion and circulation, on signs of degradation as much as on elements shaped by the film's production process, on forces that spell an inevitable destruction of the film as well as potentialities that point toward new aesthetic formation. Thus, the crack-up in all its ambiguities presents an invisible glue that, by means of initial separation, shows the figurative and material elements as necessarily tied to each other.

For these reasons, any examination of *Grand Consecration*'s aesthetic function cannot be done without addressing its material and media properties, including those that partake in the film's destruction. Excursions into theoretical accounts of filmic matter and its ever-changing ontology (from André Bazin and his correlation between materiality and indexicality[10] to contemporary concerns about the entanglement of analog and digital, human and nonhuman, living and nonliving entities) and archival research on film technology (especially that which focuses on the issues of digital preservation and restoration) are necessary to assess the role of the color veil in the distribution of figurative and material elements across the moving image. And conversely, the materialist-inclined approaches need to acknowledge that various deformations of filmic matter have their own figurative merit, whether intentional or unintentional. This is why the found footage phenomenon, with its aesthetic possibilities and affective qualities, also becomes a valuable factor in the present discussion.

Thus, face to face with archival artifacts whose matter is distributed between photochemical and digital elements, as well as deformations of diverse origins, the following questions arise: Where does the distorted color veil in *Grand Consecration* stand regarding the inevitably transforming ontology of film and the often-presumed death of cinema? Is it a sign of loss and ruination or a symptom of the creativity of hybrid filmic matter? How can the crack-up between figuration and materiality instigated by the involuntary veil be exploited for aesthetic purposes in archival film and experimental found footage? And which specific weird shapes can emerge when we analyze the film frame by frame? This chapter addresses these

---

[10] Bazin himself does not use the term "indexicality." The one who contextualized Bazin's thought in semiotics was Peter Wollen, see Peter Wollen, "Ontology and Materialism in Film," in *Readings and Writings: Semiotic Counter-Strategies* (London: Verso, 1982), 189–207.

questions in four respective parts. *Grand Consecration* and its idiosyncratic material-technological qualities serve to flesh out these issues *from below* in a miniature yet condensed manner.

The Mummy Complex and the Death Drive of Cinema

As already noted, *Grand Consecration* presents one of the most severe cases of material deformation within *Digital Kříženecký*. As far as concealment of the figurative content goes, none of the digitized materials reach quite the same level, yet the preserved nitrate prints—particularly *Midsummer Pilgrimage in a Czechoslavic Village* (Svatojanská pouť v českoslovanské vesnici; 1898, source: nitrate print), *An Assignation in the Mill* (Dostaveníčko ve mlýnici; 1898, source: nitrate print), or the fragment *Coach Transport* (Kočárová doprava; 1898, source: nitrate print)—more or less share with *Grand Consecration* the tension between the recognizable world once captured by the camera, the fluctuating color veil, and various signs of mechanical damage, image instability, and temporal ruination. At the same time, these prints were practically invisible for a hundred years; when the films appeared in compilations, TV shows, and documentaries about the history of Czech cinema, the source materials were later-generation prints.[11] From one point of view, this obscurity seems logical—due to the nonstandard single pair of round perforations,[12] the original prints are no longer screenable, the decaying nitrate base is at permanent risk of burning, and the films' pioneering status makes them treasured artifacts that need to be preserved for future generations. On top of that, the yellowish-orange veil might have been considered undesirable for its tendency to occlude what is happening in the image, as well as colliding with the ingrained (albeit nowadays firmly disproved) idea that early films were black-and-white. However, as the case of *Grand Consecration* demonstrates quite clearly, a vintage nitrate print from the early 1900s and its later-generation copy make for altogether different aesthetic meanings and effects. If we compare the dance of colors in the digitized vintage print with indistinct black stains in, for example, Bohumil Veselý's compilation

---

[11] On the provenance of Kříženecký's films, see Jan Trnka, "Provenance filmových materiálů: Původ a životaběh negativů a kopií s kinematografickými díly Jana Kříženeckého," in *Digitální Kříženecký: Nový život prvních českých filmů*, ed. Jiří Anger (Praha: Národní filmový archiv, 2023), 108–43.

[12] The films were shot on film stock from the Lumière brothers with specific perforation—one round sprocket hole on each side of the film frame, instead of the now standard four rectangular perforations: Pommeau and Anger, "The Digitization of Jan Kříženecký's Films," 105.

Jan Kříženecký (1968),[13] taking into account alterations caused by decay and digital compression, we see completely different films. The color veil became a full-fledged aesthetic feature and simultaneously a materialized metaphor for the destructive impulses lying at the heart of the film.

The decision not to efface any signs of filmic physicality and mortality, even with the most high-end technology at hand, can be better understood within the "death of cinema" debates that have, for the last roughly thirty years, tried to make sense out of the changing materiality of film. Spelling the end of cinema has always been a popular sport among all professions involved in film, particularly in times of crisis or technological change. André Gaudreault and Philippe Marion counted as many as eight deaths of cinema since its advent[14]—from Antoine Lumière's denouncement of his sons' invention as one "with no future"[15] to the digital crisis—the panic amidst the shutdown of cinemas due to Covid-19 could be considered number nine.[16] Before that, the last wave started in the 1990s with the advent of digital technology and the fears about photochemical film becoming obsolete, and, in a less apocalyptic fashion, it is still present in today's thinking, including in archival, scholarly, and artistic circles.[17] The death of cinema debate has

---

[13] Bohumil Veselý, "Jan Kříženecký," *YouTube*, 2013, accessed December 31, 2022, https://www.youtube.com/watch?v=Rk2OrOXEmnM.

[14] André Gaudreault and Philippe Marion, *The End of Cinema? A Medium in Crisis in the Digital Age* (New York: Columbia University Press, 2015).

[15] I am referring to his famous statement: "Cinema is an invention with no future." He allegedly said it when Georges Méliés, who was present at the Grand Café screening on December 28, 1895, asked him to sell him the Cinématographe patent. See Maurice Bessy and Lo Duca, *Louis Lumière inventeur* (Paris: Éditions Prisma, 1948), 49.

[16] See, for example, Kong Rithdee, "Corona and the Death of Cinema (Again)," *Bangkok Post*, March 30, 2020, accessed December 31, 2022, https://www.bangkokpost.com/life/social-and-lifestyle/1889185/corona-and-the-death-of-cinema-again-.

[17] For the debate on the death of cinema in the archival circles, see, for example, Gian Luca Farinelli and Nicola Mazzanti, eds., *Il Cinema ritrovato: Teoria e metodologia del restauro cinematografico* (Bologna: Grafis, 1994); Paolo Cherchi Usai, *The Death of Cinema: History, Cultural Memory, and the Digital Dark Age* (London: BFI, 2001); Roger Smither and Catherine A. Surowiec, eds., *This Film Is Dangerous: A Celebration of Nitrate Film* (London: FIAF, 2002). Some of the most influential contributions to the respective debate in film theory and history are these texts: Anne Friedberg, "The End of Cinema: Multimedia and Technological Change," in *Reinventing Film Studies*, ed. Christine Gledhill and Linda Williams (London: Arnold, 2000), 438–52; Mary Ann Doane, "The Indexical and the Concept of Medium Specificity," *Differences* 18, no. 1 (2007): 128–52; D. N. Rodowick, *The Virtual Life of Film* (Harvard: Harvard University Press 2007); Barbara Flueckiger, "Material Properties of Historical Film in the Digital Age," *NECSUS European Journal of Media Studies* 1, no. 2 (2012): 135–53; Richard Grusin and Jocelyn Szczepaniak-Gillece, eds., *Ends of Cinema* (Minneapolis: University of Minnesota Press, 2020). From the variety of artists thematizing the role of photochemical film in the digital age, we could name Bill Morrison, Tacita Dean, Yervant Gianikian and Angela Ricci Lucchi, or DJ Spooky. For an examination of the aesthetic aspects of the return to analog,

multiple levels, related to issues such as verisimilitude (indexical linkage to reality vs. computer-generated imagery), spectatorship (collective "going to the cinema" vs. individual viewing practices throughout digital platforms), production (physical relation to film vs "manipulation" through mediating software), or temporality (photochemical image as indicative of the past versus electronic images that collapse temporal differences into real-time instantaneity).[18] One factor that brought the concerns of archivists, scholars, and artists together is, to quote Jihoon Kim, the "loss of film's celluloid-based materiality and its subsequent erosion of the value of the filmic image as causally linked to the passage of time in reality."[19] Although this essentialist view of the marriage between materiality and indexicality as a basis of the analog (or, in more concrete terms, photochemical) film has often been challenged,[20] it served its role in redrawing attention to the ontology of film. Considering all the transformations and redefinitions of the film medium, did any specific features persist? If yes, how can we deal with their (seemingly unavoidable) demise? What shall we do to preserve at least the remnants of these unique qualities? And how do we come to terms with the loss of those that cannot be saved?

Once again, a return to André Bazin, especially to his essay "Ontology of the Photographic Image" (1945), comes off as fruitful for such discussion. Bazin describes how all plastic arts share a fundamental motivation of "embalming" the dead, preserving corporeal bodies from the ravages of time. The "mummy complex" satisfies the need to "defend against time," for "death is nothing more than the victory of time."[21] The specificity of photography, compared to sculpture and painting, lies in its objectivity: "For the first time, the only thing to come between an object and its representation is another object. For the first time, an image of the outside world takes shape automatically, without

---

see, for example, Katherine Groo and Paul Flaig, "Historicity Begins with Decay and Ends with the Pretense of Immortality: An Interview with Paolo Cherchi Usai," in *New Silent Cinema*, ed. Katherine Groo and Paul Flaig (London and New York: Routledge, 2015), 53–62; Scott Mackenzie and Janine Marchessault, eds., *Process Cinema: Handmade Film in the Digital Age* (Montreal: McGill-Queen's University Press, 2019); Kim Knowles, *Experimental Film and Photochemical Practices* (London: Palgrave Macmillan, 2020).

[18] For a general overview, see Jihoon Kim, *Between Film, Video, and the Digital: Hybrid Moving Images in the Post-Media Age* (New York: Bloomsbury Academic, 2018), 20–8.

[19] Ibid., 21.

[20] See, for example, Tom Gunning, "Moving Away from the Index: Cinema and the Impression of Reality," *Differences* 18, no. 1 (2007): 29–52; Berys Gaut, *A Philosophy of Cinematic Art* (New York and Cambridge: Cambridge University Press, 2010); Rachel Schaff, "The Photochemical Conditions of the Frame," *Cinéma & Cie* 16, no. 26–27 (2016): 55–64.

[21] André Bazin, "Ontology of the Photographic Image," in *What Is Cinema?* (Montreal: caboose, 2009), 3.

creative human intervention, following a strict determinism."[22] Photography, thus, earns a "degree of credibility absent from any painting" in virtue of the fact that it "transfers reality from the object depicted to its reproduction." The image is "capable of relieving our need to substitute for the object something more than an approximation. That something is the object itself, but liberated from its temporal contingencies."[23] Bazin's ontology of film is not materialist per se—his focus on the material properties of film is governed by the belief in the mummy complex, which is essentially psychological and subjective.[24] Marxist-oriented film theory of the 1960s and 1970s even criticized Bazin's conception for being idealist—for example, Peter Wollen argued that Bazin saw the material processes of photographic registration as mere vehicles of transcendent meaning and thus "transferred the burden of meaning outside the cinema, to the non-cinematic codes."[25] Nevertheless, Bazin's grounding of filmic ontology in the photochemical process, indexically tied to the "reality" shot by the camera and preserved on the celluloid base to fight off our fear of death and decay, is something to which the materialist-oriented theories of film explicitly or intuitively keep returning.

Where would be the place of films such as Kříženecký's *Grand Consecration* in this ontology? Of particular interest is this quote, related to the material quality of photography: "The image may be out of focus, distorted, devoid of colour and without documentary value; nevertheless, it has been created out of the ontology of the model. It is the model."[26] A case in point for Bazin are old photo albums, whose "grey or sepia shadows, ghost-like and almost indiscernible, are no longer traditional family portraits; they are the troubling presence of lives halted in time and liberated from their destiny [. . .]."[27] The fact that the color veil significantly obscures the reality of the depicted event, or, more precisely, that it puts the represented figures on one plane with the endlessly variating marks of deterioration (from torn sprocket holes to rotting red stains), would not make the film any less authentic or indexical. Maybe the reverse is true—Blandine Joret, referring to the "Ontology" essay and also to a later article on Thor Heyerdahl's expedition documentary

---

[22] Ibid., 7.
[23] Ibid., 8.
[24] See especially: Philip Rosen, *Change Mummified: Cinema, Historicity, Theory* (Minneapolis and London: University of Minnesota Press, 2001), 3–42.
[25] Wollen, "Ontology and Materialism in Film," 206. For a general overview of semiotic-materialist criticism of Bazin, see D. N. Rodowick, *The Crisis of Political Modernism: Criticism and Ideology in Contemporary Film Theory* (Berkeley: University of California Press, 1995), 147–79.
[26] Bazin, "Ontology of the Photographic Image," 8.
[27] Ibid.

Kon-Tiki (1950),[28] shows how "extremely poor quality," "uninviting shooting conditions," or "huge gaps" in the films may paradoxically work as proofs of authenticity—provided that they relate to the original circumstances of filming.[29] The presence of the color may have been undesired by Křiženecký and, due to its lack of recognizable content, may have led to the film being accused of lacking in documentary value; nevertheless, it is also an indexical sign that harkens back to the conditions that shaped the film's coming into existence. In a way, it can be seen as a more radical example than anything Bazin ever came up with. Unlike the family photographs, the color veil, by means of unmasking the multiplicity of deformations on its surface, threatens to disfigure even the last straws of reality that was once meant to be captured. Furthermore, there is a strong possibility that, unlike the sepia tone, the yellowish-orange color is not just a trace of decay but an integral feature of the material.

A reflection of films that are defined by their material dimension to such an extent demands injecting the Bazinian ontology with an archival impulse. Bazin's mummy complex, especially in its darker contours, resonates with the perspective of film archivist and curator Paolo Cherchi Usai, one of the pioneers of the "death of cinema" debate in the archival circles,[30] whose approach continues to inspire creative policies and solutions in film preservation and restoration (including those applied by the National Film Archive in Prague),[31] as well as new approaches to film history.[32] In his most well-known book, aptly named *The Death of Cinema: History, Cultural Memory, and the Digital Dark Age* (2001), he directly states that

---

[28] André Bazin, "Le Kon-Tiki ou grandeur et servitudes du reportage filmé," *France Observateur*, April 30, 1952, 23-4. See also André Bazin, "Cinema and Exploration," in *What Is Cinema?* Vol. 1 (Berkeley: University of California Press, 2005), 154-63.

[29] Blandine Joret, *Studying Film with André Bazin* (Amsterdam: Amsterdam University Press, 2019), 49–50. See also Oliver Gaycken, "Through the Body with Laser Gun and Camera," in *Cinema of Exploration: Essays on an Adventurous Film Practice*, ed. James Leo Cahill and Luca Caminati (New York and London: Routledge, 2020), 40–56.

[30] Cherchi Usai has been publishing texts on this topic since the 1980s, in both English and Italian. For his early views on the materiality of (especially silent) cinema, see Paolo Cherchi Usai, *Una Passione Inflammabile* (Turin: UTET, 1991).

[31] The discourse on film preservation and reservation in the Czech archival and scholarly scene is significantly influenced by Usai, at least ever since Anna Batistová brought his thoughts to the Czech audience. See, for example, Anna Batistová, "Poezie destrukce: Typologie, periodizace a reflexe destrukce filmových pohyblivých obrazů," *Iluminace* 17, no. 3 (2005): 27–46.

[32] See, for example, the recent works of Katherine Groo: Katherine Groo, *Bad Film Histories: Ethnography and the Early Archive* (Minneapolis: University of Minnesota Press, 2019); Katherine Groo, "Let It Burn: Film Historiography in Flames," *Discourse* 41, no. 1 (2019): 3–36.

"cinema is the art of moving image destruction."³³ From the moment it is produced, the film begins its decomposition process. Each run of a film print through a projector signals mechanical damage; the chemical substrate is in a permanent risk of decay, if not immolation (in the case of nitrate); and even the best storage conditions do not save the image carrier from a host of cancerous nonhuman agents such as bacteria and fungi.³⁴ As if the mummy's defense against the passage of time were predestined to fail—due to the fragile bindings of its body, it is already a thing that is in a state of decay. In this situation, for Cherchi Usai, "the ultimate goal of film history is an account of its own disappearance, or its transformation into another entity."³⁵

Among other things, Cherchi Usai's notions teach us about the film's entwinement in the material universe. First and foremost, Cherchi Usai's apocalyptic vision demonstrates one key aspect: the death of cinema is not reducible to the digital turn, nor even to the other seven deaths mentioned by Gaudreault and Marion—it constitutes an immanent principle. The correlation of materiality and indexicality introduced by Bazin makes sense only within this "will-to-death"—the fact that as soon as film is not busy being born, it starts being busy dying. If we take Bazin's mummy complex seriously, we may ask, along with Bernd Herzogenrath, what happens if "the corruption and entropy [. . .] also eat at the mummy's bandages"³⁶ as in many films of Jan Kříženecký? Sepia-toned family albums may preserve traces of indexical presence, but still, are they not a paltry thing in comparison with the punctured surface of *Grand Consecration*? Are the signs of time that passed between the film's birth and the present moment really on the same level as the color veil that more than likely participated in the film's very origin? If such an image still shares "the ontology of the model" out of which it was created,³⁷ does the opaque color veil signal that the reality captured on film has been doomed right from the start? Faced with such extreme artifacts, the "materiality-indexicality" alliance needs to be reconceived (and radicalized) with regard to the death drive of (not only) filmic matter and its transgression of the thin line that separates the figurative universe from annihilation.

---

³³ Cherchi Usai, *The Death of Cinema*, 6.
³⁴ Ibid., 13.
³⁵ Ibid., 89.
³⁶ Bernd Herzogenrath, "Aesthetics of the Archive: An Introduction," in *The Films of Bill Morrison: Aesthetics of the Archive*, ed. Bernd Herzogenrath (Amsterdam: Amsterdam University Press, 2017), 16.
³⁷ Bazin, "Ontology of the Photographic Image," 14.

Slow Decay versus Vibrant Creation

Two notions in Cherchi Usai's theory, when confronted with *Digital Kříženecký* and its weird shapes, need to be adjusted. First, Cherchi Usai's emphasis on materiality is inseparable from its subjection to historical decay. On the one hand, moving images are ontologically auto-destructive; on the other, the destruction takes place under the condition that they have already been produced and started aging. To quote Cherchi Usai, "once it has been projected, the film [. . .] is subject to the physical decay of its images and the memory of perfection lost,"[38] as if the process of the film's coming into being (manufacturing, shooting, processing, printing) happened in a vacuum. The existence of a moving image "as it goes through the process of being created" is played down as "hypothetical."[39] The primacy of degradation would imply that all forms of material distortion are ontologically homogeneous regardless of their origin—not that their differences are not recognized or taken into account during preservation, but philosophically, they are understood as subject to the same immanent principle of slow death. In this sense, films that contain elements that are inseparable from the film's production process would be no different from "ordinary" aging films with dots, scratches, and dust. The only thing that escapes this fate is the "Model Image," "the summation of all the optical illusions presented [. . .] in such a way that each viewer can perceive them in their totality," or, to put it more simply, a hypothetical image that would be immune to decay and history.[40] It is not entirely clear where the color veil in *Grand Consecration* would fit into this story, as it does not necessarily come out of deterioration, nor does it qualify as a feature of the Model Image (more like a thing that prevents us from seeing the figures represented in the film in bright contours). In this particular case, the crack-up is not something that would have to wait for damages to be indicted upon the finished film—the yellowish-orange is engraved in the figurative content and the material carrier to such an extent that the idea of the film as ever having existed without it becomes less and less tenable.

Second, although Cherchi Usai links the destruction of moving images to their attachment to the material world, his insistence on medium specificity—even refusing to call electronic moving images cinema[41]—narrows the scope of his radical argument. Not that his viewpoint is necessarily nostalgic—

---

[38] Cherchi Usai, *The Death of Cinema*, 39.
[39] Ibid.
[40] Ibid., 40-3.
[41] Ibid., 7.

although his thoughts were generally interpreted as a plea for saving analog cinema, or at least coming to terms with its loss and decay, the death impulse he talks about affects all matter, not just analog nor even cinema. Moreover, the book came out when the massive digitization of archival films was only slowly beginning, and Cherchi Usai certainly paid more nuanced attention to it later.[42] Yet, he continues to see the digitization of photochemical films as little more than a necessary evil or a production of "facsimiles."[43] He has many valid arguments to support these claims—for example, that digitization cannot reproduce the material properties of the photochemical image nor its presentation through a mechanical apparatus in a theatrical setting, and also that it does not involve a long-term plan for preservation, as the digital images are anything but immune to degradation. It is particularly his emphasis on the irreversibility of decay in both analog and digital images, as well as his criticism of the idea of digital restoration,[44] that resonate with the decision of the National Film Archive not to refer to the Křiženecký project as digital restoration. Still, Cherchi Usai's essentialism makes it hard to account for various hybridized forms of moving images to which the digitization of analog cinema gave birth—be it through pure conversion, circulation in the online space, or artistic appropriation. If we take materials such as *Grand Consecration* and other Křiženecký's films that are digitally transcoded yet visibly marked by ontological deformations of the nitrate negatives or prints (such as the yellowish-orange color), the complex dialectic between their crisp imagery and the pervasive deterioration of various order would most likely be shrugged off as a (however useful) simulation. Furthermore, their death would be conceivable exclusively in the singular, without any hope of distinguishing between photochemical and digital deformation (as the former presumably no longer exists in digitized films) or creatively reworking one through the other. If we want to study the digitized materials for what they are and not for the untouchable and unscreenable originals, we need to consider the plurality of elements contained within them—photochemical

---

[42] Paolo Cherchi Usai, "The Digital Future of Pre-digital Film Collections," *Journal of Film Preservation*, no. 88 (2013): 9–16; Groo and Flaig, "Historicity Begins with Decay and Ends with the Pretense of Immortality: An Interview with Paolo Cherchi Usai"; Paolo Cherchi Usai, *Silent Cinema: A Guide to Study, Research and Curatorship* (London and New York: BFI - Bloomsbury Publishing, 2019), 6–20.

[43] Cherchi Usai, *Silent Cinema*, 7–8.

[44] "Turning silver grains into pixels is not right or wrong per se; the real problem with digital restoration is its false message that moving images have no history, its delusion of eternity." Paolo Cherchi Usai, "The Lindgren Manifesto: The Film Curator of the Future," in *Work/s in Progress: Digital Film Restoration Within Archives*, ed. Kerstin Parth, Oliver Hanley and Thomas Ballhausen (Vienna: SYNEMA - Gesellschaft für Film und Medien, 2013), 28–9.

and digital, intrinsic to its production process or imposed by decay, steering toward annihilation or endlessly renewing themselves.

With these actualizations, Cherchi Usai's vision of the death of cinema may serve to open the filmic matter toward different forms of materiality, with their own modes of dying and, consequently, with their own modes of shaping the crack-up between figuration and materiality. While from Cherchi Usai's viewpoint, films are allowed, paraphrasing Reza Negarestani, to die only in certain ways,[45] inherent to decay and their photochemical condition, rediscovering the inherent heterogeneity of filmic matter bears the potential to widen the scope of its death(s). The color veil in *Grand Consecration* enables us to see a variety of deaths—the death of figures frozen in time and obscured by deformed shapes; the death instilled by historical decay (scratches, tears, splices); the death of the Lumière nitrate print embroiled in torn perforations and unstable movement; the death of the colors themselves, turning from bright yellow and orange to rotting red; and, potentially, the death of digital compression and circulation—each of which contributes to the blurring of the film's material character, as well as to its figurative and aesthetic potentialities.

The distribution of media elements that are alien to each other within a single domain demands an approach that would entail the multiplicity of nonidentical materialities yet would not result in some abstract, nondifferentiated plenitude. For this purpose, Jihoon Kim's theory of "hybrid moving images" mentioned in the Introduction is a useful bridge. His vision of an "array of impure image forms characterized by the interrelation of the material, technical, and aesthetic components of existing moving image media"[46] enables us to conceptualize hybridized forms of analog and digital images within a single work—in the sense that this interaction serves as an end in itself. Kim's conception, while not entirely new,[47] also allows for a concrete "dialectic of medium specificity and hybridity"—"what makes a hybrid cannot be understood if the individual properties being combined

---

[45] See Negarestani's critique of "necrocracy," a system which determines the possibilities and limits of death and therefore negates its emancipatory potential: Reza Negarestani, "Drafting the Inhuman: Conjectures on Capitalism and Organic Necrocracy," in *The Speculative Turn: Continental Materialism and Realism*, ed. Levi R. Bryant, Nick Srnicek, and Graham Harman (Melbourne: Re.Press, 2011), 182–201.

[46] Kim, *Between Film, Video, and the Digital*, 3.

[47] Ontological hybridity of contemporary moving images is accented, for example, by Rodowick, *The Virtual Life of Film*; Lev Manovich, *Software Takes Command* (New York: Bloomsbury Academic, 2013); Iain Macdonald, *Hybrid Practices in Moving Image Design: Methods of Heritage and Digital Production in Motion Graphics* (New York: Springer International Publishing, 2016); Giovanna Fossati, *From Grain to Pixel: The Archival Life of Film in Transition*, 3rd Revised ed. (Amsterdam: Amsterdam University Press, 2018). Gaudreault and Marion, *The End of Cinema?*

cannot be distinguished."⁴⁸ Rather than being satisfied with the affirmation of diverse elements mixing and mingling together, we should acknowledge that hybrid moving images do not necessarily erase conventions associated with either photochemical or digital practices but highlight their relational character. Thus, hybrid moving images accentuate that any notion of medium specificity can be identified only in comparison—by means of how the figurative and material components of other mediums are adopted and what new properties are added to them in the resulting image.⁴⁹

Even though Kim focuses primarily on contemporary media art—from video art through found footage to multichannel installations—his perspective proves handy for *Digital Křiženecký* as well. Nevertheless, the hybridity of Křiženecký's works does not manifest in the same way it does in some other types of digitized photochemical works. While we can argue that formerly photochemical films that are "restored" through digital retouching and stabilization are technically hybrid, many of the specificities associated with their photochemical condition (grain of the image, camera trembling, perforations, marks of static electricity, and others) may become suppressed or even invisible. Conversely, the visibility of photochemical deformation in materials that are "only digitized" depends significantly on the level of compression. As Katherine Groo reminds us, many digitized archival films circulating on the internet make photochemical (resulting from the decaying print) and digital (resulting from compression) degradation overlap, at least for a nonprofessional audience. Using an example of ethnographic cinema from the collections of the EYE Film Institute Netherlands, she mentions that "the processes of digitization and compression contribute yet another layer of visual noise to a collection of already badly damaged films."⁵⁰ Thus, we could say that these artifacts are still hybrid but too blurry with regard to the specificity of individual properties.

Křiženecký's films, especially *Grand Consecration*, differ in two subtle but key respects. First, due to scanning in 4K resolution, the level of compression and digital noise is much lower. While a certain degree of loss obviously remains, as well as the tendency of all matter toward degradation, the formerly photochemical deformations become more visible. Simultaneously, the digital code turns out to be more of a general framework that simulates their specific appearance. The digitized color veil may only approximate its nitrate model, but the high-resolution digital image ensures that the photochemical features can be seen as structuring elements of the work, not as an indistinct mass of stains. Second, every single element that appears on the

---

48 Kim, *Between Film, Video, and the Digital*, 6–7.
49 Ibid., 9.
50 Groo, *Bad Film Histories*, 256.

colored surface can be extracted and put under individual scrutiny in video-editing software, thereby allowing for the examination of differences and connections between grain and pixel but also nuances between deformations intrinsic to the material and deformations arising from decay or external intervention. As this coexistence and interrelation of different analog and digital, intrinsic and extrinsic, human- and non-human-induced features of the moving image, as well as transformations of one type of element through those of the other, inevitably translates into the figurative universe of the films, it demands seeing *Digital Kříženecký* in the context of hybrid moving images that play with such intrusion on purpose.

Contemporary practices of appropriating archival or found footage deserve special attention precisely because they put the clashes between diverse material elements and images that once meant something different intentionally on display.[51] Despite its focus on experimental rather than archival appropriation, what Kim terms "transitional found footage practices" allows us to grasp the role of hybrid materiality in shaping the figurative aspects of *Digital Kříženecký*. Of interest are particularly films that work with early cinema and old nitrate prints and/or those that address the death of cinema issue. For example, Bill Morrison's film *Decasia: The State of Decay* (2002) may offer what Kříženecký as of yet lacks—an appropriation that would not let the material disfiguration go that far away from meaning, that would follow the folds of the crack-up in *Grand Consecration* and extend it to provoke new insight. And conversely, the encounter may show that even such canonical found footage artworks do not result primarily from artistic genius or traces of passing time—each *Decasia* needs a raw, autonomously creative piece of archival footage like *Grand Consecration* to establish itself in the first place. Seeing *Grand Consecration* through *Decasia* and vice versa allows us to perceive the ontological death of cinema as mutually involved with the aesthetics of the moving image.

Decasia and the Horror of Hybrid Matter

Once labeled "the most explicit cinematic homage to the death of film,"[52] Bill Morrison's *Decasia: The State of Decay* stands as a symptom of the transitional

---

[51] Kim, *Between Film, Video, and the Digital*, 145–95. Kim's notion of found footage's transitionality was preceded by Canadian filmmaker Malcolm Le Grice, who perceived found footage as the ideal bridge between analog and digital technologies. Malcolm Le Grice, *Experimental Cinema in the Digital Age* (London: BFI, 2001), 312.

[52] Chuck Tryon, *Reinventing Cinema: Movies in the Age of Media Convergence* (New Brunswick: Rutgers University Press, 2009), 73.

period between analog and digital—both in terms of what was meant to be saved and what was supposed to lie ahead.[53] This fascinating audiovisual symphony, consisting of deteriorating nitrate pictures and accompanied by Michael Gordon's apocalyptic music, unveils the forces of decay and rot that penetrate into the figurative content of nitrate films. It creates a physical feeling of watching the people, places, and things we know vanishing before our eyes, yet without disappearing altogether. The film has been appearing frequently in the death of cinema debates[54] and also influenced discussions within archival circles: whenever one feels the urge to digitize or even restore decomposing archival footage, especially of the nitrate era, shades of this film cannot help but reemerge. *Decasia* reminds us of the extent to which the figurative and conceptual value of a film can change when the images delve into the depths of filmic matter. The indexical bond to the once photographed reality is put under permanent threat—in a perverse conjecture of Bazin's mummy complex, it is time that triumphs over film rather than the other way around.[55]

This destructive impulse is not exclusive to the photochemical film, let alone nitrate prints. Of course, Morrison assembled his film solely out of archival footage on nitrate film stock, but the material shape of the prints he used varies greatly. Not all of them have their origin in the so-called silent era—some were allegedly produced as late as the 1950s.[56] Despite being smoothed out by montage and immersed in the same black and white through duplication, the differences in the level of decay at times shine through. Furthermore, the appearance of the footage was not insignificantly determined by Morrison's use of an optical printer for duplication. The

---

[53] Other symptomatic archival/found footage films of this era include *Lyrical Nitrate* (Lyrisch Nitraat; Peter Delpeut, 1991), *Transparences* (Trasparenze; Yervant Gianikian and Angela Ricci Lucchi, 1998), *Crack, Brutal, Grief* (R. Bruce Elder, 2000), *Passio* (Paolo Cherchi Usai, 2006). For later "death of cinema" films, see *Chemical Intervention in (Film) History* (Jürgen Reble, 2019) or *The Philosophy of Horror: A Symphony of Film Theory* (Péter Lichter and Bori Máté, 2020).

[54] For analyses specifically related to the "death of cinema" issue, see, for example, Doane, "The Indexical and the Concept of Medium Specificity"; Sean Cubitt, "The Shadow," *MIRAJ Moving Image Research and Art Journal* 2, no. 2 (2013): 187–97; Michael Betancourt, "Dread Mechanics: The Sublime Terror of Bill Morrison's Decasia (2002)," *Bright Lights Film Journal*, January 14, 2015, accessed December 31, 2022, https://brightlightsfilm.com/dread-mechanics-the-sublime-terror-of-bill-morrisons-decasia-2002/; Bernd Herzogenrath, "Decasia. The Matter | Image: Film is also a Thing," in *The Films of Bill Morrison: Aesthetics of the Archive*, ed. Bernd Herzogenrath (Amsterdam: Amsterdam University Press, 2017), 84–96.

[55] For the issues of temporality in Morrison's films, see: Matthew Levine, "A Poetic Archeology of Cinema: The Films of Bill Morrison," *Found Footage Magazine* 1, no. 1 (2015): 6–15.

[56] Betancourt, "Dread Mechanics."

optical printer is a device that "re-photographs the image on an existing, processed film element onto unexposed, new film stock."[57] Unlike the contact printer, "an image of the source element is projected through a lens onto the emulsion of the destination stock, without any physical contact between the two."[58] While the duplication results in "a significant loss in contrast, definition and (if applicable) color saturation,"[59] it allows for the introduction of special effects such as dissolves, mattes, or slow/fast motion—this is where the hypnotic glacial movement in *Decasia* comes from.[60] Thanks to the optical printer, it is even harder to distinguish whether we really see the archival films in their "Model Image" state, especially considering that most of the prints—similar to the vintage prints with Křiženecký's films—are nowadays impossible to project. Also, the film was digitized in order to edit to Michael Gordon's score[61] and distributed not only on 35 mm film and as a multi-screen installation but later also as a digital file,[62] a form in which it is increasingly likely to be watched—this way, even a film that is supposedly tied to the photochemical condition seals its hybridity. Sean Cubitt describes this multiplicity of degrading materialities quite convincingly:

> the clash of the slicing of time into frames in film and frame-by-frame scanning, and the furring of rot that pierces through the tight-wound film; both of which are crisscrossed by the step-motion that punctuates Morrison's account of their movement, and the interlace that electronic imaging brings into play. Add to these the micro-temporality of compression and decompression, and the vicissitudes of the circulation of moving images via the Internet, and surprising new effects appear.[63]

Crucially, though, this hybrid decay also translates into the figuration of a distinctive fictional world—a world that leaves signs of recognizable reality yet is always already infiltrated by elements of obscurity. As Michael Betancourt

---

[57] Leo Enticknap, *Film Restoration: The Culture and Science of Audiovisual Heritage* (London: Palgrave Macmillan, 2013), 96.
[58] Ibid., 97.
[59] Ibid.
[60] The optical printer allowed him to re-photograph each frame multiple times. For the creative possibilities of the optical printer in avant-garde cinema, see: John Powers, "A DIY Come-On: A History of Optical Printing in Avant-Garde Cinema," *Cinema Journal* 57, no. 4 (2018): 71–95.
[61] This paradox is investigated by Nessa Johnston: Nessa Johnston, "Sounding Decay in the Digital Age: 'Audio-Visions' of *Decasia* (2002) and *Lyrical Nitrate* (1991)," in *The Music and Sound of Experimental Film*, ed. Holly Rogers and Jeremy Barham (New York: Oxford University Press, 2017), 219–32.
[62] *Decasia* was first released on DVD in 2004 by plexifilm.
[63] Cubitt, "The Shadow."

argues, "what unites the materials of *Decasia* is the presentation of a world on film that is undergoing fragmentation, dissolution, decay"—most visibly in the "gaping white void" that obliterates what was once perhaps an interior in Japan.[64] The figures, places, and objects in front of us are being disintegrated by various "glitches" of filmic matter, but they are also continuously asserted as belonging to a discernible, often familiar reality—though it may not evoke a specific place in time. As Bernd Herzogenrath recalls, Morrison deliberately chooses sequences in which "the representation engages in direct contact with the material carrier."[65] For example, he refers to the scene that I already mentioned in the Introduction, where "a boxer is seen fighting against an amorphous blob (once presumably the image of a punching ball) threatening to swallow him."[66] There are numerous similar weird shapes throughout the film, sometimes even strangely metaphorical. In one instance, we see a newly born baby covered by grey-to-black mottles, reminiscent of plague spots or cancerous lesions. These emblems of destruction, watched in slow motion, indicate that even the beginning of existence is already infiltrated by forces of extinction, making any attempts to return to an imaginary before-state doomed to failure. In other words, the (dis)figurative force of material deformations that "twist faces, burn bodies, and cut holes" becomes inherent to the fictional world, and consequently to "our world that produced these images."[67] The inherent formal and diegetic linkage between the people, objects, and places seen in the film and the omnipresent physical distortions (as in the case of *Digital Kříženecký*, even more visible when watched in high-resolution picture quality), as well as crawling glitches of a digital kind, manifest in creating an entropic world hidden in the surface reality we inhabit.[68]

What is significant in terms of film aesthetics is that Betancourt delineates the world that emerges from this encounter through a language of terror and horror: "This horrific poetry brings us into a contemplation of just how small humans really are, how we inhabit an inhuman, alienating and indiscriminately hostile universe where all our endeavors will ultimately come to dust."[69] One wonders whether such inhuman horror can be extended into a concept that

---

[64] Michael Betancourt, *Glitch Art in Theory and Practice: Critical Failures and Post-Digital Aesthetics* (London: Routledge, 2017), 115.
[65] Herzogenrath, "Decasia," 86.
[66] Ibid.
[67] Betancourt, *Glitch Art in Theory and Practice*, 115.
[68] Ibid., 116–17. The role of *Decasia* and Morrison's other films in depicting an "inhospitable world" was also analyzed by Jennifer Fay, through a perspective resonant with contemporary debates on the Anthropocene. Jennifer Fay, *Inhospitable World: Cinema in the Time of the Anthropocene* (New York: Oxford University Press, 2018), 201–7.
[69] Betancourt, *Glitch Art in Theory and Practice*, 116.

would highlight the entanglement of figurative processes within the material phenomena in a language that evokes a specific aesthetic mode and, at the same time, a specific ontology beyond the death drive of cinema alone. Eugene Thacker's notion of the "world-without-us" could be the missing piece of the puzzle, standing not only for the universal decay of *Decasia* but also for the alien existence of the color veil in *Grand Consecration*—strangely twisted yet integral to the figurative world of the film. In the first volume of his "Horror of Philosophy" trilogy,[70] *In the Dust of This Planet* (2011), Thacker distinguishes three distinctive worlds. First, there is the "world-for-us" (the human-centric view of the world), then the "world-in-itself" (the world as it exists in essence), and finally, the "world-without-us": "the world-without-us lies somewhere in between, in a nebulous zone that is at once impersonal and horrific."[71] The world-without-us becomes a platform that allows us to speak of the withdrawn dimension of the world that, nevertheless, intrudes into our lived reality in the form of constitutive otherness.

In this regard, Thacker talks explicitly about "those blind spots" at the presuppositions of our philosophical inquiry (that is, the world being there for us) and the aim to express them "not in abstract concepts but in a whole bestiary of impossible life forms—mists, ooze, blobs, slime, clouds, and muck."[72] Curiously, these forms recall the weird shapes that emerge not only in classical or arthouse horror films, on which Thacker focuses, but even more literally on the surface of archival and found footage films (for instance, the blobs and mottles in *Decasia*). Examining their unfolding within (and prior to) the figurative space reveals the moving image as a world infiltrated by something that withdraws from us yet strives to make itself visible in this withdrawal. Archival footage constitutes a platform that highlights this struggle between two inherently intertwined yet mutually hostile dimensions. Thus, what if the "horror ontology" of Thacker speaks manifested directly in the filmic matter, as in the boxer's clash with the amorphous blob in *Decasia*? What if the color veil in *Grand Consecration* constituted a battleground of impossible life forms of the world-without-us, a space of ontological obscurity that, nevertheless, cannot be separated from the way we see the shadowy figures on the bridge? The crack-up, then, would serve as proof of a fundamental rupture between the world as we know it and the world that will always be beyond the scope of human thinking and action—yet a rupture that also confirms that one world cannot exist without the other.

---

[70] Eugene Thacker, *In the Dust of This Planet: Horror of Philosophy*, Vol. 1 (Winchester: Zero Books, 2011); Eugene Thacker, *Starry Speculative Corpse: Horror of Philosophy*, Vol. 2 (Winchester: Zero Books, 2015); Eugene Thacker, *Tentacles Longer Than Night: Horror of Philosophy*, Vol. 3 (Winchester: Zero Books, 2015).
[71] Thacker, *In the Dust of This Planet*, 11.
[72] Ibid., 14.

The crack-up actualizes in both *Decasia* and *Grand Consecration*; however, the difference between their weird shapes (besides the fact that one is in black and white and the other is in color) lies in their origin and unfolding. Whereas *Decasia*, as a work with artistic ambition, assembles shots with various cracks on purpose and then shapes them to evoke a certain aesthetic response, the crack-up in *Grand Consecration* arises unintentionally. One can only speculate in what form the film was seen by Kříženecký and the audience of the time, which depended significantly on technical conditions in each specific exhibition venue (particularly on lighting), but thus far nothing suggests that the author employed color for artistic purposes. Even if it were a product of additional tinting or toning, it is highly dubious that such major concealment of visible figures by material actors would have been desired. There, the world-without-us intrudes accidentally, and without any artistic or archival guidance, it may just as quickly turn back into chaos. The opening seconds of the film are particularly telling in this matter—the image is governed by a multiplicity of bursting shapes and blurs that look as if they came from an abstract experimental film, and only pausing or slowing down can reveal that there are some people and objects amid the disarray. Throughout the film, there are brief instances, particularly toward the end, when the figures are more discernible, yet even when the yellowish-orange veil is at its most transparent, the crack-up is in a permanent risk of reversing this development, dissolving into the hybrid matter, and letting the world-without-us overflow everything else. How, then, can we contain and exploit this materialized death drive lying behind every effort to transform a cluster of material-technological elements into animated figurative images of our world? How can we participate in an unfolding of the crack-up that is simultaneously emancipatory and terrifying? Instead of letting it overwhelm us, we need to examine it *from below*, which in this case means *frame by frame*. That is how the most aesthetically generative, weird shapes can be discovered.

Seeing the World-Without-Us Frame by Frame

To bracket this fluctuating and reversible unfolding of the crack-up in *Grand Consecration*, we need to inspect it "independently of [its] placement in a phase of motion."[73] As the film involves a rich multitude of material elements with varying effects on the figurative content, watching it in 24 frames per

---

[73] Mihaela Mihailova, Jen Bircher, Robert Bird, Mariana Johnson, Ian Bryce Jones, Ryan Pierson, Alla Gadassik, and Tim Palmer, "Teaching (Like) Hannah Frank (1984–2017): A Tribute," *The Moving Image: The Journal of the Association of Moving Image Archivists* 18, no. 1 (2018): 84–92.

second and in its feeble length of 46 seconds runs the risk of engulfing the spectator with abstract noise—some of the individual specificities, including the figures walking on the bridge, may get lost. For example, the color veil evokes an impression of continuous, indivisible flux when watched "properly," but the individual frames tell a slightly different story—when examined in the digital software, the nuances of different colors, from the clearest yellow to the most degraded red, become more pronounced, as well as the degree to which they are disclosing or unclosing the diegetic reality. Thus, echoing the materialist aesthetics of animated cartoons conceived by Hannah Frank, we should "inaugurate a study of the single frame, the single document, in which the tiniest of details—a brushstroke, a shadow, an errant speck of dust—is freighted with historical and, ultimately, political weight."[74] In her account, the instances of fuzziness, distortion, and discoloration Bazin talks about are not barriers that we pass to satisfy our need for the material object but parts and parcels of the image's own materiality.[75] Considering that the weird shapes in Kříženecký's film are no mere "mishaps" or details that seem out of place[76] but much more encompassing phenomena, much more inherent to its technological and aesthetic character, they should thus be guaranteed special attention. As our main interest is the emergence of the crack-up from the depths of filmic matter, choosing the first seven frames for a closer view seems appropriate. They show the crack-up at its most fragile, the material (particularly color) phenomena at their most diverse, and the filmed figures and objects at their most vulnerable, and therefore bring the horrors of the intruding world-without-us to the spotlight (Figures 1.5–1.11).

As we can see from the stills, the unpredictable dance of colors creates an involuntary veil, an alternative surface that, nevertheless, cracks from within: "volcano replaces the porcelain."[77] The crack-up actualizes between figuration and materiality in the form of the yellowish-orange veil, which varies in its shades and hues, and any potential consistency is ruined by the intruding red blots and clouds of rot. If the crack-up cannot be ascribed to artistic appropriation, as in *Decasia*, or to any other intentional intervention, and there is a strong suspicion that it has always been present in the image, how can we make sure that it does not become reduced to noise or disposable decay? Using the words of Gilles Deleuze, what are we supposed to do "if the order of the surface is itself cracked, how could it not itself break up, how is

---

[74] Hannah Frank, *Frame by Frame: A Materialist Aesthetics of Animated Cartoons* (Berkeley: University of California Press, 2019), 15.
[75] Ibid., 48.
[76] Ibid., 52.
[77] Gilles Deleuze, "Porcelain and Volcano," in *The Logic of Sense* (London: The Athlone Press, 1990), 154–61.

Keep That Image Burning 53

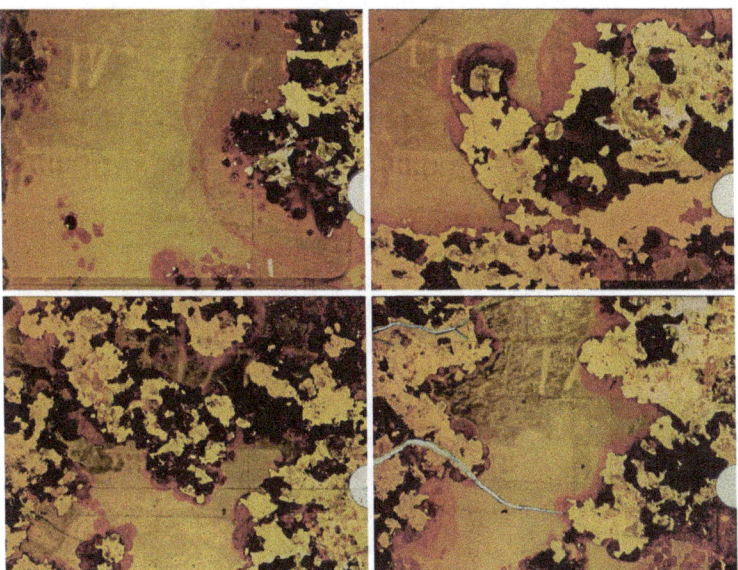

Figures 1.5–1.8 *Grand Consecration of the Emperor Franz I Bridge* (Slavnostní vysvěcení mostu císaře Františka I.; 1901, source: nitrate print) © Národní filmový archiv.

it to be prevented from precipitating destruction, even if it meant losing all accompanying benefits—the organization of language and even life itself"?[78]

The answer I propose is that we must imagine the color veil not as a cipher of death, destruction, and the world-without-us in general but as a plurality of color modes of which each one keeps the figurative and material elements living and dying on their own measure. Contemplating their play of differences frame by frame, one may, for example, discover the yellowish-orange veil as a semi-transparent "baroque" texture, transcending the depth-surface boundary and spreading out the figurative and material elements across an immanent horizontal axis. In the case of additionally tinted or toned films, we could speculate whether the applied colors originally fulfilled sensual or indexical, spectacular or naturalistic, emotional or realistic functions,[79] but here, the existence of the color veil predates its essence.

---

[78] Ibid., 157.
[79] Jennifer Lynn Peterson, "Rough Seas: The Blue Waters of Early Nonfiction Film," in *The Colour Fantastic: Chromatic Worlds of Silent Cinema*, ed. Giovanna Fossati et al. (Amsterdam: Amsterdam University Press, 2018), 75–93.

Therefore, we must not stipulate a hierarchy of effects and functions and instead show how the veil contributes to the distribution of elements on the surface of the image. Not only does the texture stage a dialectical tension between the diffused veil and the forms in the background, but it also enacts a multitude of material forms with their own ways of making their dying perceptible and resonant. Thanks to the filtering veil, the anachronistic yet persistent features of the original nitrate film stock (for instance, the shifting single round perforations), the damages imposed by the passing of time (scratches, tears, and burns, as well as products of color degradation), and the occasional pixelation caused by digital compression (visible while enlarging the frames or jumping between them in the media player) intertwine without losing their distinctive qualities. The remaining silhouettes of the figures and objects lose their privileged position and get swallowed by the veil as well—what they lack in discernible individual characteristics, they gain by being enmeshed in the material surface of the film strip, becoming one of the things waiting to be "touched" by the grazing eye of the spectator. Thus, the respective scene gains an aesthetic shape that is not as chiseled as in *Decasia* but all the more diverse precisely because of the ambiguity arising from the unintended and unpredictable.

Conversely, the red color, oscillating between lighter and darker tones, signals the breaking point at which the material carrier stops being a membrane onto the world-for-us and intrudes upon it like a disease, manifesting in small circular dots, which are often organized into denser clusters. Again, one can encounter such blots within the decaying tinted or toned films (though rarely in this scope and frequency), but they can be at least identified as signs of degradation within an otherwise intentionally designed and uniformed color structure. In *Grand Consecration*, there is no such hierarchy between purposeful and unpurposeful color elements, and the yellowish-orange color cannot be totally exempt from decay, so the role of red blots in the aesthetic function of the film cannot be automatically perceived as secondary or derivative. As the color veil's origin remains unknown, the red dots may no longer be recognized as aliens within a prescribed color veil but reinterpreted as inherent features of the multilayered color world of every single frame. Furthermore, we cannot underestimate their figurative function: for example, in the fifth frame (Figure 1.9), we can see how the assemblies of red dots encircle two characters on the bridge—symbolically highlighting their potential annihilation by otherworldly forces yet also foregrounding them as discernible subjects within the diegesis. The closer we zoom in on the red blots, the more we are inclined to acknowledge how even the most homogeneous surface is made out of tiny dots (grains or pixels) that can easily turn into something else and may potentially lead to redrawing the surface of the image. Deciding where to put the red dots would then mean deciding which figures and objects in the background should keep living and which ones should die.

Finally, in a few places, the mixing and blurring of colors with the figures gives way to sprawling clouds that seem as if they were indifferent both to the image's content and the speculative meaning of the veil. At this point, the world-without-us, in its formlessness and color indistinguishability, fossilizes the swarming of figurative and material signs on the veil and dissolves them into the abstract humming of the geological world. However, even these seemingly dead zones of the image reveal a peculiar double movement, with the darker colors spiraling toward inert matter and the lighter ones toward a certain kind of X-ray vision, which reveals that the basest level of color is still that (curious) yellow, not black and white. The veil cannot be scraped away, regardless of whether by artists, archivists, or ravages of time, and if we wanted to get closer to the world we know (or once knew), we would have to erase all the figures and objects along with it. Maybe moments such as this prove that even when the death drive of cinema is reaching toward its return to the inorganic state, certain capacities for figuration still remain.

Where is the place of the human in this material universe? At first glance, the features of the world-for-us appear hijacked from their natural environment—buried deep within the phantasmagoria of whirling colors, appearing "so ancient [they are] alien."[80] The contours of the bridge, flags waving in the wind, and the occasional passing figures do not belong to the three-dimensional space they once inhabited; instead, they are immersed in the multi-color assemblage of the print's surface. Even when the figures are at their most visible (as in Figure 1.11), they are no more than anonymous walking suits appearing or disappearing. The model situation of Frank's frame-by-frame method thereby gets reversed: now we do not discover flies zigzagging across the screen, nor even accidental brushstrokes of the animators,[81] but the human figures who once served as protagonists of the film. Thanks to the possibility to zoom in on particular places in the frame, enabled by digital technology, the people can be "rescued" from being annihilated by the folds of the color veil, despite the pixelation that zooming brings even with better-quality digital files. Later in the film, when the number of people crossing the bridge grows exponentially, lots of things can be discovered within the mass, notably the slight differences in the behavior of the characters toward the apparatus or, by extension, toward the unseen

---

[80] Eugene Thacker, *After Life* (Chicago and London: The University of Chicago Press, 2010), 2.
[81] Frank, *Frame by Frame*, 51–2.

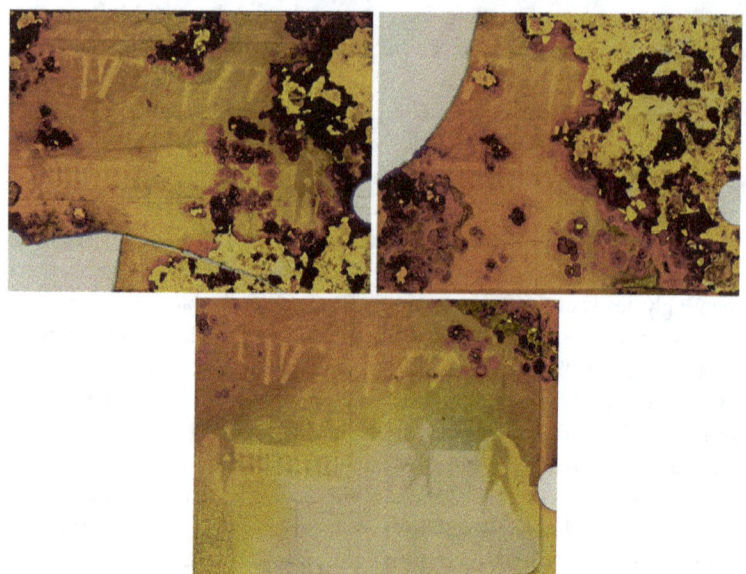

Figures 1.9–1.11 *Grand Consecration of the Emperor Franz I Bridge* (Slavnostní vysvěcení mostu císaře Františka I.; 1901, source: nitrate print) © Národní filmový archiv.

and yet unthinkable deformations of the world they occupy. And maybe one day we could find even the Austro-Hungarian emperor Franz Joseph I, who was supposedly present at the consecration.

Coda: The Death of Cinema Extended into Eternity

The examination of Kříženecký's *Grand Consecration* taught us that even in its most dangerous phase, the crack-up does not equal pure destruction. It kneads the figurative and material elements into weird shapes that reconfigure our idea of what the death of cinema truly means. Watching the destruction of nitrate film through a veil, through a web of blobs, blotches, and wounds that appears all the more diversified due to the unmotivated presence of colors, enables us to finally appreciate the death of cinema and the horror ontology of matter in the plural, as a mix of elements, each of which has its own way of dying. The first seven frames affirm the color veil as a matrix, with yellowish-orange, red, and black motives as distinctive modes of distributing the film surface among figurative and material, photochemical and digital, extrinsic and intrinsic, human and nonhuman entities. This hybridity plays a noteworthy aesthetic role in multiplying the spectrum of elements that can participate in figuration and enacting numerous interminglings between figurative content and technological properties that produce weird shapes of the most terrifying order.

The mysterious presence of the color veil in *Grand Consecration* may not yet have a clearly known origin, but the hypothesis about a unique, possibly even undesired quality of the Lumière nitrate print stipulates that any hopes of separation between the material carrier and figurative content are doomed right from the start—possibly even before the specific film was developed. Although it would be foolish to say that the National Film Archive presents the film exactly as it was, the veil of distortions without any predefined cause has once again brought attention to the fundamental nonidentity of film—its chronic indecision in what it is going to be, either in terms of which material components support it or what (or whether at all) it is supposed to represent. This way, we can rethink the tension between figurative and material elements, visible in experimental found footage films such as *Decasia*, as inseparable from the struggle that has always been part of the endlessly variable existence of the moving image and does not necessarily have to be added to it. If there is anything original or authentic in *Digital Kříženecký*, it is its variations of the crack-up, and the available digital technology makes this quality better discernible than ever before.

The digitized *Grand Consecration* becomes another emblem not only of the death of cinema but also of what comes ahead. The ability to examine the operations of inhuman and hybrid filmic matter, as well as to search for the remnants of the human world, surrenders death to eternal repetition. One can hear the echoes of Nietzsche, Deleuze, and Blanchot, or, more specifically, the good old Godardian dictum, "cinema is ending, but never stops ending."[82] Nevertheless, *Digital Kříženecký* employs this perpetual motion of destruction in a less metaphoric, more literal sense. Katherine Groo employs the figure of fire to describe this ontological role of death and destruction for film history and theory, stating that rather than trying to overcome or ward against the flames of film history, we should "let it burn."[83] The case of *Grand Consecration* provokes us toward radicalizing this gesture as its weird shapes wait to be replayed, remixed, and pushed forward. The color veil signals not only the inevitable death of cinema but also its possible

---

[82] Quoted from: Hillary Radner and Alistair Fox, *Raymond Bellour: Cinema and the Moving Image* (Edinburgh: Edinburgh University Press, 2018), 80.

[83] Groo, "Let It Burn."

"prolongation," or "extension into eternity," as Johannes Binotto would say.[84] Rather than merely expressing fascination with these destructive impulses or even fetishizing them, we should intervene—open the digital files in our video-editing software, discern and isolate the places that may seem the most threatened by material evisceration, and seek to turn their death(s) into an alternative figuration of a life force to come. Since we are dealing with colors, we should, for instance, change the settings of our screens to explore the sustainability of the veil with different shades and hues. Echoing the title of Rainer Kohlberger's experimental film, we should ensure that the images "keep burning."[85]

---

[84] Johannes Binotto, "Tributes—Pulse: A Requiem for the 20th Century: Death | Drive | Image," in *The Films of Bill Morrison: Aesthetics of the Archive*, ed. Bernd Herzogenrath (Amsterdam: Amsterdam University Press, 2017), 241.

[85] I am referring to the film *keep that dream burning* (Rainer Kohlberger, 2017).

2

Do Archivists Dream of Electric Horses?

Static Electricity and the Quadruple Logic of Indexicality

May 10, 1908. The first day of the horse races at Velká Chuchle near Prague, captured on film by Jan Kříženecký. At first glance, we see a relatively straightforward attempt to report what is going on during a notable social event: crowds of people marching toward the stadium, horses and jockeys getting ready, audience in-between watching the action and goofing around, honorary persons being photographed, the fury of the sport itself. Nevertheless, there are other, nonhuman actors entering the image and congesting the visible world. Black-and-white dots, scratches, and holes all point to the fact that the film covered a long distance in time to get to the present form. What also comes into view are curious lightning bolts that sometimes hit even the horse racers. Could these marks transform our notion of the technological and aesthetic reality of the filmed occasion? (Figures 2.1–2.4)

While features such as the yellowish-orange veil on the vintage print of *Grand Consecration* clearly distort the figurative content of the films, others, such as the lightning bolts in *The First Day of the Spring Races of Prague* (První den jarních dostihů pražských; 1908, source: original negative), are more subtle, almost waiting to be discovered (Figure 2.4). They appear even in films that survived in a remarkable technical condition with a beautiful and clear photographic image. These signs gain particular visibility in the digitized original negatives, inverted into a positive form, in which the photographic qualities (soft black-and-white contrast, depth of field, and grain of the image) are preserved to the fullest extent.[1] Again, the decision not to retouch was significant as it would make the photographic features

---

[1] Jeanne Pommeau and Jiří Anger, "The Digitization of Jan Kříženecký's Films," *Iluminace* 31, no. 1 (2019): 105. See also Jeanne Pommeau, "The Digitisation of Kříženecký's Films" [videocommentary], in *Filmy Jana Kříženeckého/The Films of Jan Kříženecký*, ed. Jiří Anger, DVD/Blu-ray (Praha: Národní filmový archiv, 2019).

Figures 2.1–2.4 *The First Day of the Spring Races of Prague* (První den jarních dostihů pražských; 1908, source: original negative [digitally inverted]) © Národní filmový archiv.

of the original negatives disappear.[2] The digitization of the films "as they exist today" does not necessarily make them more "authentic," but it draws attention to how even the slightest technological feature can transform the aesthetic effects of film and also its presumed bond to reality or, more specifically, to the original event that was being filmed.

Along with the signature round sprocket holes or remnants of fuzz,[3] marks of electrical discharge in *Spring Races* are windows onto the real world of the Lumière film technology, which were hard to get rid of even if one wanted to. Seeing that the amount of film stock was very limited, especially for filmmakers who had to buy all their materials from abroad (such as Jan Kříženecký),[4] the operators must have thought twice before

---

[2] Pommeau and Anger, "The Digitization of Jan Kříženecký's Films," 106.

[3] The Lumière film stock had one pair of perforations (one round sprocket hole on each side of the film frame), instead of the four pairs of rectangular perforations that became standard. The remnants of fuzz derive from the velvet strip placed at the projector gate. Ibid., 105.

[4] According to the invoices preserved in the National Technical Museum Prague, Kříženecký bought film stock from the Lumière brothers at least three times—twice in 1898, then once in 1901.

doing multiple takes. Also, creative postproduction as we know it today was practically nonexistent, so editing out frames with undesirable elements was a risky endeavor, particularly when they covered a sequence of images.[5] Remember the words of Bolesław Matuszewski: "Perhaps the cinematograph does not give history in its entirety, but at least what it does deliver is incontestable and of an absolute truth. Ordinary photography admits of retouching, to the point of transformation. But try to retouch, in an identical way for each figure, these thousand or twelve hundred, almost microscopic negatives . . . !"[6]

From our current perspective, this comment may seem naïve when there are so many possibilities to manipulate images according to our needs and when the idea of an "incontestable and absolute truth" sounds ridiculous, but in one key respect, it can still teach us a lesson. The "reality" that we see on the screen does not result only from verisimilitude but also from respecting the technological conditions that shaped the filmed event. From this viewpoint, *Digital Křiženecký* may draw its connection to past reality from two seemingly contradictory things. First, we must recognize the filmed figures, objects, and places as belonging to a lived world that was once captured by the camera. Second, we must acknowledge that due to the nonintrusive approach to digitization, the signs of film technology used during the production process remained visible in the image.

This chapter aims to investigate how the inconspicuous physical signs in *Digital Křiženecký*, most notably the lightning bolts as the marks of static electricity (the so-called "static marks"), can actualize the crack-up in images that visibly allude to their "indexical" relationship to the lived reality. The indexicality of film, generally understood as a causal connection between the object of reality and its photographic reproduction, remains one of the defining concepts that serve to distinguish what cinema was and how (or whether at all) it persists in the (post)digital age. Despite many accounts spelling its demise, indexicality still haunts the contemporary production of moving images and not just those shot on analog film.[7] Processes such

---

[5] On "provisional" forms of editing in early cinema, see, for instance, Scott Higgins, "The Silent Screen, 1895–1927: Editing," in *Editing and Special/Visual Effects*, ed. Charlie Keil and Kristen Whissel (New Brunswick: Rutgers University Press, 2016), 22–36, or Genevieve Yue, *Girl Head: Feminism and Film Materiality* (New York: Fordham University Press, 2021), 73–101.

[6] Boleslas Matuszewski, "A New Source of History," *Film History* 7, no. 3 (1995): 323.

[7] See, for example, Mary Ann Doane, "The Indexical and the Concept of Medium Specificity," *Differences* 18, no. 1 (2007): 128–52; D. N. Rodowick, *The Virtual Life of Film* (Harvard: Harvard University Press, 2007); Dan Streible, "Moving Image History and the F-Word; Or, 'Digital Film' Is an Oxymoron," *Film History* 25, no. 1–2 (2013): 227–35; Miriam De Rosa and Vinzenz Hediger, "Post-what? Post-when? A Conversation on the 'Posts' of Post-media and Post-cinema," *Cinéma & Cie* 16, no. 26–27 (2016):

as digital restoration, online circulation, or artistic appropriation give birth to various forms of hybrid moving images that make us see formerly photochemical films and their supposedly privileged bond to reality in a different light. Among other things, these forms make us consider the role of specific technological agents in determining the recognizability of profilmic reality and the extent to which their visible presence in the image is desirable.

Whereas in *Grand Consecration*, any indexicality depended on a temporary resolution of the horrors of filmic matter, the digitized films with comparatively clear image quality let any signs of materiality emerge within a recognizable fictional world. As I argue, *Spring Races* and other films by Křiženecký that preserve clear contours of the world that was once photographically reproduced yet also contain multiple marks of material intervention neither erase indexicality nor do they necessarily transform it. Rather, they show it in a kind of convex mirror that highlights the concept's fundamental ambiguity. The indexicality of film involves the capacity to preserve "real" figures, objects, and places that were once captured by the camera, as well as the material-technological conditions that allowed for such capture. What happens when one form of indexicality starts to interfere with the existence of the other? When even seemingly nonessential elements such as the static marks disturb the purity of the represented world or even impact upon the figurative processes and aesthetic effects of the films, indexicality reveals itself in its multifaceted form.

The moment when the bifurcations of indexicality become visible is also the moment in which the crack-up finds itself at home. This time, though, its deformative impulses are more delicate and dependent on a more or less coherent nonfictional representation of reality. The crack-up's reliance on indexical reality becomes even more convoluted due to the fact that it owes its origin to a phenomenon that is technological as well as natural—electricity. The questions are: Wherein lies our sense of reality that was originally captured and preserved on film? Do static marks disturb or deform this reality, or do they constitute a surplus that the film medium adds to the represented world? Are they signs of the irreducibility of a spontaneous encounter between reality and the technological dispositif of its time, or does their intrinsic relation to electricity indicate a grounding of any realistic representation in the entwined worlds of nature and technology? The following analysis includes four parts: a theoretical grounding of

9–20; Christopher Ball, Meghanne Barker, Elizabeth Edwards, Tomáš Kolich, W. J. T. Mitchell, Daniel Morgan, and Constantine V. Nakassis, "Opening Up the Indexicality of the Image, Again: A Virtual Roundtable," *Semiotic Review*, 2020, accessed December 31, 2022, https://semioticreview.com/ojs/index.php/sr/article/view/62.

the indexicality of film, a distinction between various indexical signs, an outlining of the distinctive indexical function of static marks, and an analysis of Křiženecký's film *The First Day of the Spring Races of Prague* and the weird shapes of horse racers hit by lightning (or, in a shortened punchline, "electric horses"). The answers to the aforementioned questions will, however, be only provisional and lead in an "and . . . and" rather than "either-or" direction.

Cinematic Indexicality and Its Relation to Reality

The notion of film as an indexical medium has its theoretical roots in the thoughts of André Bazin, particularly in his essay "Ontology of the Photographic Image" (1945). To build upon the previous chapter, Bazin argues that our belief in the causal link between reality and its photographic reproduction does not reside primarily in the iconic resemblance between photographed and real objects but in the automatic, apparently noninterventionist, and unbiased character of the photographic record. The photographic and, by extension, cinematic image may not exactly reproduce the object "as it was," but none of our critical objections can deny that the things we see in the picture were once present to the anonymous eye of the camera and that, by means of our act of watching, they affirm and prolong their existence.[8] The principle of indexicality[9] ensures that the image establishes a connection between the past encounter and the present spectatorial experience. No matter how stylized the image appears or to what extent it succumbs to decay, it links the reality that was being captured in the past to the present moment of recognizing which aspects of this original event prevailed and how they conform to our current perception of reality.

This primacy of indexicality constitutes a framework that allows us to understand any photographic image as real or realistic. As Dudley Andrew, one of Bazin's chief interpreters, claims, "realism to [Bazin] is not primarily a stylistic category. It is an automatic effect of photographic technology drawing on an irrational psychological desire."[10] For Bazin, the mechanical causality

---

[8] André Bazin, "Ontology of the Photographic Image," in *What Is Cinema?* (Montreal: caboose, 2009), 3–12.
[9] As indicated in Chapter 1, the one who contextualized Bazin's thought in semiotics was Peter Wollen, see Peter Wollen, "Ontology and Materialism in Film," in *Readings and Writings: Semiotic Counter-Strategies* (London: Verso, 1982), 189–207.
[10] Dudley Andrew, "Foreword to the 2004 Edition," in André Bazin, *What Is Cinema?* Vol. 1 (Berkeley: University of California Press, 2005), xv. See also Philip Rosen, *Change Mummified: Cinema, Historicity, Theory* (Minneapolis and London: University of Minnesota Press, 2001), 3–41; Dudley Andrew, *What Cinema Is! Bazin's Quest and*

between the object and its reproduction functions as indexical only insofar as it "satisfies our appetite for illusion by means of mechanical reproduction in which there is no human agency at work"—the reason why photography fulfills our obsession with realism lies "not in the resulting work but rather in its genesis."[11] To put it more precisely, we read images as indexical because they fulfill our longing for presence and our desire to preserve moments that we can no longer experience directly. As we affirm the bond between film and reality, and also between subject and object, we are able to reassure our place in the lived world as perceiving subjects who can control the ravages of time.

Nonetheless, as Philip Rosen reminds us, this psychological complex (which Bazin generally calls the "mummy complex") is, in essence, contradictory. On the one hand, the specific contours of reality are halted in time and preserved in the form of rectangular frames, in a way that lets us experience the real without direct participation and within a controlled environment. On the other hand, the reality that we perceive on screen is itself taking place in time, and therefore it can "paradoxically open the spectating subject to the concrete, hence the flow of time and the fact of change."[12] Therefore, our belief in the indexicality of the film medium derives from our trust not only that the moment once happened but also that its capture exists in time. This paradox may cause that the indexed reality may include more elements than it was meant to be preserved: those that infiltrated into the image due to aging (for example, those white dots, scratches, and holes in *Spring Races*) or those that come from the film's manufacturing, shooting, processing, or printing (for instance, perforations, fuzz, and static marks).

Among other things, the paradox of "change mummified" effectively brings to question which components and properties of the image enable the film to be perceived as a historical document of the real. Does such a document result solely from a credible approximation of the filmed objects, or also from elements that were added to it by means of the production process? Daniel Morgan focuses on Bazin's argument that "photography has an effect upon us of a natural phenomenon, like a flower or snowflake whose beauty is inseparable from its earthly origin,"[13] or, similarly, "that photography plays

---

Its Charge (New York: Wiley-Blackwell, 2010); Burke Hilsabeck, "The 'Is' in *What Is Cinema?*: On André Bazin and Stanley Cavell," *Cinema Journal* 55, no. 2 (2016): 25–42; Jeff Fort, "André Bazin's Eternal Returns: An Ontological Revision," *Film-Philosophy* 25, no. 1 (2021): 42–61.

[11] Bazin, "Ontology of the Photographic Image," 6.
[12] Rosen, *Change Mummified*, 39.
[13] Bazin, "Ontology of the Photographic Image," 7.

a real part in natural creation, rather than substituting for it."[14] Quotes such as these would imply a continuity between photography and objects in the world, and thus that its creation adds something to the captured reality rather than just copying it or alluding to it. In other words, the camera does not only represent the figures, objects, and places in front of it—by the very act of making a recognizable technological reproduction of reality, it creates a surplus that enriches our vision of this reality with a distinctive nonhuman perspective.

Consequently, Křiženecký's film *Spring Races* does not have to be understood as realistic just because it is an actuality, a supposedly authentic report on a current event—accidental looks into the camera, as well as many physical details that come into view, evoke a certain reality effect on their own terms. Denis Diderot's concept of the "little wart" is the perfect example of how an unintended, seemingly unaesthetic detail contributes to the perception of realism.

> A painter executes a head on his canvas. The outlines are all strong, bold and regular; it is a collection of the most rare and most perfect traits. Looking at it, I feel respect, admiration and awe. [. . .] But let the artist show me a small scar on the forehead of this portrait, a mole on one of the temples, a barely perceptible cut on the lower lip, and although it seemed an imaginary portrait only a moment before, now it becomes the likeness of a real person.[15]

These details appear so inconspicuous, banal, and pointless that they take the work of art away from the ideal and the imaginary toward the experience of so-called life. Whereas Diderot considers such details as affirmative of the writer's skill,[16] if we followed Bazin's logic, the "little warts" would account for indexes of mechanical, nonhuman reproduction of reality. In both cases, weird shapes, as long as they do not significantly cloud the contours of figures we know from our everyday perception, add realism to the image, not subtract it. Framing the static marks as surplus elements of indexical reality would therefore make sense; the question is what these signs actually point to.

---

[14] Ibid., 9. Daniel Morgan, "Rethinking Bazin: Ontology and Realist Aesthetics," *Critical Inquiry* 32, no. 3 (2006): 443–81.
[15] Denis Diderot, "The Two Friends from Bourbonne," in *Rameau's Nephew and Other Works* (Indianapolis: Hackett, 2001), 244.
[16] Noa Merkin, "Little Patch of Yellow: On the Detail in Film" (PhD diss., The University of Chicago, 2020), 26.

Between Trace and Deixis

In this context, it is worth pointing out that the term "index," coined by semiotician Charles Sanders Peirce,[17] has always been torn between two different, seemingly incompatible meanings. Mary Ann Doane demonstrates that the original index has two definitions: index as trace and index as deixis.[18] First, the index as trace, exemplified by the footprint or the photograph, "implies a material connection between sign and object as well as an insistent temporality—the reproducibility of a past moment."[19] This understanding of the index necessarily aligns it with historicity—the notion that at one point the represented object actually existed—and as such, it also stresses the temporal distance that the sign had to cover to get from its origin to the present reception. Second, the index as deixis, "the pointing finger," "does exhaust itself in the moment of its implementation and is ineluctably linked to presence. There is always a gap between sign and object, and touch here is only figurative."[20] It is more like a gesture that expresses nothing but its own unfolding, that points to the context of the sign's occurrence and its impact on the signified object. While the interpretation of index as trace has been prevalent in film studies for many decades, examining its deictic function might help us imagine the "surplus" that film brings to reality by capturing it. This surplus may consist in diegetic details that seem out of place, weird gestures or looks, accidental interventions of figures and objects into the frame, but also in the intrusions of the filmic matter itself. As Peirce explains, some indices exceed the operation of merely guaranteeing that an object exists; they also show something of the object (for instance, the outline of a foot or the lines of a fingerprint). These signs do not just assure us that something once was; they enact the presence of a past moment in its physical unfolding.[21]

Given this chapter's focus on the impact of physical intrusions on cinematic reality, is there a way we could distinguish traces and deixes in the material dimension of Kříženecký's *Spring Races*? For Doane, the trace-deixis

---

[17] Charles Sanders Peirce, *The Essential Peirce: Selected Philosophical Writings*, Vol. 1, ed. Nathan Houser and Christian Kloesel (Bloomington: Indiana University Press, 1992).
[18] Doane, "The Indexical and the Concept of Medium Specificity."
[19] Ibid., 136.
[20] Ibid.
[21] Charles Sanders Peirce, *Collected Papers of Charles Sanders Peirce*, Vol. 4 (Cambridge: Harvard University Press, 1933), paras. 447–8. See also Katherine Groo, "Let It Burn: Film Historiography in Flames," *Discourse* 41, no. 1 (2019): 13. Sybille Krämer's distinction between "trace" and "index" is also relevant here. See also Sybille Krämer, *Medium, Messenger, Transmission: An Approach to Media Philosophy* (Amsterdam: Amsterdam University Press), 174–86.

duality serves to distinguish index as a trace of recognizable reality and index as a "hollowed-out sign," "limited to the assurance of an existence" and providing "no insight into the nature of its object"; it simply indicates that "something is 'there.'"[22] Katherine Groo, building upon Peirce's and Doane's arguments, claims that these hollowed-out signs assure the vulnerability of filmic matter to "a whole range of external forces, interactions, and accidents."[23] Do the dots, dust, and scratches necessarily correspond to these hollowed-out signs? Although they are extrinsic both to the film stock and the reality that was initially filmed on camera, they are firmly tied to a film's historicity: "the properties of film that contribute to its being historically meaning bearing and the particular relationship that film bears to past time."[24] Thus, they contribute to our belief in the existence of film in time. The dots, dust, and scratches in particular have established themselves as markers of the distance footage covered to get to the present state; would it not be possible, then, to treat them as traces of past reality? In comparison, signs that point to the film's production process, such as the static marks, tend to be less immediately recognizable and attributable to meaning on their own. Although they tell us almost nothing about the reality that was meant to be depicted, they participate in the expressive event that is the film's coming into being. Due to this link to presence, their deictic quality should be considered.

Furthermore, how can the duality between traces and deixes account for the moments when the filmic matter and the figurative dimension of the image encounter each other, that is, when the crack-up emerges? Groo talks about bringing the "internal" features of ethnographic cinema—its images, cinematography, and compositional patterns—into conversation with its "external" qualities, with the "rips, tears, and textures."[25] She pursues this argument by "comparing the landscapes we see in ethnographic cinema to the landscape, or physical surface, that film itself actually is."[26] She also mentions a few examples of archival films in which the communication between figurative and material landscapes affects the aesthetic meaning, such as *Between the Nile and the Congo* (Tusschen Nijl en Congo; Paul Julien, ca 1930), where a flock of swarming locusts on the horizon gradually fills the frame and creates a texture that "imitates the shimmering pockmarks of

---

[22] Doane, "The Indexical and the Concept of Medium Specificity," 133, 135.
[23] Groo, "Let It Burn," 13.
[24] Katherine Groo, *Bad Film Histories: Ethnography and the Early Archive* (Minneapolis: University of Minnesota Press, 2019), 8.
[25] Ibid., 42.
[26] Ibid.

celluloid deterioration."[27] As intriguing as Groo's account is, it would make the weird shapes of the crack-up virtually indistinguishable as long as matter collides with the represented reality. Could the electric horses show us what makes the weird shapes caused by deictic physical signs different from the weird shapes induced by material traces?

To address the questions above, I propose a quadruple logic of indexicality, in which the original double logic is multiplied by the existence of two interrelated registers that can be indexed—one related to the represented reality that is portrayed in the figurative content and the other to the technological reality that springs to the surface through material interventions. Thus, the manifestations of indexicality in the most transparent and "realistic" of Kříženecký's digitized films are conditioned by two blocs of concepts—figuration-materiality and trace-deixis—whose mutual relationship conditions the appearance of the crack-up. Let us return to the opening description of *Spring Races* and start with its figurative content. What we see on a superficial level are traces of what happened during the horse race. Tracking and panning shots, allowed by the additions Kříženecký made to the original Lumière Cinématographe,[28] alternate with static shots, scenes of everyday life and the audience intertwine with scenes of the races, in order to construct a realist quasi-narrative of the event.[29] Yet, there are also profilmic moments that do not conform to this narrative entirely: men swiftly withdrawing from the camera, photographers jumping into the frame, or blurred horses jumping over fences. Such moments may not come to the foreground but maintain deictic glimpses of the original experience of catching life unaware. From the materialist point of view, various signs of wear and tear (black and white dots, scratches, and holes) inevitably congest the visible world, all of them pointing to the gap between the past and present. They may not provide information about the figures and events once captured by the camera, yet they bear traces of the decay and aging of this reality. Meanwhile, the intrinsic signs of the used technology (perforations, fuzz, and static marks) constitute idiosyncratic gestures that signify the film's

---

[27] Ibid., 274.

[28] The new additions that enabled him to film longer shots, and also to film more consecutive shots, were primarily the double exchangeable magazines for film stock (instead of a single magazine for 17.5 meters of film) and the viewfinder, which allowed him to watch the action while shooting. Petr Kliment and Jeanne Pommeau, "The Presentation of Kříženecký's Cinematograph" [videocommentary], in *Filmy Jana Kříženeckého / The Films of Jan Kříženecký*, ed. Jiří Anger, DVD/Blu-ray (Praha: Národní filmový archiv, 2019).

[29] Kateřina Svatoňová, "Kříženecký's Films in the Context of Industrial Exhibitions" [videocommentary], in *Filmy Jana Kříženeckého/The Films of Jan Kříženecký*, ed. Jiří Anger, DVD/Blu-ray (Praha: Národní filmový archiv, 2019).

coming into being, the original event of capturing and transforming reality by technological means. Still, none of these elements can be understood as exclusive to one of the concepts nor can they exist in isolation from others; the real point of interest is their mutual "interference and interfacing"[30] that, at the same time, presupposes a specificity of all the figurative and material entities involved.

What makes this assemblage of signs in Kříženecký's film different from found footage films in which the issue of indexicality often comes under scrutiny?[31] Consider, for example, the found footage films of Gustav Deutsch, Peter Forgács, Yervant Gianikian and Angela Ricci Lucchi, and other artists who appropriate decaying archival fragments to highlight the temporal distance between then and now,[32] or, more precisely, between figures from the past and signs of wear and tear that circulate across the image. No matter how respectful and nonintrusive their approach to the recycled footage is, anytime we see traces of decay or deixes of the filming process, they always come in quotation marks. Bill Morrison's *Decasia*, which I addressed at length in the previous chapter, offers a variety of indexical signs, yet the images we see are dispersed between different materials from different eras and disconnected from their original sources to such an extent that distinguishing traces and deixes becomes a challenge. Not that it is necessarily a bad thing, of course, but as long as the images are taken out of their context and reassembled for artistic purposes, the indexical signs of the "original" images inevitably blur and become more abstract, which makes the variability of signs within the quadruple logic of indexicality less pronounced. In comparison, the unnerving movement of both sprocket holes within and out of the frame in *Spring Races* signifies that the film strip once passed through the fluctuating cinematographic apparatus—as the images were being created. A trace of reality could have been preserved only because the film stock submitted to the violence of the feeding mechanism, which was even stronger because of

---

[30] Gilles Deleuze, "Porcelain and Volcano," in *The Logic of Sense* (London: The Athlone Press, 1990), 155.

[31] See, for instance, the discussion of *Decasia* in Doane, "The Indexical and the Concept of Medium Specificity" or Bernd Herzogenrath, "Decasia. The Matter | Image: Film is also a Thing," in *The Films of Bill Morrison: Aesthetics of the Archive*, ed. Bernd Herzogenrath (Amsterdam: Amsterdam University Press, 2017), 84–96.

[32] See, for example, Jeffrey Skoller, *Shadows, Specters, Shards: Making History in Avant-Garde Film* (Minneapolis: University of Minnesota Press, 2005); Jaimie Baron, *The Archive Effect: Found Footage and the Audiovisual Experience of History* (London: Routledge, 2014); Jihoon Kim, *Between Film, Video, and the Digital: Hybrid Moving Images in the Post-Media Age* (New York: Bloomsbury Academic, 2018), 145–95.

the original violence of the perforations.[33] Such an example indicates that the act of photographing or filming could really add something notable to the figurative image, something that might actively participate in the figurative processes, and, crucially, something that does not have to be discovered or manufactured "ex post." In the case of *Digital Kříženecký*, the trace-deixis issue can be examined concretely *from below*, through the minute details of the films, with attention to their technological as well as aesthetic dimensions.

Of course, the fact that the digitization of Jan Kříženecký's films left the deictic material gestures unretouched does not make them identical to the analog originals as primary historical sources.[34] However, we can still argue that the indexical bond perseveres. As Tom Gunning claims, storage of information in terms of numerical data does not eliminate indexicality: digital images, just as their photochemical predecessors, "can serve as passport photographs and other legal evidence or documents, which ordinary photographs supply."[35] He argues that both digital and analog photographs depend on elaborate procedures that take place prior to the resulting imprint of reality. Just as digital photography transforms its data into an intermediary form, the analog one involves complicated mediation of lens, film stock, exposure rate, type of shutter, and other elements, not to mention processes of developing and printing.[36] In the case of electrostatic discharge in *Spring Races*, digital compression and possible alterations during scanning play only a minor role. Due to the crisp high-definition image and susceptibility to being examined frame by frame, the deictic static marks can be reconstructed as technological actors that took part in the film as an expressive event. They disclose the encounter between the film stock, the unplugged Lumière apparatus, and static electricity, or between the lightning bolts and the human and animal actors being captured on camera

---

[33] At the outset of cinema, perforations were often perceived as a "weakening" of film: the single pair of sprocket holes Lumière brothers used was a compromise, ensuring that the perforated film strip "would be less susceptible to tear or break from the impact, however minimal, of the claws" while still being able to advance steadily through the film gate. Benoît Turquety, *Inventing Cinema: Machines, Gestures and Media History* (Amsterdam: Amsterdam University Press, 2019). See also Chapter 6 of this book.

[34] Franziska Hellerová, "Proč se zabývat dějinami filmu? Několik poznámek k otázce, jak digitalizace mění náš obraz minulosti," *Iluminace* 27, no. 2 (2015): 41–56.

[35] Tom Gunning, "What's the Point of an Index? or, Faking Photographs," *Nordicom Review* 25, no. 1–2 (2004): 40. See also Tom Gunning, "Moving Away from the Index: Cinema and the Impression of Reality," *Differences* 18, no. 1 (2007): 29–52; Julia Noordegraaf, "The Analog Film Projector in Marijke van Warmerdam's Digitized Film Installations," in *Exposing the Film Apparatus: The Film Archive as a Research Laboratory*, ed. Giovanna Fossati and Annie van den Oever (Amsterdam: Amsterdam University Press, 2016), 211–22.

[36] Gunning, "What's the Point of an Index?," 40.

and mummified on film, respectively, in the making. The following passages examine the implications of this encounter for indexicality—first generally, to present the issue of static electricity as a technological as well as natural phenomenon, then specifically, to showcase the weird shapes imposed by the static marks as particular actualizations of the crack-up that enrich our notions of cinematic reality.

Pleasures and Threats of Static Electricity

Static electricity marks (or just static marks) on the film emulsion are typical symptoms of the fragility and instability of the cinematographic apparatus during the early days of cinema. They could be described as "physical defects in a film image caused by exposure to the light from the discharge of static electricity before raw film is processed, especially in areas with low humidity."[37] The way the film strip fluctuated through the hand-cranked camera, and also the sensitivity of the raw nitrate stock during handling, made film particularly vulnerable to electrostatic charges. "Rolls of negative would often release these charges as they were unwinding in the camera and cause exposure of the film which results in lightning-like streaks after processing."[38] These marks were generally understood as technological mishaps or malfunctions waiting to be overcome; the first official organization of cinematographers in the United States even named itself The Static Club of America, and one of its initial goals was to "diagnose and troubleshoot" the dilemma with static electricity charges.[39] In the case of the Lumière Cinématographe and film emulsion, the "problem" seemed even worse. One may recall the elementary

---

[37] Richard W. Kroon, *A/V A to Z: An Encyclopedic Dictionary of Media, Entertainment and Other Audiovisual Terms* (Jefferson and London: McFarland & Company, 2010), 645. See also Paul Read and Mark-Paul Meyer, eds., *Restoration of Motion Picture Film* (Oxford: Butterworth-Heinemann, 2000), 175, 338.

[38] "Static Mark," *Glossary of the National Film and Sound Archive of Australia*, accessed December 31, 2022, https://www.nfsa.gov.au/preservation/preservation-glossary/static-mark.

[39] "Introduced in the early 1900s, the iconic Pathé Studio was the primary camera used from the early to mid Silent Era, based on a patented Lumière design," *The American Society of Cinematographers*, accessed December 31, 2022, https://theasc.com/asc/asc-museum-pathe-studio. The Static Club of America served a variety of functions. One of the Club's early members, Arthur Miller, mentioned that the Club "provided the chance for members to discuss problems of lighting, standardisation of frame-line, and other matters concerned with the art of cinematography" and also served as a "social-gathering place." Quoted in David Bordwell, Janet Staiger, and Kristin Thompson, *The Classical Hollywood Cinema: Film Style & Mode of Production to 1960* (London: Routledge, 1998), 109.

school mantra: "When an ebonite rod is rubbed with fox fur, electrostatic charge is created," that is, electrons move from fur to the ebonite rod; hence, ebonite becomes negatively charged, and fur gets a positive charge. Now imagine that the film roll is the ebonite rod and the velvet strip placed at the projector gate is the fox fur, and you get the idea. Even in their most polished form to date, resulting from the digital restoration led by Thierry Frémaux,[40] white static marks in Lumière's films remain visible—whether in the form of singular lightning bolts or larger tree-branch shapes.[41]

Despite their presence in numerous films of that period, these marks remain an understudied phenomenon, often described as signs of decay and destruction—one source even speaks of "ruination."[42] On the other hand, they seem hard (perhaps even undesirable) to get rid of. For example, see a 2019 video of The Museum of Modern Art called *The IMAX of the 1890s | HOW TO SEE the First Movies*. While clearly designed to highlight the startlingly crisp and stable quality of the digitally restored 68mm nitrate prints from the MoMA collections, the film still takes static marks into account, albeit as mere flies in the ointment.[43] If we return to the digitized Lumière films, whereas other signs of intrinsic deformation, such as image instability or a monochromatic layer on some of the surviving prints, are nowhere to be seen, static electricity persists. It may be because the static marks are difficult to retouch without damaging the image's content or that the "general public" does not find them as disturbing as, for example, a trembling image. The static marks are more of a curiosity that becomes lost in otherwise crystal-clear imagery, soothing music, and Thierry Frémaux's nostalgic voice-over that sutures all the works into a single narrative.[44] Still, they are there—as fleeting signs of a past encounter between the Cinématographe, the film

[40] See the DVD/Blu-ray collection: Bertrand Tavernier and Thierry Frémaux, eds., *Lumière ! Le cinématographe 1895–1905*, DVD/Blu-ray (Lyon: Institut Lumière, 2015), and also the film *Lumière!* (Lumière! L'aventure commence; Thierry Frémaux, 2016).

[41] See, for example, *Automobile Accident* (Accident d'automobile; 1903–1905) for the first type of static electricity, and *Westminster Bridge* (Pont de Westminster; 1896), *Concorde Square (obelisks and fountains)* (Place de la Concorde (obélisque et fontaines); 1897), or *Indochina: Children Gathering Rice Scattered by Western Women* (Enfants annamites ramassant des sapèques devant la Pagode des Dames; 1900) for the second type.

[42] "Introduced in the early 1900s" (footnote 110). See also Brian Wright, "Film's Worst Enemies (7 Common Film Issues)," *CineStillfilm*, February 24, 2017, accessed December 31, 2022, https://cinestillfilm.com/blogs/news/film-s-worst-enemies-7-common-film-issues.

[43] Sean Yetter, "The IMAX of the 1890s | HOW TO SEE the First Movies," *The Museum of Modern Art*, 2019, accessed December 31, 2022, https://www.youtube.com/watch?v=BBNwiPgknn8&feature=youtu.be. The static electricity footage comes from the film *Queen Victoria's Last Visit to Ireland* (1900).

[44] See Benoît Turquety, "Lumière ! Le Cinématographe 1895–1905. Les films Lumière présentés par Bertrand Tavernier et Thierry Frémaux," *1895*, no. 78 (2016): 209–14.

strip passing through the camera, the operator who is turning the crank (or anyone who is handling the film before processing), and the filmed figures in their environment. Nonetheless, what importance do we ascribe to them? Are they obstacles to seeing the past reality or documents of how this reality has always been shaped by technological actors?

The static marks do not just evoke fear of tainting the captured reality—they also recall the ambiguous attitude of the Lumière film technology toward electricity in general. On the one hand, the Cinématographe itself, unlike the apparatuses designed by Thomas Alva Edison, functioned independently of electrical energy. As a hand-cranked machine, it functioned solely on the interaction between the camera and its operator, and it could be used in any setting. According to Benoît Turquety, the unplugged apparatus was paradoxically more autonomous and versatile; he sees the resistance to electrification as something that allowed the machine to operate in symbiosis with any environment in which it found itself. In terms of capturing the contingent reality, it presented an advantage, albeit difficult to maintain and orchestrate. Nadia Bozak sums it up aptly: "The cameraman circulated freely outdoors, catching life on the street, with its conflicting planes of activity," relying on natural light that, in the words of Georges Bataille, "gives energy without demanding payback."[45] Sure, many advocates of modernity and scientific progress in the late parts of the nineteenth century mobilized artificial light to "conquer the dark, disenchant the night, and create new media and art,"[46] and eventually succeeded. Nonetheless, the "primitive" cinema of the Lumière brothers and Kříženecký proves that Bazin's idea of indexicality, tied to the notion of light-sensitive chemicals as mediators between an object and its depiction, may be better off with the sun. Even in their digitized form, static marks are a powerful reminder of this unplugged indexicality, particularly resonant in an age when the ecological impact of filmmaking becomes more pressing than ever.[47]

Are static marks more than just inconspicuous curiosities for archivists and film historians? Casual spectators may not even notice static marks; cinephiles and theorists may perceive them as instances of Barthesian "punctum."[48] However, they may also serve as models for film technology's

---

[45] Nadia Bozak, *The Cinematic Footprint: Lights, Camera, Natural Resources* (New Brunswick: Rutgers University Press, 2010), 33.
[46] Noam M. Elcott, *Artificial Darkness: An Obscure History of Modern Art and Media* (Chicago and London: University of Chicago Press, 2013), 4.
[47] Laura U. Marks, "Let's Deal with the Carbon Footprint of Streaming Media," *Afterimage* 47, no. 2 (2020): 46–52.
[48] Roland Barthes, *Camera Lucida: Reflections on Photography* (New York: Hill and Wang, 1982).

struggle to capture ephemeral reality with as much detail as possible while disclosing its entanglement with that same reality. With regards to indexicality, they bring both the limits and benefits of the mummified change to the foreground. On the one hand, static marks illustrate what happens when the cinematographic event captures more of reality than originally intended. It may cause the figures that were meant to be filmed to become contaminated with other shapes and subsequently lose their privileged position in the profilmic reality. On the other hand, the variable presence of the marks, or even their interference with the figurative content, indicates that the cinematographic event might involve significant processes that cannot be limited to the mimetic representation of visible objects. It signals that the camera has captured more than meets the human eye, and therefore creates a more diffused reality, spread among a multitude of distinctive actors. Rather than dismantling this mutual entanglement, we should embrace it and see what it can do when confronted with a specific figurative formation—notably that of the racing horses themselves.

Horse Racers Struck by Lightning

It is not known how static marks were perceived in the Czech lands or specifically in the films of Jan Kříženecký. Throughout his short and fragmented filmmaking career, Kříženecký was entirely dependent on film material bought from abroad, concretely from the Lumière brothers. As a filmmaker from a small nation who did not even have the privilege to be a classified Lumière operator, his access to film material was severely limited; therefore, he presumably could not have afforded to manipulate with the static marks in any significant way. Nevertheless, at least we know that the marks were preserved in the surviving nitrate materials and continue to be visible in the digitized films. Similar to the digitally restored Lumière films, they appear in several forms. For example, *Exhibition Sausage Seller and Bill-Poster* (Výstavní párkař a lepič plakátů; 1898, source: original negative, take A) contains extensive tree-branch-like shapes which at certain moments cover the entire image; in *Old Town Firemen* (Staroměstští hasiči; 1898, source: original negative), the marks look alike, but they are visible only on the left side of the frame.[49] *Spring Races* represent probably the most specific

---

[49] Static marks are also perceptible on the vintage prints; see, for example, *Exhibition Sausage Seller and Bill-Poster* (Výstavní párkař a lepič plakátů; 1898, source: nitrate print, take B).

Figures 2.5–2.8 *The First Day of the Spring Races of Prague* (První den jarních dostihů pražských; 1908, source: original negative [digitally inverted]) © Národní filmový archiv.

case for two reasons. First, the electric bolts appear more isolated—instead of convoluted threads, there are usually only one or two lines—yet they seem all the more visible in the images, due to the bright background and sharpness of the white streaks. Second, they come to the fore during the racing sequence (*c.* between 02:00 and 02:30, usually on the right side of the frame), in a way that transcends the boundary between figuration and materiality and establishes provisional contact. The way horses and jockeys, and, to a lesser extent, the photographer trying to take pictures and the ladies working on the hurdles, seem to be struck by lightning, compels one to delve into a more speculative dimension of that indexical encounter (Figures 2.5–2.8).

In many ways, the presence of static marks within the horse-racing microcosm reflects the fantasy of showing and at the same time disciplining the contingencies of the visible world, manifest in the endeavors of cinematic precursors and early practitioners, from Eadweard Muybridge and Étienne-Jules Marey to the Lumière brothers and Křiženecký.[50] Unlike

---

[50] Mary Ann Doane, *The Emergence of Cinematic Time: Modernity, Contingency, the Archive* (Cambridge, MA: Harvard University Press, 2002).

Muybridge's and Marey's scientific exercises,[51] the movements of the galloping horses are not subordinated to isolation and fragmentation. They are shown within a recognizable reality that is in constant flux, without discernible phases or gaps, diffusing our attention among diverse figurative and material phenomena. Thanks to the camera's ability to film longer tracking shots with a viewfinder, the horses can be followed throughout their trajectory, and the rudimentary editing possibilities push their actions further into narrativity. And yet, both liberating and constricting forces entailed within this fascination with the real come to a halt when facing the physical, seemingly unworldly gestures of fleeting electricity. These intrusions remind us that the newly championed contingency reaches beyond the actual accidents caused by the profilmic reality. It starts to invite accidents that stem from things that were supposed to be extracted from that reality. The crack-up that emerges denies any possibility of figuration outside the event that gives it birth—an event that is co-realized by untamed technological actors.

Such an intrusive appearance of electricity creates a paradox that reminds us of the role technological accidents play in the photographic representation of reality as well as in the figurative content of the image. As already mentioned, static electricity was deemed disturbing in its period due to its unpredictability and uncontainability. Even those who championed contingent reality considered it a threat—a chaotic, alien force whose intrusion risks the integrity of the represented reality. In *Spring Races*, the lightning bolts signal a reality that is simultaneously artificial, tied to the unique construction of the Cinématographe, and natural, stemming from its envelopment in the lived world. The traces of galloping horses and their riders are visibly there, but devoid of their exclusive right to be represented, while the apparatus loses its privilege to remain anonymous. From this perspective, static electricity seems like "the natural force of artifice and the artificial force of nature at the same time," as Jacques Ranciére would say.[52] On one level, electricity invades the profilmic reality with lightning streaks that seem out of place, setting the contours of the human world temporarily ablaze; on the other, as the digital form of the film lets us see even clearer, this electricity constitutes an immanent potentiality of the material universe that makes the forms emerge.

---

[51] I am referring to Muybridge's famous study of horses in motion, *Sallie Gardner at the Gallop* (1878), and Marey's numerous chronophotographic images of horse trotting and galloping.
[52] Jacques Ranciére, *Aisthesis: Scenes from the Aesthetic Regime of Art* (London and New York: Verso, 2013), 104.

Thus, we can perceive static electricity as a force that mediates the relation between the Lumière equipment, the filmed figures and objects, and their representation, and consequently broadens our notion of cinematic reality and indexicality. Not only does Kříženecký's film confirm the objectivist dimension of Bazin's ontology, with the primacy of a nonliving agent that intervenes between the originating object and its reproduction. The static marks present a distinctive actor, a surplus that enhances reality with its underlying technological dimension, and also evokes what the film's figurative content owes to the event of its own making. Yet, as tempting as it would be to see this as a step toward an object-oriented film theory, with Bazin as its precursor, we should listen to Luka Arsenjuk's reservations about such an endeavor. He claims that "contrary to OOP [object-oriented philosophy]'s sharp metaphysical distinctions, film theory has always depended on its ability to establish the (moving) image in terms of a dialectic (rather than sheer unmediated separation) of being and appearance, of reality and sensuousness, of the object and its representation."[53] He argues that despite his "object-oriented" account of cinematic ontology, Bazin is "well aware of the paradox of the image: even the filmmakers who place their 'faith in reality' must find a way to work with appearances. They must invent something like a nonmanipulative manipulation of sensuous relations and representations of reality capable of revealing to the spectator the new sense of reality's being."[54] In other words, Bazin's idea of realism has an intrinsic tie to the activity of material and technological actors, but only as long as they are grounded within a perceptually recognizable, artistically shaped reality. As an early film that marries a pre-documentary, fly-on-the-wall approach with rudimentary technological means of the unplugged cinematographic apparatus, *Spring Races* underlines this paradox, leaving room for both figurative and material reality, as well as for their diverse traces and deixes.

The intermingling of these realities and processes can be even more visible when confronted with specific frames in which the lightning bolts hit the horse racers. Leaving aside factors such as framing, tracking shots, or staging in depth, or, from the other end, the speed of hand-cranking, the visibility of static marks in Figures 2.9–2.12 is highlighted because the content particularly encourages it. The galloping horses' movement is so frenetic that seeing it frame by frame in editing software inevitably causes the racers to turn blurry and therefore more vulnerable to the deformative forces of filmic matter. As continuous as the horses' movement seems, the blurred figures

---

[53] Luka Arsenjuk, "On the Impossibility of Object Oriented Film Theory," *Discourse* 38, no. 2 (2016): 206.
[54] Ibid.

Figures 2.9–2.12 *The First Day of the Spring Races of Prague* (První den jarních dostihů pražských; 1908, source: original negative [digitally inverted]) © Národní filmový archiv.

demonstrate that even this continuity has its limits. However, the frame-by-frame investigation may also reinvent these constraints as windows onto an altogether different sphere of the contingent reality, and, consequently, a different notion of movement that implies human and nonhuman factors together (Figures 2.9–2.12).

Film theory has generally linked blur to low-definition quality and to the fact that "inappropriate" conditions of recording, storing, and screening can significantly tamper with our ideas of order and clarity. For example, Asbjørn Grønstad champions blurry, low-resolution practices as a challenge against transparency, immediacy, and sharpness in contemporary art.[55] According to him, low-definition images "function like tropes, in that they make visible,

---

[55] Asbjørn Grønstad, *Rethinking Art and Visual Culture: The Poetics of Opacity* (Cham: Palgrave Macmillan, 2020). For the recent discourse on blurry images, see Martine Beugnet, Allan Cameron, and Arild Fetveit, eds., *Indefinite Visions: Cinema and the Attractions of Uncertainty* (Edinburgh: Edinburgh University Press, 2017); Beugnet, Martine and Richard Misek, "In Praise of Blur," *[in]Transition: Journal for Videographic Film & Moving Image Studies* 4, no. 2b (2017), accessed December 31, 2022, http://mediacommons.org/intransition/2017/07/11/praise-blur.

and italicize, the inherent opacity of all images,"[56] their "constitutive thickness" akin to "a kind of semiotic crust whose inevitable presence always makes the content of the image generative rather than reflective."[57] Nonetheless, in the digitized original negative of *Spring Races*, the sharpness of the images scanned in 4K does not erase this thickness but enriches it. Considering there is such a moment when the galloping stops being divisible and measurable on screen, a blurred focus may be an appropriate expression of a dynamic movement that is no longer tied to individual figures and enters into a flux of material beings—as Sergei Eisenstein would say, first the movement, and then what moves.[58] The represented reality turns into a rhythmic interplay of deictic forces, oscillating between the blurry figures and the sharp white streaks on an immanent plane, and thereby it is revealed as composed of small, loosely assembled particles of light. Gilles Deleuze offers a nice generalization of this principle: "visibilities are not forms of objects, nor even forms that would show up under light, but rather forms of luminosity, which are created by the light itself and allow a thing or object to exist only as a flash, sparkle or shimmer."[59] In other words, the distorted figures and the lightning bolts would be just particular instances of a universal luminosity that structures the moving image and, by extension, the whole reality.

Still, the crack-up guarantees that the weird shape of electric horses does not delve too far into abstraction. Without a trace left in the form of a figure, both of these vectors of movement would vanish into an indistinguishable noise of light particles. As Jacques Aumont comments, the most interesting intrusions of natural or artificial light into the image are those that "do not occult it absolutely" and rather "hover on it, as if hesitating to be a part of it."[60] For the weird shape to remain discernible, even in its blurred form, the crack-up needs to navigate between the technological gestures through which it invades the profilmic reality and the traces of this reality, which is shaped by electrostatic energy in a broader sense. This way, we gain a

---

[56] Grønstad, *Rethinking Art and Visual Culture*, 48.
[57] Ibid., 5.
[58] Sergei Eisenstein, "Conspectus of Lectures on the Psychology of Art," in *The Eisenstein Collection*, ed. Richard Taylor (Calcutta: Seagull Books, 2006), 237. See also Luka Arsenjuk, *Movement, Action, Image, Montage: Sergei Eisenstein and the Cinema in Crisis* (Minneapolis: Minnesota University Press, 2018), 26–31.
[59] Gilles Deleuze, *Foucault* (Minneapolis: University of Minnesota Press, 2006), 52. See also Hanjo Beressem, "Local Color: Light in Faulkner," in *Media|Matter: The Materiality of Media|Matter as Medium*, ed. Bernd Herzogenrath (New York: Bloomsbury Academic, 2015), 69–95.
[60] Jacques Aumont, "The Veiled Image: The Luminous Formless," in *Indefinite Visions: Cinema and the Attractions of Uncertainty*, ed. Martine Beugnet, Allan Cameron, and Arild Fetveit (Edinburgh: Edinburgh University Press, 2017), 30.

better understanding of the entanglement between the figurative world and its material-technological underpinnings without marginalizing their differences.

Coda: In Praise of Impure Reality

The encounter between horse racers and static electricity reflects how even inconspicuous enactments of the crack-up through minuscule physical marks can question and enrich the age-old problem of cinema and its relation to reality. Not only does the presence of technological actors in the image distort our view of the represented event of a horse race, but it also enriches our awareness of how many various phenomena that event initially entailed. Electricity emerges as an indexical force of technology that disturbs the formation of a coherent diegetic reality but also as a constitutive factor of nature that co-determines the film's coming into being. Such a role of electrical energy is even more paradoxical due to the fact that it raises in the context of the Lumière apparatus that was operated by hand. Seeing the marks of this encounter in the digitized artifacts reminds us that no matter how many layers of technological transformation and external damages accumulate in the moving image, the indexical reality in all of its meanings finds a way to make itself visible.

In *The First Day of the Spring Races of Prague*, the quadruple logic of indexicality—expressed by the interrelated doubles of figuration and materiality and trace and deixis—allowed us to approximate why elements tied to the film's production process, such as static marks, stand out from just any other indexical signs. They point neither to the represented world as it was nor to its changes in time but to the expressive encounter that shaped the original filming event in the first place—an encounter that has both technological and natural dimensions. Regarding the crack-up, the static marks appear less pronounced than the yellowish-orange color in *Grand Consecration of the Emperor Franz I Bridge* (Chapter 1), yet they are more directly targeted. The frames with electric horses in particular show how deictic gestures can produce weird shapes of indexical presence without drowning the images into nothingness. In this endeavor, the film clearly belongs to a family of other films with a Lumière signature mark, yet the sharp, individuated white streaks aimed at the horse racers affect the form and content of the images to such an extent that the scene can be perceived as a highly specific (if not entirely unique) variation of the static marks.

What changes can the electric horses undergo in their newly acquired digital form? The digitization in 4K may distance the images from the immediate contact with the light that "existed, right then and there, at the moment the photograph was taken."[61] However, it also allows us to bracket the scenes in which lightning bolts instigate a crack-up and experiment with how they can alter our notion of what the film surface is and can be. An inspiration can come from Sami van Ingen's short found footage film *Flame* (Polte; 2018). This work, based on damaged frames from the only remaining nitrate reel of a lost Finnish melodrama from the 1930s,[62] bears many resemblances with the films of Bill Morrison, particularly in the way it lets the signs of decay communicate with the diegetic action in slow motion. However, van Ingen's approach is more interventionist, experimenting with the newly acquired puzzle-like structure of the film as a digital file. The author treats the deformations like masses of pixels, disassembling and reassembling them across the frames and using the editing software as a divining rod that searches for places where it could generate the biggest amount of energy, the most developed crack-up. If we applied this tactic to Kříženecký's *Spring Races*, the static marks would finally have the privilege to circulate in a pronouncedly electric sea of pixels and search for a spot where the crack-up could hit the hardest and where the quadruple logic of indexicality would become truly visible and meaningful. In this manner, digital technology may become something more than an empty shell or an eraser/retoucher—a full-fledged agent in investigating how many notions of the index even a single frame can contain.

---

[61] Bozak, *The Cinematic Footprint*, 19.
[62] The film is *Fallen Asleep When Young* (Silja; Teuvo Tulio, 1937). All screening prints and the negative of the film were destroyed in a 1959 studio fire. A sequence from the middle of the film was found at La Cinémathèque française in Paris in 2015. Sami van Ingen, "Flame," *Vimeo*, 2018, accessed December 31, 2022, https://vimeo.com/ondemand/flamefilm.

3

Trembling Meaning

Camera Instability and Transduction in Archival Moving Images

June 6, 1908. The opening ceremony of the Čech Bridge in Prague. A group of local bureaucrats, all dressed in black and neatly arranged into rows, is ready to make the first walk across the bridge. The Lumière Cinématographe, operated by Jan Kříženecký, waits on the other end. The goal is to capture the parade with as much precision and as much grandeur as possible. However, as the figures are slowly approaching the apparatus, the camera starts trembling, both horizontally and vertically. The jerky movement escalates and eventually transforms the distinguished, fine-hatted gentlemen into a vibrating black wave of barely differentiable shapes. In the end, the threat of the fourth wall is literalized by an uncanny synchronization between the image content and the defects of the Cinématographe device. Is this menacingly approaching black wave reconcilable with an equilibrium of sorts? (Figures 3.1–3.4)

This captivating yet oddly disturbing scene comes from Kříženecký's short actuality *Opening Ceremony of the Čech Bridge* (Slavnost otevření nového Čechova mostu, 1908) or, more precisely, from what we are allowed to see of the film 115 years after its creation, in the form of a high-resolution video that was digitized from the original negative. Alternatively, we can at least watch the specific fragment in a condensed GIF format that demonstrates the motion of trembling in a way the film stills above cannot.[1] In this moment, the crack-up, albeit for a little while, functions like a well-oiled machine, connecting two notions of trembling and, by extension, two distinctive worlds—the world of representation and figuration and the world of matter and technology—into an automatized system of making meaning. Even within Kříženecký's body of work, such moments are quite rare. The uncannily well-timed translation of material trembling into the figurative

---

[1] The camera trembling in *Opening Ceremony* is better visible in GIF format. You can access the GIF at krizenecky.nfa.cz or download it here: https://drive.google.com/file/d/1GWoVHgksDT01mnghFA2rFWMCZH_JwC_n/view?usp=sharing.

Figures 3.1–3.4 *Opening Ceremony of the Čech Bridge* (Slavnost otevření nového Čechova mostu; 1908, source: original negative) © Národní filmový archiv.

one postulates a notion of the crack-up that not only mediates the encounter between the figurative and material dimensions but also synchronizes them to pursue a specific meaning. How do the raw, tectonic rupture of the color veil in *Grand Consecration* or the invasion of lightning streaks in *Spring Races* turn into a regulative mechanism between seemingly separated spheres of signification?

The bridge scene presents another case in point of a noninterventionist approach to digitization, preserving the dispositions of the camera Kříženecký obtained from the Lumière brothers (*Cinématographe-type*). Due to the fact that the images were left trembling rather than being corrected and stabilized, the film can shake our own ideas of how aesthetic effects may emerge. It creates an impression that the trembling is an aftereffect—the moment when the quivering of the apparatus becomes the quivering of the figures approaching the screen (and vice versa) seems as if it has been set up, amplified, or even added artificially by a later filmmaker who appropriated these images. Indeed, there are many found footage filmmakers who might utilize such image instability for artistic ends. In other words, they would use the trembling of the camera to pull the figurative image out of joint in order to highlight the extent to which its form and content depend on their material-technological underpinnings and investigate, in the words of found footage filmmaker Peter Tscherkassky, the possibilities of "walk[ing] the line between figuration and abstraction."[2]

However, an archivist or historian of film technology would (rightly) surmise that the trembling reflects the original properties of the Lumière Cinématographe, which was infamous for its horizontal and vertical instability,[3] or, more generally, the instability inherent to most cinematographic apparatuses of that period.[4] The trembling would be assessed as something that pertained to the early cinematic experience but not as a desirable or aesthetically pleasing element—rather as a disturbance waiting to be overcome, operating on an altogether different plane of existence, oblivious to the specific content of the image. Although there were very specific audiences that found a certain poetry in the trembling,[5] the idea of acknowledging its aesthetic appeal or even exploiting it for artistic purposes was not generally deemed plausible.[6] Kříženecký himself must have been aware of the trembling moment and tolerated it enough to authorize it, but there is nothing that would suggest that he staged it for aesthetic purposes—certainly not those imagined by today's audiences trained in watching experimental film and video art. In the case of digitizing or restoring such quivering images, the decision whether or not to stabilize them (or to what degree) would be more guided by a respect for their historical context or by a desire to make them more accessible to the contemporary public rather than by any presumed aesthetic intention.

Yet, neither of these interpretations by themselves accounts for the unintentional aesthetic meaning that arises out of the interaction between the gentlemen walking on the bridge and the unstable Lumière camera. Particularly, the way the shaking of the apparatus intensifies and escalates just as the figures are approaching the camera presents a fascinating exercise in accidental aesthetics that, even for an archival/found footage aficionado,

---

[2] Alejandro Bachmann, "The Trace of Walk That Has Taken Place—A Conversation with Peter Tscherkassky," *Found Footage Magazine* 4, no. 4 (2018): 30.
[3] Laurent Mannoni, "Les Appareils cinématographiques Lumière," *1895*, no. 82 (2017): 52–85; Jeanne Pommeau and Jiří Anger, "The Digitization of Jan Kříženecký's Films," *Iluminace* 31, no. 1 (2019): 105.
[4] Paolo Cherchi Usai, *Silent Cinema: A Guide to Study, Research and Curatorship* (London and New York: BFI – Bloomsbury Publishing, 2019), 63–6.
[5] Yuri Tsivian, *Early Cinema in Russia and Its Cultural Reception* (Chicago: The University of Chicago Press, 1998), 88–9.
[6] Benoît Turquety, *Inventing Cinema: Machines, Gestures and Media History* (Amsterdam: Amsterdam University Press, 2019), 231–48.

holds many surprises. There are many experimental found footage films that employ image instability for (de)formative ends, and even more archival films where camera trembling subtly or abruptly infiltrates figuration, but significantly rarer to encounter are film moments in which the instability resonates with the diegetic action to such an extent—and when they do emerge every once in a while, we lack proper conceptual instruments to describe and analyze them.

This leads to key questions that the present chapter addresses: What does it mean when the crack-up reaches an equilibrium? What happens when two heterogeneous spheres—the figurative one (the gentlemen crossing the bridge and the formal composition of the scene) and the material one (the Lumière camera and its fluctuating film feeding mechanism)—cooperate toward a common aesthetic meaning and effect without any prior intention or expectation? Is the weird shape of a trembling black wave reconcilable with some form of stability? And how could such moments be perceived as more than mere deviations or bits of comic relief, and further pursued for aesthetic or scholarly ends?

To answer these questions, the archival and artistic perspectives need to join forces with film theory and, to a larger extent than in previous chapters, with the philosophy of technology. While contemporary film and media theory offers tools to scrutinize the role of technology and filmic matter (analog or digital) in creating aesthetic effects, the paradoxical marriage of instability and equilibrium in *Opening Ceremony* is so abstract (in its ontological groundlessness) and so concrete (in its relative aesthetic uniqueness) that it benefits from a particular philosophical intervention. Therein lies the importance of Gilbert Simondon, whose ontogenetic philosophy of technology is becoming increasingly relevant in film studies, especially in the research of film technology.[7] His line of thinking enables us to conceive of the dialectic between instability and equilibrium in archival/found footage as not necessarily dependent on the intervention of external actors—whether by artistic manipulation or temporal degradation—but as possibly emanating from an autoregulative mechanism of the archival moving image itself. In the words of Adrian Mackenzie, "what was thought to be merely added on to something more primary turns out to be irreversibly

---

[7] Francois Albera and Maria Tortajada, eds., *Cinema Beyond Film: Media Epistemology in the Modern Era* (Amsterdam: Amsterdam University Press, 2010); Turquety, *Inventing Cinema*; Benoît Turquety, *Medium, Format, Configuration: The Displacements of Film* (Lüneburg: meson press, 2019).

and inextricably presupposed in the constitution of what is said to be added on to."[8]

Here, I specifically employ Simondon's concept of "transduction,"[9] which in many ways resonates with the Deleuzian crack-up,[10] yet also enables us to be more precise concerning situations in which its operations between figuration and materiality reach an equilibrium. The importance of this term lies precisely in its double logic of multiplicity and stability. On the one hand, it designates a process that resides in the intersection and knotting together of diverse realities within a domain, a process that highlights the transitionality and transversality lurking behind the individuation of all living and nonliving entities. On the other hand, it also stresses the necessity of balance (however provisional)—although the intermingling of different spheres within a system introduces chaos, this chaos has its own way of achieving "metastability," a temporary state in which the potentialities hidden in the diverse realities are kept in mutual tension without being actualized. Therefore, transduction allows us to grasp not only a processual encounter between heterogeneous actors but also the ability of this encounter to sustain without any of the actors withdrawing or eliminating the other.

Considering that this chapter dedicates such a huge role to an established philosophical concept, one might ask if this approach remains true to *film theory from below*. The point of confronting transduction with the trembling bridge scene lies not in one-way application but in mutual transformation. Simondon's concept is imagined as a mechanism operating within a machine that does not function according to any preestablished plan, and its role is thus to find some sort of balance from within. As the trembling scene in *Opening Ceremony* comes together by way of a technological accident and the black wave lasts only for a few seconds, transduction highlights its capacity to function even within the bounds of the most chaotic and inconspicuous detail and still achieve (meta)stability. Moreover, the unpredictability and

---

[8] Adrian Mackenzie, *Transductions: Bodies and Machines at Speed* (London: Continuum, 2002), 7.
[9] Gilbert Simondon, *On the Mode of Existence of Technical Objects* (Minneapolis: Univocal Publishing, 2017); Gilbert Simondon, *Individuation in Light of Notions of Form and Information* (Minneapolis: University of Minnesota Press, 2020).
[10] For a specific Deleuzian interpretation and application of transduction, see Audronė Žukauskaitė, "Deleuze, Simondon, and Beckett: From Being to Becoming," in *The Dark Precursor: Deleuze and Artistic Research*, ed. Paulo de Assis and Paulo Guidici (Leuven: Leuven University Press, 2017), 272–8. Overall, Deleuze's philosophy was highly influenced by Simondon, particularly by his notion of individuation, which helped him articulate his theory of differentiation and actualization. For treatments of the Deleuze-Simondon relation, see, for example, Emmanuel Alloa and Judith Michalet, "Differences in Becoming: Gilbert Simondon and Gilles Deleuze on Individuation," *Philosophy Today* 61, no. 3 (2017): 475–502.

unintentionality of the trembling moment give us room to speculate about how transduction can involve human intervention in a non-anthropocentric and non-mastering way. A human (scholarly) operator may not only examine the scene for the subtle interchanges between figuration and materiality but also isolate the black wave and make it last.

The argument for the connection between Simondon's notion of transduction and the trembling black wave in *Opening Ceremony* shall progress in three stages. First, I demonstrate the relevance of transduction for understanding the relationship between figuration and materiality as partly independent from external intervention and capable of staging and regulating their mutual entanglement and differentiation in archival moving images. Second, I examine the usefulness of the concept when applied to various examples of image instability as a phenomenon that brings the figurative and material spheres together in experimental found footage. Third, I return to the case of *Opening Ceremony* in order to show how transduction can emerge and operate by serendipity, examining the key moment of the approaching black wave through isolation, repetition, and slow observation frame by frame (or, more precisely, between the frames).

Transduction as a Mechanism of Distribution and (Meta)Stability

Throughout his works, Simondon defines transduction in numerous ways,[11] but always with the same general principle in mind. Instead of imagining reality as composed of preexistent substance, stable identities, and binary oppositions, he portrays reality as inherently processual, as something that is in constant flux. Transduction consists in "following being in its genesis, in carrying out the genesis of thought at the same time as the genesis of the object."[12] Simondon's ontogenetic rather than ontological account of the world manifests itself in a new notion of man's relation to technology. He

---

[11] See, for example, Adrian Mackenzie, "Transduction: Invention, Innovation and Collective Life," Unpublished manuscript, 2003, accessed December 31, 2022, http://www.lancs.ac.uk/staff/mackenza/papers/transduction.pdf; Muriel Combes, *Gilbert Simondon and the Philosophy of the Transindividual* (Cambridge: MIT Press, 2012), 6–9; Paulo de Assis, "Gilbert Simondon's 'Transduction' as Radical Immanence in Performance," *Performance Philosophy* 3, no. 3 (2017): 695–716.

[12] Gilbert Simondon, "The Position of the Problem of Ontogenesis," *Parrhesia* 7 (2009): 4–16. For a broader account of Simondon's view on ontogenesis, see Jean-Hugues Barthélémy, *Life and Technology: An Inquiry Into and Beyond Simondon* (Lüneburg: Meson Press, 2015).

opposes the common view, which understands technology and nature as separate entities or, more precisely, sees technical objects as tools designed to manipulate nature. Instead, technology (or technicity) is conceived as a mode of "being in the world" that can only exist as a continually evolving network of relations—not only between different tools and machines but also between machines and their elements, between machines and their associated milieu, and between machines and the human beings who use them.[13] Transduction plays a key role in the processes by which both humans and technical objects are becoming "individuated," meaning they are never given in advance but are continuously produced.[14] It enables individuation to be both relational and distributive, in that individuation always happens at the interface between two or more different realities and is paradoxically stable in the sense that it maintains an immanent distribution of potential energy between the diverse spheres. In a nutshell, transduction is the invisible glue that holds a multiplicity of potentially individuating processes together without erasing the differences between them and without denying that the whole system is non-coincident with itself.

More specifically, Adrian Mackenzie demonstrates how transduction manages to bring together phenomena that are usually seen as contradictory. It shows us how "conceptually opposed terms such as form and matter can be seen as abstract husks of the transductive interactions from which they derive."[15] Mackenzie refers to Simondon's example of making a brick—what we perceive as an imposition of a "parallelpiped" form on a raw clay involves "linking realities of heterogeneous domains."[16] The capacity of the material to be molded is itself the outcome of a "series of transformative operations," and the resulting shape comes from a "state of internal resonance in the mass of clay" by which the mold "limits and stabilizes" matter; rather than creating forms, it "gives an end to the deformation."[17] Thus, rather than a linear progression from two isolated materials toward a finished product, we have a set of complicated mediations and interactions, which in this case culminate in matter-taking-form, but do not always necessarily have to result in this way.

If we imagine the figurative space in *Opening Ceremony* as form and the apparatus as matter, we can discern a similar yet not so finalized process in the trembling moment of the bridge scene. From a strictly Simondonian

---

[13] Simondon, *On the Mode of Existence of Technical Objects*.
[14] Simondon, *Individuation in Light of Notions of Form and Information*.
[15] Mackenzie, *Transductions*, 46.
[16] Ibid.
[17] Ibid., 47.

perspective, it would also make sense to conceive of the figures, the bridge, and the camera as an assemblage of material actors from which form emerges through a process of transduction, which brings the assemblage together in the moment of filming and transforms the potential energy into an actual one.[18] However, this approach would struggle to account for the presupposed hierarchy between the figurative and material spheres in the film's meaning-making process, which is overcome only by means of an accident. While describing transduction in *Opening Ceremony*, the emerging assemblage of figurative and material elements should be thought of in relation to the preexisting crack-up between the two dimensions—even though they finally interact and operate toward the same aesthetic goal, the material level becomes visible (and meaningful) only through a perceived failure. For these reasons, the distribution of components in the scene is more fragile and reversible than in Simondon's and Mackenzie's examples, but as we will see later, these qualities help us broaden the scope of shapes and assemblages of figurative and material elements that may unfold.

Besides its capacity for transversal distribution, transduction also offers a certain degree of regulation and stability. One of the definitions Simondon provides for transduction is "a regulative function in all machines with a margin of localized indeterminacy in their functioning."[19] In its mediation between different spheres, each with its own specific energetic potentials, it also has to find at least a temporary way to keep one group of elements from actualizing at the expense of erasing the other. To keep this from happening, transduction presupposes a "metastable" state, a "provisional equilibrium established when a system rich in potential differences resolves inherent incompatibilities by restructuring itself topologically and temporally."[20] In other words, metastability involves a plurality of latent energetic potentials whose interaction does not end in one thing becoming another but still keeps going, maintaining an elementary form of the incompatibility and irreducibility of their differences.[21] This notion resonates with Jihoon Kim's dialectic of specificity and hybridity described in previous chapters,[22] and it finds its particular variation in the bridge scene of *Opening Ceremony*: despite the chaotic eruption of the trembling apparatus that immediately translates into the trembling figures on the bridge, the image neither eliminates the

---

[18] Simondon, *On the Mode of Existence of Technical Objects*, 155.
[19] Ibid.
[20] Mackenzie, *Transductions*, 103.
[21] Combes, *Gilbert Simondon and the Philosophy of the Transindividual*, 3–6.
[22] See Introduction and Chapter 1.

figures nor does it efface the apparatus—at one brief moment, they work together toward a single aesthetic effect.

What humans bring to these processes is giving the most distinguished shape to the "margin of indeterminacy." This is the margin that "brings potential energy to its actualization," which allows the technical object to be individuated and integrated into its milieu and to exchange information with other technical objects.[23] This aspect reveals a certain privileging of the human perspective, which, due to the progressively autonomizing technical agency in the modern age, may seem less and less tenable. Nevertheless, the primacy of the human element in transduction is not necessarily a given— for example, the hierarchy has been reconsidered by Shane Denson. In his book *Postnaturalism: Frankenstein, Film, and the Anthropotechnical Interface* (2014), which aptly focuses on situating media beneath the evolutionary split between the human and the technical, Denson understands transduction according to the principle of "distributed embodiment" rather than human embodiment. He speaks of a "transduction of materially intersecting entities, each with their own form of embodiment, their own manner of marking the boundary, embodying the membrane, between material flux and the emergent realm of discrete objects."[24] In other words, the role of transduction resides in navigating the transitions between entities across the human-technological spectrum while also acknowledging the irreducibility and nonidentity of these entities. The regulation of the margin of indeterminacy would thus be distributed between the human and the nonhuman as well, which grants us the possibility to see human intervention (including the artistic one) as potentially less authoritative and more subtle and relational.

To provisionally sum up, transduction is important for two main reasons. First, it is a principle that enables us to account for transmissions and transformations between two qualitatively distinct yet communicating dimensions within a system. Second, at the same time, it is a mechanism that still entails a certain degree of stability, holding these two spheres in balance, making their movements perceptible in their nuances, and not letting either of them actualize at the expense of the other. In this way, it allows us to conceptualize hybridity and specificity together and let the crack-up gravitate toward a (however temporary) equilibrium.

The distinctive shaping of transduction through camera instability in archival and found footage films demands an analysis from two interrelated

[23] Simondon, *On the Mode of Existence of Technical Objects*, 18, 156.
[24] Shane Denson, *Postnaturalism: Frankenstein, Film, and the Anthropotechnical Interface* (Berlin: Transcript Verlag, 2014), 328. See also Shane Denson, *Discorrelated Images* (Durham: Duke University Press, 2020), 21-2.

perspectives. The first approach investigates the uses of camera trembling in the context of experimental found footage, where it often plays the role of highlighting the ongoing deformation of existing images to reveal potential energy within them as well as to show the mutual imbrication of figuration and materiality. The cases of intentional transduction demonstrate that the image instability in *Opening Ceremony* can be seen as a supremely aesthetic phenomenon with a discernible afterlife in media art. The second approach entails a close reading of the bridge scene in *Opening Ceremony* itself, examining the images frame by frame or, more specifically, between the frames, since the trembling becomes visible only through movement from one frame to another. This process of submitting the scene to a specific "slow observation" that "highlights operational and material shifts over time"[25] enables us to track and guide the margin of indeterminacy that keeps the tension between figurative and material elements from disappearing.

Image Instability—Technological Problem or Aesthetic Potentiality?

Camera instability was one of the defining features of the earliest cinema, and haunted cinema well into the 1910s. To quote Benoît Turquety, "the perception of trembling, in all its forms and variations—vibration, wavering, shaking—was foremost and fundamental. It was only through effort that the eye could overcome this pulsatile state and see something."[26] More specifically, Paolo Cherchi Usai mentions that the vertical shift of the image is, in its slight form, considered normal in all analog cinema, but "the phenomenon was often more pronounced and severely disruptive in the earliest years of cinema."[27] Cherchi Usai claims that jittery images were considered disturbing both by spectators and film producers,[28] which leaves all restorers with a dilemma: should they "correct" a defect which was almost universally acknowledged as disruptive to the film experience, or remain faithful to the history of film technology?[29] And even if they choose to preserve the trembling, is it even

---

[25] Denson, *Postnaturalism*, 331–2. Although Denson uses the term "slow observation" more in the vein of examination over a longer time period, the concept fits the idea of a slow-motion study as well.
[26] Turquety, *Inventing Cinema*, 241.
[27] Cherchi Usai, *Silent Cinema: A Guide*, 66.
[28] Cherchi Usai mentions the example of one Italian production company, Itala-Film, which included the French word *fixité* in its trademark logo to signify that their projected images were rock-steady. Ibid.
[29] Paolo Cherchi Usai, *Silent Cinema: An Introduction* (London: BFI, 2000), 60.

possible to maintain it in a digital medium which, again using Turquety's words, lacks "movement in the machine?"[30]

Each of these approaches can have its merit under given circumstances, and while film archives tend to lean more toward historical authenticity, there are many degrees of stabilization that the digital restorer might opt for.[31] In some cases, though, stabilization may significantly interfere with the figurative content of the image. David Francis gives an example of one restored print of Lumière's *Boat Leaving the Port* (Barque sortant du port; 1895), which was "stabilised so effectively that you d[id]n't see the rocking of the boat"[32]—and the most recent digital restoration of the film supervised by Thierry Frémaux and Bertrand Tavernier more or less follows suit.[33] A more recent example involves a segment from the ongoing digital restoration of D. W. Griffith's *The Stolen Jewels* (1908, nitrate print), conducted by the Film Preservation Society within The Biograph Project, that demonstrates how the stabilization of a crowd scene eliminates the vertical trembling that amplified the represented chaos of the marketplace and thus also the crack-up between figurative and material elements.[34] If the decision of the archivist affects figuration to such an extent, it is debatable whether these compromises to make the films more easily digestible for the public are really worth it.

Nevertheless, the figurative effects of image instability can also be exploited for aesthetic purposes. This endeavor has a strong tradition in experimental cinema—especially when working with early cinema as found footage.[35] Of course, one cannot list all the reasons why found footage filmmakers turn

---

[30] Turquety, *Inventing Cinema*, 243.
[31] For example, the hotly debated digital restoration of the silent film *Beyond the Rocks* (Sam Wood, 1922), conducted by the EYE Filmmuseum in Amsterdam, preserved some image instability while also carrying out a minimal level of digital stabilization, "mainly due to the shrinkage of the nitrate print." See Giovanna Fossati, "The Restoration of Beyond the Rocks," in *Work/s in Progress: Digital Film Restoration within Archives*, ed. Kerstin Parth, Oliver Hanley and Thomas Ballhausen (Vienna: SYNEMA – Gesellschaft für Film und Medien, 2013), 111–20.
[32] Paolo Cherchi Usai, David Francis, Alexander Horwath, and Michael Loebenstein, eds., *Film Curatorship: Archives, Museums, and the Digital Marketplace* (Wien: Synema – Gesellschaft für Film und Medien, 2008), 104.
[33] Bertrand Tavernier and Thierry Frémaux, eds., *Lumière ! Le cinématographe 1895–1905*, DVD/Blu-ray (Lyon: Institut Lumière, 2015).
[34] This paradox is highlighted by the video clip made from the scan, which still includes the edges and perforations of the frame that freely jump around while the image in the frame remains perfectly stable. "Sorry for a Lag in Posting . . .," *The Biograph Project Facebook*, April 2, 2020, accessed December 31, 2022, https://www.facebook.com/filmpreservatio nsociety/videos/621649468415755/.
[35] Bart Testa, *Back and Forth: Early Cinema and the Avant-Garde* (Toronto: Art Gallery of Ontario, 1992); Christa Blümlinger, "Lumière, the Train and the Avant-Garde," in *The Cinema of Attractions Reloaded*, ed. Wanda Strauven (Amsterdam: Amsterdam University Press, 2006), 245–64.

to archival footage from the earliest cinema (though R. Bruce Elder offers an interesting list of six major reasons).[36] There are, however, quite a few films that exploit camera instability as a means to unravel the ontological tension between the figurative and material components of the moving image. Arguably the most famous (and extreme) example is the "aggressive passage"[37] in Ken Jacobs's *Tom, Tom, the Piper's Son* (1969), which is based on Billy Bitzer's eponymous film from 1905. According to P. Adams Sitney, in this extended section, the image jumps "in the projector gate to the point of indecipherability by vertical distortion," making it difficult for anyone seeing the film at first glance to discern "if the projectionist has misthreaded or if what they are seeing is part of the film itself."[38] Even when the strategy is revealed as deliberate, there remains a lingering feeling that this vertical blur draws attention to the mysterious, unknowable quality of cinema in its most unrefined form—Elder even calls it a "surrealistic character."[39] In other words, the artistic appropriation extracts a miniature of early cinema at its most chaotic and brackets it—not in order to tame the impulse, but rather to examine it under the microscope, to discover some sort of "equilibrium of disequilibrium" that embraces disarray as a state of things in which cinema feels most at home.

A different approach—more metaphorical yet explicitly linked to the Lumière Cinématographe—is represented by Al Razutis's film *Lumière's Train, Arriving at the Station* (1979). Described by its author as an essay on "cinema itself" as "an apparatus of representation wherein fact and fiction are recreated,"[40] this work reimagines the arrival of a train at La Ciotat Station in the legendary Lumière brothers' film[41] and other moments of alignment between train and cinema which followed it. The third section of the film depicts the iconic moment from the Lumière film, but the trajectory of the train, originally designed—similarly to the path of the crowd in *Opening Ceremony*—to break the fourth wall and "assault" the audience from within the depths of the *mise-en-scène*, no longer follows linear logic. Razutis's artistic strategies—continuous alternation between positive and negative frames at a varying speed, halting the locomotive at various phases of movement, shifting

---

[36] R. Bruce Elder, "Bart Testa: Back and Forth: Early Cinema and the Avant-Garde [book review]," *R. Bruce Elder*, 1992, accessed December 31, 2022, http://rbruceelder.com/documents/writing/bibliography/film/critical/1992_OnBartTestasBackAndForth.pdf.

[37] P. Adams Sitney, *Visionary Film: The American Avant-Garde, 1943–2000* (New York: Oxford University Press, 2002), 344.

[38] Ibid., 344–5.

[39] Elder, "Bart Testa."

[40] Al Razutis, "Lumiere's Train: Visual Essays No 1," *Light Cone*, accessed July 31, 2021, https://lightcone.org/en/film-1197-lumiere-s-train.

[41] *The Arrival of a Train at La Ciotat* (L'Arrivée d'un train en gare de La Ciotat; 1896).

the machine from place to place—aim to unveil new potentialities within the mythical event. Crucially, the rapid montage of positive and negative images simulates the vertical and horizontal instability of the apparatus. In the first case, it sets the locomotive into motion even as it stands still; in the latter, it makes the elements surrounding the train disappear and reemerge. The primal scene of film history is thereby not only confronted with its own technological underpinnings and its (de)figurative possibilities but also with the decentering power and energy embedded in the figure of the train itself, resulting in a curious multiplication of figurative and material elements that explodes in a sort of mechanistic spectacle.[42]

What these two examples demonstrate is that image instability can be used as a powerful strategy for enacting the aesthetic potential of transduction within archival moving images. However, even if the trembling in those experimental films and in Kříženecký's *Opening Ceremony* differ in degree rather than in kind, the distinction in terms of the crack-up is still substantial. Whereas with found footage it is always more or less possible to attribute the clashes between figuration and materiality to the (at least partial) control of the appropriator or the inevitable passing of time, there is no such safety net in *Opening Ceremony*. Also, found footage at least implicitly presupposes that there are meaningful ends to the process of overcoming the gap between the two spheres—but in the trembling bridge scene, such promise is clearly lacking. Transduction in Razutis's and Jacobs's films is intentionally orchestrated, amplified, and built up to the point of relative consistency, designed to regulate the margin of indeterminacy. In Kříženecký's film, on the other hand, transduction remains volatile and prone to accidents. Even when it emerges and reaches such equilibrium as in the closing moments of the scene, there persists a permanent risk that the rudimentary autoregulative mechanism will give in to the forces of entropy. When the figurative and material elements mingle by means of the distributed embodiment brought about by transduction, the pull toward abstraction becomes all too strong. The threat does not reside in the loss of form but in the excess of it—too many (de)figurative operations happen all at once, within a spatiotemporal unit that cannot contain them. However, there is something, a valve of sorts, that functions as a last resort against abstraction—and this can be observed and prolonged when looking at the images frame by frame or, in this case more precisely, between the frames.

---

[42] Mike Hoolboom, "Three Decades of Rage: An Interview with Al Razutis," in *Al Razutis Iconoclast*, ed. Mike Hoolboom (2009), accessed December 31, 2022, http://mikehoolboom.com/thenewsite/docs/601.pdf, 63–64.

If we want to differentiate the contours of transduction in the bridge scene, we must pay attention to how they take shape in the details of specific visual forms. To paraphrase Jihoon Kim, "it is on the level of their forms that the aspects of [. . .] hybridizations, including the simultaneous occurrences of their media components, become discernible."[43] As camera instability in archival moving images orchestrates an interplay between figurative and material components, every single detail visible in-between the frames can be imbued with meaning.

The Black Wave (Dis)Appearing Between the Frames

The meanings and effects that *Opening Ceremony* evokes are, in essence, straightforward. The crisp image of the digitized original negative allows us to clearly see the distinctive attributes that anchor the film in the actuality genre, as well as the popular formal features of the earliest cinema, such as frontal composition and staging in depth.[44] At the same time, we can also discern an attempt to break the fourth wall and "attack" the audience—a strategy that is in principle not dissimilar to period films in which a delegation of people walks straight toward the camera[45] or, by extension, to meta-fictional "experiments" such as *The Big Swallow* (James Williamson, 1901), in which a man, irritated by the presence of a photographer, devours the camera. Hence, the scene, while primarily invested in presenting the occasion of a significant monument being unveiled, also displays a predilection toward the disturbing experience of erasing the distance between the profilmic world (the filmed figures, places, and objects) and us (the viewing subjects).

Nonetheless, the threat of the "menacingly approaching black wave" in *Opening Ceremony* that was mentioned by Czech writer Adolf Branald[46] would hardly be thinkable without the trembling apparatus, whose horizontal and vertical instability escalates almost analogically with the characters approaching the camera. According to film restorer Jeanne Pommeau, instability was compensated during the digitization process "only when it

---

[43] Kim, *Between Film, Video, and the Digital*, 35.
[44] Thomas Elsaesser, "Louis Lumière—the Cinema's First Virtualist?," in *Cinema Futures: Cain, Abel or Cable? The Screen Arts in the Digital Age*, ed. Thomas Elsaesser and Kay Hoffmann (Amsterdam: Amsterdam University Press, 1989), 45–64.
[45] See, for example, the film *The Bey of Tunis and His Entourage Descend the Steps of the Bardo* (Le bey de Tunis et les personnages de sa suite descendant l'escalier du Bardo; 1903, filmed by the Lumière operator Alexandre Promio).
[46] Adolf Branald, *My od filmu* (Praha: Mladá fronta, 1988), 196, 197. The book is a fictionalized biography of Jan Kříženecký.

occurred as a result of the film strip fluctuation in the scanner."[47] In order to not mask the instability that was created in the apparatus during the shooting, the perforations at the edges of the strips, and not the exposed or printed image, were used as reference points.[48] As I have already pointed out, the higher-than-usual presence of not only vertical but also horizontal camera instability[49] is primarily caused by two factors. First, due to the existence of just a single sprocket hole on each side of the frame (instead of the four holes used by Edison, which soon became standard), the film strip was less prone to remain steady. Second, the film feeding mechanism that was designed to move the film strip in the camera and keep it in place at the time of exposure was highly volatile.[50] Add to this the many other types of instability that are hardly conceivable with digital technology, such as the sensibility of the crank drive to the physical movement of the operator's arm[51] or the ever-present flicker, and it is no wonder that one period Cinématographe notice warned users against the risk of "vibrations."[52] The horrifying effect therefore arises unequivocally but in a strangely twisted manner, since it is achieved by the collaboration between two dimensions—the figurative and the material— that differ in kind. Transduction brings them together while at the same time highlighting them as distinctive producers of meaning.

We can imagine the function of transduction in the scene as follows. The figurative elements in *Opening Ceremony*—the freshly built bridge, the entourage of elaborately dressed men, and a panorama of Prague, as well as the frontal composition, the staging in depth, and the risk of breaking the fourth wall—and the material elements—the Lumière Cinématographe with its fluctuating feeding mechanism and single-perforated nitrate film stock— are two communicating regimes of energy. Once transduction loosens the

---

[47] In the case of some of the materials, there is also the instability created during the printing process. Whereas the horizontal and vertical shift of the camera that is visible in the digitized originals is quick and jittery and rarely disrupts the integrity of the frame, the instability caused by inappropriate printing tends to affect the image to such an extent that it starts to "jump" in-between the frames. See Pommeau and Anger, "The Digitization of Jan Kříženecký's Films," 107.

[48] Ibid.

[49] Besides *Opening Ceremony*, the camera instability is perfectly visible in some of the digitized original negatives: *Exercises with Indian Clubs by the Sokol of Malá Strana* (Cvičení s kužely Sokolů malostranských; 1898), *Exhibition Sausage Seller and Bill-Poster* (Výstavní párkař a lepič plakátů; 1898), or *Satan's Railway Ride* (Satanova jízda po železnici; 1906). It is also present in some of the prints, such as *Coach Transport* (Kočárová doprava; 1908).

[50] Pommeau and Anger, "The Digitization of Jan Kříženecký's Films," 105.

[51] Turquety, *Inventing Cinema*, 237.

[52] Louis Lumière and Antoine Lumière, *Notice sur le Cinématographe* (Lyon: Société anonyme des plaques et papiers photographiques A. Lumière et ses fils, 1897), 19.

borders between these two groups of elements (though it does not erase them), the trembling of the apparatus slowly extends into the trembling of the bridge, progressing to the point at which the figures and the camera threaten to cancel each other. Nonetheless, the figurative and material processes do not merge but paradoxically amplify one another. On the one hand, the horizontal and vertical quivering of the apparatus, which temporarily turns the figures into a "black wave," almost beats the formal and representational elements at their own game. On the other, the reality presented on screen becomes increasingly technological, grounded in a "continuous and non-inert matter" that entangles human and nonhuman entities, both in space and in time. We could perceive this weird assemblage of figurative and material actors as an immanent space of mutual intermingling, but this would risk losing sight of the fact that it was enabled only by the prior (and unintentional) overcoming of the rupture between the two spheres. As there is no traceable artistic purpose that would guide this interplay and its reception by the audience, nothing guarantees that the mutual becoming would make the specific presence of all the individual actors meaningful in their own right. This is why a material intervention in the form of slow motion becomes appropriate for the crack-up to maintain itself.

The forming of transduction in the film must be treated with specific care. As a processual phenomenon, this transduction is perceptible only in movement (see the GIF)—no matter how blurry the characters become in the film, the individual frames still hold them in clear contours. The examiner must make do with noting the changing positions of the edges of the frames or swiftly clicking between the frames to gain at least an abstract idea of the horizontal and vertical shifts. Regarding image instability, it is not the single frame but the movement from frame to frame that is the basic unit of film. To paraphrase Sean Cubitt, the moments when one frame disappears and another one appears, "so that no single frame is ever complete enough for it to be recognized as the particular moment of origin," are the building blocks of film.[53] Therefore, a certain degree of movement needs to be maintained, but with two crucial limitations. First, in order to capture the crucial moment of transduction, the movement must occur within the short interval between the black wave threatening to swallow the camera (and, by extension, the audience) and the return to a normal state. Second, to reveal the duration hidden between the frames, the movement needs to be slowed down almost to the point of freezing. In this way, the interval is expanded, magnified, and

---

[53] Sean Cubitt, *Videography: Video Media as Art and Culture* (New York: St. Martin's Press, 1993). See also Kim, *Between Film, Video, and the Digital*, 72.

Figures 3.5–3.8 *Opening Ceremony of the Čech Bridge* (Slavnost otevření nového Čechova mostu; 1908, source: original negative) © Národní filmový archiv.

revealed as potentially inexhaustible,[54] and therefore we are able to witness the transductive equilibrium and also the crack-up in-between its appearance and disappearance (Figures 3.5–3.8).

In accordance with Vivian Sobchack's description of slow motion, watching the climax of the trembling bridge scene at a glacial tempo does not render the movement imperceptible but hyperbolizes it—it "cuts to the quick" and thus uncovers an interesting dialectic of speed and slowness, forestallment and action.[55] Slow and fast can thus be regarded not as qualitatively opposed categories—especially when considered in the context of early cinema, which notoriously lacked standard frame rate[56]—but as relative powers of the single

[54] Tom Gunning, "Interview with Ken Jacobs," in *Films That Tell Time: A Ken Jacobs Retrospective* (New York: American Museum of the Moving Image, 1989), 29–62; Rebecca A. Sheehan, *American Avant-Garde Cinema's Philosophy of the In-Between* (New York: Oxford University Press, 2020), 14.

[55] Vivian Sobchack, "'Cutting to the Quick': Techne, Physis, and Poiesis and the Attractions of Slow Motion," in *The Cinema of Attractions Reloaded*, ed. Wanda Strauven (Amsterdam: Amsterdam University Press, 2006), 338.

[56] Cherchi Usai, *Silent Cinema: A Guide*, 181–5.

category of speed. Hence, our attention is drawn to how the figurative and material elements, devoid of spatiotemporal coordinates that kept them apart from each other, each pulsate according to their specific rhythms.[57] Crucially, we can also track the transductive hybridization of characters and the apparatus as it is occurring and take note of the most minute details of the process, including those that are, in the words of Sobchack, not "for us,"[58] in other words, not normally intended for human eyes.

For example, the vertical shaking grows to monstrous proportions, lending each step of the clumsily approaching gentlemen an otherworldly, larger-than-life significance. The horizontal shaking, previously overshadowed by the vertical one, disturbs the figures in a more subtle measure, with inconspicuous, neurotic tics moving from right to left and vice versa. The men in black, increasingly paralyzed by the emerging clash of material operations, lose their seeming privilege to dictate the speed level and consequently to express meaning as well. The closer they are, the more their figurative outlines mutate into a blur; the more recognizable and individualized the crowd should be, the more it appears devoured by an inhuman black wave. To employ the words of Eugene Thacker, "the movement of such massing and aggregate forms is that of contagion and circulation, a passing-through, a passing-between, even, in an eschatological sense, a passing-beyond."[59] The equilibrium thus arises at the price of bifurcations that result from the distribution of the meaning-making process across the borderlands of qualitatively distinct worlds.

How can we make sure that transduction may still keep going? Although the slow-motion effect intensifies the spreading of all the elements across a single plane—albeit a fissured one—the figures in black never diffuse entirely; they are caught in the process of being swallowed, but they are never actually swallowed. The scene even ends on a "positive" note: for a brief moment, the image seems as if it were about to rectify itself. The shifting of the camera ebbs slightly, the characters regain their contours—one of them even takes his hat off—and the next scene starts. In order to salvage the equilibrium and the margin of indeterminacy, another intervention must occur. If we return to the examples of Jacobs's and Razutis's films, we see that their effect is so powerful because the moment of transduction is replayed over and over—in other words, the trembling of figurative and material elements does not end

---

[57] Jiří Anger, "(Un)Frozen Expressions: Melodramatic Moment, Affective Interval, and the Transformative Powers of Experimental Cinema," *NECSUS European Journal of Media Studies* 8, no. 2 (2019): 40.
[58] Sobchack, "'Cutting to the Quick,'" 346.
[59] Eugene Thacker, *Tentacles Longer Than Night: Horror of Philosophy*, Vol. 3 (Winchester: Zero Books, 2015), 54.

in a finite resolution but repeats itself, always with a little variation.⁶⁰ One experimental found footage film, Siegfried A. Fruhauf's *La sortie* (1998), demonstrates this process in a composition markedly similar to *Opening Ceremony*. Based on the first film made by the Lumière brothers—*Workers Leaving the Lumière Factory in Lyon* (La Sortie de l'Usine Lumière à Lyon, 1895)—*La sortie* shows the workers marching relentlessly through factory corridors over and over again, moving from background to foreground and foreground to background and simultaneously from left to right and right to left in a loop.⁶¹ In an ironic twist on the Lumière film, the workers are stuck inside the factory without a hope of ever leaving. What is particularly relevant is that the horizontal and vertical quivering of the camera both mimics and amplifies their movement, highlighting their entrapment not only in the context of the frame but also vis-à-vis the apparatus. In the trembling scene in *Opening Ceremony*, which stages transduction by itself, the effect of repetition-as-equilibrium is achievable through a much simpler form—for example, the animated GIF that was created to make the trembling perceptible for the readers of this book.⁶² Thus, the human actor becomes more of a curator who guides the energies and potentialities hidden within the material.

With the scene slowed down and looped, the monstrous dissolution of the approaching figures into the black mass might be a step toward another individuation—less smooth yet more adapted to the human-technological entanglement. Strangely similar to the first appearance of the monster's flattened head with stitches and neck bolts, in a close-up, in James Whale's *Frankenstein* (1931), a usually transparent composition becomes a vehicle for the human-technological transition. Echoing Denson's interpretation of this moment, the lack of resolution to the hybridization process makes the trembling of *Opening Ceremony* a "parable of anthropotechnical evolution,"⁶³ taking place in a zone of indeterminacy between the embodiment of the shifting apparatus, the uncertain and recursive embodiment of the human

---

⁶⁰ Repeating films on loop was also quite ordinary during the early days of cinema, albeit not only for the purpose of shocking the audience but also for more contemplative and meditative experience. See Charles Musser, "A Cinema of Contemplation, a Cinema of Discernment: Spectatorship, Intertextuality and Attractions in the 1890s," in *The Cinema of Attractions, Reloaded*, ed. Wanda Strauven (Amsterdam: Amsterdam University Press, 2006).

⁶¹ Nicole Brenez, "'Is This the Precise Way That Worlds are Reborn?' The Films of Siegfried A. Fruhauf," in *Film Unframed: A History of Austrian Avant-Garde Cinema*, ed. Peter Tscherkassky (Wien: SYNEMA - Gesellschaft für Film und Medien, 2012), 276–85.

⁶² Creation of GIFs from early films has found its platform on social media, see *Silent Movie GIFs Twitter*, accessed December 31, 2022, https://twitter.com/silentmoviegifs.

⁶³ Denson, *Postnaturalism*, 393.

figures, and the embodiment of the scholar who actively strives to make sense of their interactions. Transduction perceived and further enacted via slow observation ensures that both principal agents of this co-evolution remain distinguishable, and that the crack-up maintains its differential as well as relational function.

Coda: Towards a Transductive Film Scholarship

Having moved from the general problem of a diffused yet self-organizing interaction between figurative and material elements within a system to an examination of specific contours of this interaction in archival moving images, the narrative arc of this chapter is now complete. It has been argued that transduction, as a principle that involves both transversal distribution and regulative metastability, is a mechanism with significant aesthetic potential. Its appearances in found footage practices—experimental (in the films of Ken Jacobs, Al Razutis, and Siegfried A. Fruhauf) as well as archival (in the films of Jan Kříženecký)—demonstrate that the tension between the figurative and material spheres (with neither of them prevailing) can generate paradoxes that highlight the co-implication of these usually separate dimensions and also the inherent potentiality of the crack-up within the moving image. The analysis of the bridge scene in *Opening Ceremony* also shows that the transductive equilibrium can emerge accidentally, independent of artistic intervention or the ravages of time, through the autonomous creativity of a trembling camera. The only things necessary for revealing this phenomenon are a theoretically generative concept (transduction) and a slow observation of the emergence of the weird shape (the black wave)—pursued via slow motion and looping—that regulates the margin of indeterminacy and allows the moment of transduction to endure. This way, the crack-up can be localized in a moment of perfect synchronization when everything curiously falls into place (no matter how fleetingly).

It is ironic—or perhaps not ironic at all if we think in terms of the Simondonian framework—that a thorough examination of these autoregulative processes is still enabled by a human intervention, that is, isolating a fragment of the scene and subjecting it to slow motion, as if transduction, even in its most independent phase, still needed help from the operator to become sensible. Only in this case, the operator is not the artist or even the archivist (although both perspectives are still essential for inspiration), but the scholar. This shift opens up space for a sort of interventionist (yet not controlling or mastering) scholarship, which should not be content with merely speaking or writing about photochemical and/

or digital matter; instead, it should strive to translate the unique materiality of hybrid media art into a creative engagement with the moving images and sounds themselves. One fine example can be found in the work of Shane Denson himself: his videographic manifesto *The Algorithmic Nickelodeon* imagines a form of audiovisual criticism that would aim to reinvent our notion of subject-object relations. For this to happen, deformations of the image/object and displacements of the analyst/subject must take place simultaneously. Thus, Denson blurs, zooms, or slows down early films (including Lumière's *The Arrival of a Train*) that have been imported into an editing program and then, with the help of an EEG device, tracks the resulting fluctuations in brain activity that occur in the midst of observing these images. In this way, he creates a sort of media-theoretical perpetuum mobile, designed for the constant investigation into what "cinema" means in the age of algorithms.[64] A similar approach could have the chance to discover numerous aesthetic and scholarly potentialities of autonomous transduction, as well as ways in which this process can be exploited by human imagination.

---

[64] Shane Denson, "The Algorithmic Nickelodeon," *Medieninitiative*, June 22, 2019, accessed December 31, 2022, https://medieninitiative.wordpress.com/2019/06/22/the-algorithmic-nickelodeon/.

4

The Milestone That Never Happened

The Scratched Kiss and the Failed Beginning of Czech Cinema

July 3, 1898. The Czech Cinematograph pavilion introduces a novelty—a comedy scene from the Prague Exhibition Grounds staged by Josef Šváb-Malostranský. The short film—An Assignation in the Mill—shows the so-called first Czech actor unveiling the official Czech Cinematograph poster and then proceeds with a story of a failed date that escalates into a fight. However, what binds these two events together now is a glimpse of perceptual ambiguity—is it two characters in search of "the first kiss in Czech cinema" or just a scratched canvas of an abstract painting? Has the future archival milestone been torn apart right from scratch? (Figures 4.1–4.4)

Since its first screening at the Exhibition of Architecture and Engineering, *An Assignation in the Mill* (Dostaveníčko ve mlýnici; 1898, source: nitrate print) has been one of the signature films that marked the beginning of Czech cinema. It is associated with numerous pioneering achievements—the first fictional film, the first acting performance, the first shot of the Czech Cinematograph, and also the first kiss. Of course, film historians would (rightly) protest against applying the documentary/fictional divide to the earliest cinematic works and put terms such as "first," "Czech," or even "cinema" under scrutiny. Still, the film's visible bond with the specific time and place of the exhibition, as well as with the tangible bodies of Josef Šváb-Malostranský and other people who performed for the camera, makes its pioneering status in popular imagination unescapable. Far more important than the self-acknowledgely[1] primitive plot, in which any sense of order is lost in the chaotic tumult of the crowd,[2] is the film's function as an archival

---

[1] Josef Šváb-Malostranský, "Vzpomínka na prvá milování v Praze," *Rozpravy Aventina* 3, no. 18–19 (1928): 222.
[2] Jiří Anger, "The Uncertain Oeuvre of a Czech Cinema Pioneer," *Revue Filmového přehledu*, January 27, 2020, accessed December 31, 2022, https://www.filmovyprehled.cz/en/revue/detail/the-uncertain-oeuvre-of-a-czech-cinema-pioneer.

Figures 4.1–4.4 *An Assignation in the Mill* (Dostaveníčko ve mlýnici; 1898, source: nitrate print) © Národní filmový archiv.

document, a testimony to the Czech Cinematograph's existence and the people who willingly turned themselves into a spectacle. Šváb-Malostranský unfolds the poster and looks at us with a grinning expression on his face, as if he pointed toward the film becoming a historic milestone that will circulate in the collective memory for decades to come.[3]

At first sight, *Assignation* might seem like an unproblematic, authoritative archival resource—a straightforward statement of Czech cinema being born, resurfacing whenever someone wants to commemorate the anniversary of the Exhibition of Architecture and Engineering or tell a story of the beginnings of Czech cinema in retrospectives, compilations, documentaries, and TV shows. Yet, this historical overdetermination masks many contradictions, ambiguities, and paradoxes that the film entails—and, crucially, has always

---

[3] It is not without interest that Šváb-Malostranský sent a letter to Jan Kříženecký and Josef František Pokorný in which he basically invited himself to the shooting of first Czech films. He offered them to "direct a few humorous scenes." Josef Šváb-Malostranský, "Dopis Josefa Švába-Malostranského Janu Kříženeckému a Josefu Pokornému z 30. dubna 1898," Archiv Národního technického muzea, Sbírka vzpomínek a rukopisů k dějinám techniky a průmyslu, inv. č. 338.

entailed. What undergoes not insignificant variations is not just the film's content—with the two parts often presented separately[4] or missing a few seconds—but also the physical carrier. The commemorative films that survived[5] never present the original nitrate materials but later-generation prints. Similar to other surviving film materials from Kříženecký's estate, the vintage print has been difficult to screen for more than a hundred years owing to the single pair of round perforations,[6] the fragility and flammability of the nitrate film stock, and its reputation of belonging to the collection of the oldest archival artifacts of Czech cinema. However, even if we put the history of film technology and fascination with nitrate patina in brackets, it should be acknowledged that such treatment involves losing many specific qualities of the image. For example, the grain of the original negative or the mysterious color on the vintage print significantly impact what can or cannot be seen from the image content and, consequently, also its archival and documentary function. In other words, what would a casual early cinema aficionado say if he found out that the first screening of Šváb-Malostranský unveiling a Czech Cinematograph poster may not have been in black and white as he had always thought? Even should he not pay much attention to filmic materiality, his experience of the cinematic milestone without the ingrained marker of "oldness" would change drastically.

When we look at the recently digitized film materials (an original negative and a vintage print) of *Assignation* more thoroughly, we realize that the problem lies deeper. In particular, the print involves moments that make the notorious images harder to discern, including one segment that curiously responds to the blind spot that has been associated with the film all along—the gap that happens between the poster unveiling and the failed tryst. The newly added opening titles state: "The print survived in two distinct rolls.

---

[4] Karel Smrž, the film historian who "rediscovered" Kříženecký's films in the 1920s, initially argued that the material presented two films—"A Scene at the Mill" (Scéna ve mlýnici) and "Failed Assignation" (Překažené dostaveníčko). See Zdeněk Smejkal, "Rané práce Karla Smrže o dějinách českého filmu," in *Otázky divadla a filmu*, ed. Artur Závodský (Brno: Universita J.E. Purkyně, 1970), 277.

[5] See, for example, *Jan Kříženecký* (Bohumil Veselý, 1968), *How It Started* (Jak to začalo; Květa Lehovcová, 1968), *Thank You, Mr. Kříženecký* (Díky, pane Kříženecký; Oleg Reif, 1978), *Jan Kříženecký* (Vojtěch Trapl, 1983) or various episodes of a TV show *In Search of Lost Time* (Hledání ztraceného času; Pavel Vantuch, 1991–2012), particularly "The First Czech with a Crank" (1993). The list of films and TV shows about Jan Kříženecký and the beginnings of Czech cinema is available here: Jiří Anger, ed., *Digitální Kříženecký: Nový život prvních českých filmů* (Praha: Národní filmový archiv, 2023), 282–7.

[6] *An Assignation in the Mill* was one of the films that were already duplicated in the 1920s onto the classic Edison perforated film stock (with four rectangular perforations on each side of a frame). See Jeanne Pommeau and Jiří Anger, "The Digitization of Jan Kříženecký's Films," *Iluminace* 31, no. 1 (2019): 104–7.

The fragments were scanned separately and assembled back to the original order." This intervention could be understood as restorative, but due to the decision not to retouch, the bridge between the two parts is anything but seamless. Whereas in the previously seen instances of the film, it was either invisible or highlighted by wipes,[7] here it is marked by disruptive scratches at the beginning of the second roll, sharp vertical grooves that almost erase the figurative content of the image, that is, the characters approaching each other and leaning in for a kiss. What some will consider a threat to the film's archival function, others will consider true to its material history. To conceptualize *Assignation*'s "archive effect"[8] in its complexity, both points of view need to come together.

Again, we encounter a filmic artifact whose meaning, effect, and status depend vitally upon the crack-up arising between figuration and materiality by serendipity and without intention. This time, though, the positions of both meaning-making spheres shift. First, unlike the color veil, static marks, and camera trembling, the vertical scratches cannot be assigned as inherent characteristics of the film's production process. Being most probably caused by later mishandling of the print, their existence is inseparable from the complex dynamic between materiality and circulation that leads us to perceive physical interventions as ravages of time. The primary function of signs of decay and degradation—such as the well-known dots, dust, and scratches—is to remind us that the archival artifact has covered a long distance between then and now. In this interpretive scheme, it is harder to ascribe to the scratches any specific signification other than the passing of time—unless they communicate with the figurative content in an aesthetically generative manner or speak about something strangely resonating with the history and memory of filmed events. Unfortunately, even when they do, they usually present a rewarding resource for found footage filmmakers and rarely stand on their own.[9]

Second, the real mystery of *Assignation* does not lie in the origin of a specific technological intervention—which in the case of the vertical scratches cannot ever be fully known—but in the origin of the filmed event,

---

[7] This is the case of compilations or documentaries such as *50 Years of Cinema* (50 let kinematografie; František Sádek, 1946), *When Photographs Came to Life* (Když oživly fotografie; Ivo Novák, 1958) or *History of Czechoslovak Cinema, Part I* (Dějiny československé kinematografie I; Vojtěch Količ, 1967).

[8] Jaimie Baron, *The Archive Effect: Found Footage and the Audiovisual Experience of History* (London: Routledge, 2014). See also Rebecca Swender, "Claiming the Found: Archive Footage and Documentary Practice," *The Velvet Light Trap* 64 (2009): 3–10.

[9] Katherine Groo's book *Bad Film Histories* presents a notable exception. Katherine Groo, *Bad Film Histories: Ethnography and the Early Archive* (Minneapolis: University of Minnesota Press, 2019).

whose (both narratively and literally) divided character turned the scratches into forces shaping its place in history. It is undoubtedly possible to reimagine the yellowish-orange color in *Grand Consecration of the Emperor Franz I Bridge*, static marks in *The First Day of the Spring Races of Prague*, and camera trembling in *Opening Ceremony of the Čech Bridge* through the perspective of the depicted events upon which they intruded and examine how they disrupt their unity, recognizability, and ability to bear witness. Nevertheless, none of the respective films portray such a pregnant and contested historical moment as *Assignation*—none of them are tied to the official film history and the official archive of cinematic milestones to nearly the same extent. When scratches arise in moving images that are so inherently recognizable, not only is the perceptual shock stronger—as anyone familiar with psychoanalysis would tell, the "unheimlich" needs the "heimlich"[10]—but the crack-up becomes more dependent on our recognition of what is represented in the image (and also the context of its making) than in the previous cases. No matter how distorted the frames are, our interpretation of the scratches is filtered through our knowledge and memory of Czech cinema's primal scene (and vice versa).

To address these differences in terms of the crack-up, special attention to questions of epistemology and perception is necessary. Not that the experience of reception in the previous chapters was irrelevant, but the weird shapes (color veil, electric horses, black wave) were connected to the films' innate material and media characteristics. Although they depended on certain psychological automatisms and benefited from selective bracketing operations, the physical deformations have, in a way, always been there, making way for the crack-up to be actualized once the proportion of figurative and material elements results in their visible interaction. When the emphasis leans to the filmed event as an archival document of a historic milestone, with all the ambiguities such a document brings, and when the physical intrusions owe their presence to decay, the emergence of the crack-up rests on the problem of historicity, "the properties of film that contribute to its being historically meaning bearing and the particular relationship that film bears to past time,"[11] to a larger extent than before. And because each cinematic event owes its archival function not just to what was initially put into the scene but also to the pioneering status cemented through circulation

---

[10] I mean unheimlich (uncanny) in the Freudian sense. Sigmund Freud, "'The Uncanny,'" in *Penguin Freud Library*, Vol. 14 (Harmondsworth: Penguin, 1991), 339–76. For understanding the concept in found footage and video essays, see Johannes Binotto, "In Lag of Knowledge: The Video Essay as Parapraxis," in *Practical Aesthetics*, ed. Bernd Herzogenrath (New York: Bloomsbury, 2020), 83–94.

[11] Groo, *Bad Film Histories*, 8. See Chapter 2.

and repetition, the crack-up is at its strongest when the physical deformation makes us question whether the depicted reality is what it seems to be. Of course, the shift of emphasis from a technological given to a structuring event is not absolute, and the phenomena analyzed in Chapters 1–3 and here differ in degree rather than in kind; nevertheless, it still has to be stated to provide a more nuanced picture of the crack-up that *Digital Kříženecký* offers.

The argument shall progress through four stages. First, I lay the groundwork for studying the historicity and archival function of the earliest cinematic artifacts by exploring Jaimie Baron's "archive effect," a concept that anchors archival documents in the experience of reception. Second, I turn attention to the affective aspects of Baron's conception, demonstrating and problematizing the causality between nostalgia and decaying materiality in found footage films. Third, I wonder whether the crack-up of the pregnant moment in *Assignation* is not a sign that the archive effect is always already riddled with the powers of the false. Fourth, I analyze the three functions that form the (false?) archive effect of the scratched kiss. In line with the rest of this book and its approach *from below*, a weird shape unfolding from a clash between figurative content and accidental material intervention (scratched kiss) opens up a theoretical/historical problem (what makes us accept certain images as archival documents?) that forces us to see many well-established concepts of film history and theory (the archive effect or, more broadly, historicity and its relation to nostalgia) as well as practice (repetition and variation of pregnant moments in found footage) in a new light.

The Archive Effect of Cinematic Firsts

The epistemological aspects of the crack-up in archival films demand to be anchored in the existing research on archives and their ability to evoke contact with the past. The so-called "archival turn" was aptly summed up by Ann Laura Stoler as a "move from archive-as-source to archive-as-subject" that has resulted in "a rethinking of the materiality and imaginary of collections and what kinds of truth claims lie in documentation."[12] The archival turn has provoked a reconsideration of the role of the archive as an institution and its relationships with power structures, as well as the value of archival documents as historical evidence.[13] As Marlene Manoff claims,

---

[12] Ann Laura Stoler, "Colonial Archives and the Arts of Governance," *Archival Science* 2, no. 1–2 (2002): 93, 94.

[13] Efrén Cuevas, *Filming History from Below: Microhistorical Documentaries* (New York: Wallflower Press, 2022), 41.

"many scholars [. . .] have come to understand the historical record [. . .] not as an objective representation of the past, but rather as a selection of objects that have been preserved for a variety of reasons. [. . .] Whatever the archive contains is already a reconstruction—a recording of history from a particular perspective."[14] Thanks to mass digitization, historical documents have reached beyond the dusty contents of archival institutions, and the range of audiovisual phenomena that can be considered archival has increased significantly, as has the number of techniques by which we can manipulate images to alter the past that is etched within them. Film and media studies have generally paid more attention to these shifts in the context of found footage films that reuse archival documents;[15] however, with the increasing number of archival materials being circulated and appropriated in the online space, the border between archival footage and found footage becomes less and less tenable.

Debates on what makes film a reliable (or unreliable) source of history have been going on since cinema's birth.[16] Boleslaw Matuszewski's celebratory text "A New Source of History" (1898), already mentioned in Chapter 2, inevitably comes to mind, with its belief in film as "ocular evidence that is truthful and infallible par excellence."[17] As C. G. Olesen claims, his vision of film has more in common with criminal evidence than with indexical documents of duration, echoing the scientific positivism of its time as well as certain epistemological naivety of contemporary audiences.[18] When moving images entered public consciousness, any notion of potential manipulation or retouching was less important than their novel ability to "make the dead and gone get up and walk."[19] No matter how disturbing, uncanny, or mysterious this sensation of "seeing movement fossilized for the first time" might have

---

[14] Marlene Manoff, "Theories of the Archive from Across the Disciplines," *Portal: Libraries and the Academy* 4, no. 1 (2004): 14.

[15] See, for example, Jay Leyda, *Films Beget Films: A Study of the Compilation Film* (New York: Hill and Wang, 1964); Patrik Sjöberg, *The World in Pieces: A Study of Compilation Film* (Stockholm: Aura, 2001); Jeffrey Skoller, *Shadows, Specters, Shards: Making History in Avant-Garde Film* (Minneapolis: University of Minnesota Press, 2005); Steven F. Anderson, *Technologies of History: Visual Media and the Eccentricity of the Past* (New Hampshire: Dartmouth College Press, 2011); Marcia Landy, *Cinema & Counter-History* (Bloomington and Indianapolis: Indiana University Press, 2015); Catherine Russell, *Archiveology: Walter Benjamin and Archival Film Practices* (Durham: Duke University Press, 2018).

[16] For an overview, see C. G. Olesen, "Film History in the Making" (PhD diss., Amsterdam University, 2017), 40–92.

[17] Boleslas Matuszewski, "A New Source of History," *Film History* 7, no. 3 (1995): 323.

[18] Olesen, "Film History in the Making," 43–6.

[19] Matuszewski, "A New Source of History," 323.

been,[20] every gesture, expression, or movement of wind in the trees was endowed with meaning, with the idea that "something happened." In this vein, Šváb-Malostranský holding a Czech Cinematograph transparent, sometimes understood as a mere opening title, bears more importance than any more or less comical plot that was orchestrated. In addition, his manic gestures and mimics throughout the film do not primarily want to persuade us that we are watching a character with feelings and motivations—first, he must make us aware that an event worthy of being preserved or even canonized is taking place. Time was limited to a few tens of seconds, space reduced to an immobile rectangle, editing virtually nonexistent (except for splices),[21] and the nitrate carrier in ever-present danger of being burnt or destroyed—that is why the gesturing needed to be as pronounced and unambiguous as possible. The film's place in history grows from contextually and materially imposed limitations, and the impossibility of their overcoming contributed to its turning into a contested and overdetermined archival document right from the beginning.

This instant historicity needs to be considered when theorizing the earliest filmic artifacts and their "archive effect." Jaimie Baron's influential monograph *The Archive Effect: Found Footage and the Audiovisual Experience of History* (2014) introduced this term to rethink archival footage and its various uses as an "experience of reception,"[22] something that resides in the activity of the spectator. Films evoke the archive effect as long as they "offer us a glimpse of the world that existed but has been erased and overlaid with different faces, current fashions, and new technologies."[23] Baron's shift toward reception helps us ask questions regarding the factors that make us understand the crack-up as revealing something important about history. Crucially, when confronted with an idiosyncratic archival artifact such as the digitized nitrate print of *Assignation*, the author's impulse can be prolonged to show that the archive effect does not have to result solely from the distance between then and now or creative appropriation but from something that is engraved within the archival document itself.

As anyone familiar with Jaimie Baron's conception will know, one of the basic triggers of the effect is "temporal disparity," the perception of a distance

---

[20] For more on this topic, see Murray Leeder, *The Modern Supernatural and the Beginnings of Cinema* (Cham: Palgrave Macmillan, 2017).
[21] See, for example, "escamontage," a formal practice whereby cuts were made without any apparent break in the framing, described in Genevieve Yue, *Girl Head: Feminism and Film Materiality* (New York: Fordham University Press, 2021), 73–101.
[22] Baron, *The Archive Effect*, 7.
[23] Ibid., 1.

between "then" and "now" generated within a single text.²⁴ Such disparity can be evoked by juxtaposing shots perceived as produced at different moments in time, as in Alain Resnais's Holocaust documentary *Night and Fog* (1955), but also by the fact that we are watching remnants of reality that were once captured by the camera and covered some distance in time to get to the present moment of reception.²⁵ When confronted with films from the pioneering days of cinema, this disparity becomes all the more convoluted. The paradoxical character of early cinematic events—spatiotemporally limited yet pregnant with historic meaning—questions the distance between then and now in minimally two respects. First, there is the idea that the first cinematic attempts—especially those that proclaimed themselves as milestones—bore a special responsibility not only to preserve real events and gestures but also to make their filmic capture historically relevant. Whether the depicted events were festive or quotidian, contingent or carefully planned, it can be intuited that each shooting during the early days involved a certain overestimation of what was about to happen. Making the most out of a brief temporal interval materialized in a static tableau required mastering the art of condensation, realizing, to quote the narrator of Honoré de Balzac's *The Wild Ass's Skin* (1831), "how many events crowd into the space of a second, and how many things hang on the throw of a dice!"²⁶ In his famous description of the "pregnant moment," Roland Barthes spoke of "a hieroglyph in which can be read at a single glance [. . .] the present, the past and the future; that is, the historical meaning of the represented action," a "presence of all the absences (memories, lessons, promises) to whose rhythm History becomes both intelligible and desirable."²⁷ In the earliest cinema, pregnant moments were constantly escaping in-between frames, due both to the relentless movement of the film strip and to the flux of life. What remained was visible evidence of history caught in the making, a larger-than-life anticipation that what was happening transcended a specific place in time, a specific "then." Under these circumstances, how can we redefine temporal disparity if the distance between then and now was already predicted in the film's creation?

The second pitfall relates to the material carrier. Baron mentions that the temporal disparity must be visible either "at the level of profilmic object" or "at the level of the filmstrip itself—the type of film stock, the color or lack thereof, its degree of damage or disintegration, and so on," or at both

---

[24] Ibid., 18.
[25] Ibid., 17–22.
[26] Honoré de Balzac, *The Wild Ass's Skin* (Oxford: Oxford University Press, 2012), 8.
[27] Roland Barthes, "Diderot, Brecht, Eisenstein," in *Image, Music, Text* (London: Fontana Press, 1977), 73.

levels at the same time.²⁸ A familiar question of what occurs when physical deformation makes the content barely recognizable resurfaces, but even if both figurative and material actors participate simultaneously and more or less equally, the recipient most often lacks information to what extent the signs of physical degradation were part of the original "then." Rips, dots, and dust are accepted as universal marks of a film being old, worn-out, or archival, but they were already pretty typical in the early years of cinema. For example, Yuri Tsivian describes how "the rain effect," "scratch marks on worn prints that show up as specks flickering vertically down the screen," became such an established feature of film reception in the beginnings of Russian cinema that it was often difficult to tell how the film would have looked like without it.²⁹ Also, the previously discussed issues of coloration, static electricity, or camera trembling, which were in some form already accessible to period spectators, owe their present archive effect more to how uncanny or alien they look like compared to both what we usually see in the available early films and what we usually see in contemporary cinema than to any conviction that they reveal the past as it was. The contemporary audience may have seen *Grand Consecration of the Emperor Franz I Bridge* through the yellowish-orange filter; however, this memory has been washed down in black and white so many times that any notion of "then" must first compete with deeply sedimented ideas of greyscale beginnings of cinema.

This instability of "then" and "now" is further deepened by the afterlife of early cinema in later contexts. Although Baron focuses primarily on the temporal disparity in found footage and appropriation films, her categorization leaves room for it to arise by circulation through various contexts and in various material states.³⁰ The situation becomes even more complicated in the online space,³¹ in which we encounter numerous works and formats that promise to erase the distance between past and present yet fail. However much some more extreme forms of digital retouching attempt to return the films to the state in which they were screened for the first time, or however much internet amateurs attempt to colorize and upscale early films into a

---

[28] Baron, *The Archive Effect*, 20–1.
[29] Yuri Tsivian, *Early Cinema in Russia and Its Cultural Reception* (Chicago: The University of Chicago Press, 1998), 85–6. Raúl Ruiz also talks about how the Kawéskar indigenous people of Chile and Argentina saw scratches on the screen in early films as rain. Raúl Ruiz, "Folklore," in *Poéticas del cine* (Santiago: Ediciones Universidad Diego Portales, 2013), 429–30.
[30] Joanne Bernardi, Paolo Cherchi Usai, Tami Williams, and Joshua Yumibe, eds., *Provenance and Early Cinema* (Bloomington: Indiana University Press, 2021).
[31] Baron elaborates on the specificities of the "digital archive effect" in Chapter 5 of her book, though again she speaks mostly of appropriation films, not about archival footage in general. Baron, *The Archive Effect*, 138–72.

state of an eternal present,[32] the gap between past and present is inescapable. Temporal change and aging still manifest in the content—different clothes, architecture, even manners of behavior in front of the camera—as well as the carrier—the absence of flicker, invariable speed of projection, or no grain in the image. Of course, we could ask whether excessive intervention makes temporal disparity more visible or less—on the one hand, it demonstrates how new technology can transform the past and make it actual; on the other, it may question whether the carefully constructed smooth surface leaves any holes for remnants of the past to emerge.

To confront the notion of the archive as experience with a larger historiographic project, Katherine Groo's book *Bad Film Histories: Ethnography and the Early Archive* (2019) is a useful companion. What she calls a "particularist approach to film historiography"[33] teaches us to take "the absences, imperfections, and discontinuities [. . .] as crucial concepts and methodological coordinates rather than obstacles to be overcome or resolved."[34] "Bad film histories" remind us that "the historiographic process will be messy, imperfect, and open to revision, especially as our artifacts change, degrade, and disappear from the archives."[35] While Groo focuses on forgotten, nameless, and discarded ethnographic films, and we have at our disposal a treasured artifact of Czech cinema, those two are not as incompatible as they might seem. The nitrate print of *Assignation* has been deemed just as unworthy of public attention as the Dutch travelogues and consequently almost invisible until its digitization. Albeit the reasons for neglect were different—there is the single Lumière perforation that made the prints difficult to screen[36] and also the understandable claim that the oldest artifacts of Czech cinema should be protected from projection—the role of physical agents in "clouding" what was originally represented in the images was a factor as well. Its punctured and discolored surface can be perceived as an obstacle to seeing the first kiss in Czech cinema, just as much as the distorted surface-landscape of ethnographic films analyzed by Groo seems to block the beautiful view of nature. Therefore, even a privileged milestone of early cinema can become part of bad film histories and, thanks to the dynamic between official history and arbitrary deformations, make for an all the more interesting research object. *Assignation* as a bad film artifact illuminates the

---

[32] See, for example, Denis Shiryaev, "21 Old Films from 1895 to 1902 Colorized and Upscaled in 60 fps, with Sound," *YouTube*, 2021, accessed December 31, 2022, https://www.youtube.com/watch?v=YZuP41ALx_Q.

[33] Groo, *Bad Film Histories*, 8.

[34] Ibid., 9.

[35] Ibid.

[36] Ibid.

archive effect *from below*, through the weird shape of a scratched kiss as an element that unites our nostalgia for a discernible and localizable image of the past with a certain obscurity that cannot be scraped away and affects the film's materiality as much as its figuration.

In this situation, the crack-up does not necessarily resolve the general issues of the archive effect. Still, it helps us disprove the illusion that the archival object reveals a discernible and localizable moment of the past that can be clearly separated from the present and points toward the notion that a cinematic event always already entails a dimension of hiddenness. Laura U. Marks once wrote that cinematic images "do not transparently reflect [the originary event] but obscure it."[37] The archival objects, or what she calls "cultural fossils," "do not simply bring an aspect of their place of origin to a new site; they also make strange the place into which they arrive." Thus, they "bring back lost histories in which both origin and destination are implicated" and also "the radical hybridity already present at both sites."[38] Speaking of Kříženecký's and Šváb's *Assignation* and its nitrate print scratched in the middle, the goal is not to unveil specific "then" and "now"—conversely, we shall pile up layer upon layer of cracks that arise at the level of figuration, at the level of materiality, and on the boundary between them. Yet, as we deal with a canonical image of Czech film history, there is still that old desire that the original event can (re)gain brighter contours. It is precisely this dialectic between the layering of disruptions and the persistence of nostalgia that guides the following subchapter.

The Limits of Nostalgia

Not surprisingly, Baron's conceptualization of the archive effect is inextricably linked to nostalgia.[39] She emphasizes that the temporal disparity "produces

---

[37] Laura U. Marks, *The Skin of the Film: Intercultural Cinema, Embodiment, and the Senses* (Durham and London: Duke University Press, 2000), 124.
[38] Ibid.
[39] For contemporary understanding of nostalgia in film and media studies, see Svetlana Boym, *The Future of Nostalgia* (New York: Basic Books, 2001); Simon Reynolds, *Retromania: Pop Culture's Addiction to Its Own Past* (London: Faber & Faber, 2010); Katharina Niemeyer, ed., *Media and Nostalgia: Yearning for the Past, Present and Future* (Basingstoke and New York: Palgrave Macmillan, 2014); Jason Sperb, *Flickers of Film: Nostalgia in the Time of Digital Cinema* (New Brunswick: Rutgers University Press, 2016); Dominik Schrey, *Analoge Nostalgie in der digitalen Medienkultur* (Berlin: Kulturverlag Kadmos, 2017); Nicola Sayers, *The Promise of Nostalgia: Reminiscence, Longing and Hope in Contemporary American Culture* (London: Routledge, 2020).

not only the archive *effect* but also [...] the archive *affect*."[40] According to her, "not only do we invest archival documents with the authority of the 'real' past, but also with the feeling of loss."[41] The euphoric images of Šváb unfolding the formative poster of Czech cinema, kissing a girl, and fighting with local brawlers inevitably (although not exclusively) evoke such feelings—longing for the atmosphere of the end of the nineteenth century, for the glimpses of national revival, for that passion for new technological inventions, for the promises that the new medium held. Nonetheless, the digitized vintage print and the original negative both remind us, in their own ways, that this historic milestone is now lost, if it was ever possible to localize one. Ruins, cracks, and imperfections visible everywhere across the figurative and material dimensions and distinctively varying in both preserved "original" versions deny us the soothing feeling of turning back the clock, returning to the lost home, and capturing that blissful moment in a freeze-frame, or at least make it harder to achieve.

An obvious interpretive move is plain to see—we can come back to Svetlana Boym's famous double of restorative versus reflective nostalgia (also applied by Jaimie Baron). Just as a reminder, the former "stresses nostos and attempts a transhistorical reconstruction of the lost home," while the latter "thrives in algia, the longing itself, and delays the homecoming—wistfully, ironically, desperately."[42] Whereas restorative nostalgia "signifies a return to the original stasis, to the prelapsarian moment" and considers the past not a duration but a "perfect snapshot," reflective nostalgia "suggests new flexibility, not the reestablishment of stasis" and focuses on the "meditation on history and passage of time" rather than recovering absolute truths.[43] It is easy to see the digitized *Assignation* as inclining toward the reflective variant. Whereas behind many digital restoration projects lies an ambition for "total reconstructions of monuments of the past" through current technological means, the layers of decay in the *Assignation* print and negative associate nostalgia that "lingers on ruins, the patina of time and history, in the dreams of another place and another time."[44]

However plausible and intuitive this account sounds, it tells only a part of the story and risks leaving many nuances of *Assignation* as an archival document behind. Putting aside the fact that digital restorations performed by archives are increasingly more reflective of the inherent contradictions

---

[40] Baron, *The Archive Effect*, 21.
[41] Ibid.
[42] Boym, *The Future of Nostalgia*, xvi.
[43] Ibid., 49.
[44] Ibid., 41.

that attempts to reconstruct the past involve,[45] the status of *Digital Kříženecký* vis-à-vis reflective nostalgia is not as clear as it seems. As a decidedly noninterventionist project, it strove to highlight the films' historicity and the inevitability of loss by showing them as they exist today, but one could object that many subtle differences between the photochemical past and digital present remain obscured in the new files (flicker, variable speed, slightly different color hues, and so on). Is the very presentation of late nineteenth- and early twentieth-century nitrate prints in 4K digital resolution not an attempt to retrieve the irretrievable? Instead of imposing strict boundaries between reflective and restorative nostalgia, it is better to look at how both dimensions can work together. This approach resonates in Baron's specific application of Boym's heuristic. In Chapter 4, segment "The Archive Affect and Nostalgia," she employs the restorative/reflective doublet to analyze Bill Morrison's *Decasia: The State of Decay* (2002), Hollis Frampton's *(nostalgia)* (1971), and Raphael Montañez Ortiz's *Cowboy and "Indian" Film* (1958). Significantly, she describes the experience of watching the former film as "one of a constantly evoked desire for something that has been lost, since these fragments are only metonyms for a larger whole that we can never see or experience as they once were."[46] The omnipresent decay is the main reason why she perceives the aims of the film as not only restorative but also reflective: "*Decasia*'s insistence on the material presence of its appropriated images has the potential to make us aware of the materiality of all things and to remind us that every fragment is a part of a much larger whole."[47]

As intriguing as Baron's interpretation is, it seems to fall into the same trap already indicated in previous chapters—she turns the physical deformation of filmic matter into a universal sign of loss, a cipher for ruination, fragmentation, and irreversible duration, a "fleeting experience of the otherness of the past."[48] Regarding nostalgia, it makes no difference how severe the damage is, where its origin lies, and in what ways it may actively shape the figurative content of the image—the most important thing is whether the archive affect is revered (*Decasia*) or subverted by irony (*(nostalgia)* and *Cowboy and "Indian" Film*). Any film dealing with physical deformation in a serious and solemn manner is apparently destined to dwell in the irrevocable past, whether it is Morrison's

---

[45] See, for example, Olesen, "Film History in the Making," 138–43; Giovanna Fossati, *From Grain to Pixel: The Archival Life of Film in Transition*, 3rd Revised ed. (Amsterdam: Amsterdam University Press, 2018); Sonia Campanini, Vinzenz Hediger, and Ines Bayer, "Minding the Materiality of Film: The Frankfurt Master's Program 'Film Culture: Archiving, Programming, Presentation,'" *Synoptique* 6, no. 1 (2018): 79–96.
[46] Baron, *The Archive Effect*, 129.
[47] Ibid., 131.
[48] Ibid., 134.

film or Lana Del Rey's music video.[49] Baron's scenario limits the range of affects that decay can evoke and the number of ways in which it can help us breach the past/present divide. For instance, Baron underestimates the role of the devouring stains in *Decasia* in the figurative processes that give form to the "inhospitable" world of the present. Morrison's symphony stitches them together to highlight that the only whole in which the deformations can function is a world *of* decay, and not a world *in* decay—as many publications on the Anthropocene testify, there is no need to yearn for the world of decay because we might as well be living it more intensely than ever.[50] Nevertheless, there is also the decay's constitutive impact on what we perceive as the "then" in temporal disparity. Whereas Baron presupposes an imaginary whole that existed before and beyond decay, the images unfolding on the screen present us with a vision of early nitrate cinema that is diffused, obscure, and fleeting, and thus perhaps closer to how filmic artifacts circulated in the beginning. *Decasia* does not offer us recognizable images pertaining to a specific time and place, but rather the unknowable objects of the early ethnographic archive described by Katherine Groo—"untitled, unauthored, and seemingly infinite in number."[51] For every depiction of a historical monument that went as planned, there were hundreds that gave no way of knowing when the original event ended and when it began, or even how much of the event was even captured on camera and consequently made visible in the frames. In this situation, it is not entirely clear which dimension of the event we should be nostalgic about, reflectively, restoratively, or otherwise.

Of course, the case of *Assignation* is different—being a signature early Czech film with a relatively wide circulation in retrospectives, compilations, documentaries, and TV shows and a firmly established place in the collective memory. Yet, if we pay attention to the multitude of prints and versions that exist, it is difficult to state which of them presents the referential event—and, in particular, the first kiss—most faithfully. The images from later-generation prints that were used in the compilations, especially those that circulated in

---

[49] The allegiance between ruin films such as *Decasia* and Lana Del Rey's grainy Super 8 music videos is mentioned surprisingly often, considering the huge difference in the level of physical damages and their role in figurative processes. See, for example, Arild Fetveit, "Death, beauty, and iconoclastic nostalgia: Precarious aesthetics and Lana Del Rey," *NECSUS European Journal of Media Studies* 4, no. 2 (2015): 192. For a polemic with Fetveit's interpretation, see Tomáš Jirsa, "For the Affective Aesthetics of Contemporary Music Video," *Music, Sound, and the Moving Image* 13, no. 2 (2019): 187–208.

[50] Jussi Parikka, *A Geology of Media* (Minneapolis: University of Minnesota Press, 2015); Jennifer Fay, *Inhospitable World: Cinema in the Time of the Anthropocene* (New York: Oxford University Press, 2018).

[51] Groo, *Bad Film Histories*, 256.

Bohumil Veselý's *Jan Kříženecký* (1968)[52] or in the episodes of a nostalgic TV show *In Search of Lost Time* (Hledání ztraceného času; 1991–2012),[53] may be the most familiar, but they often do not even show the whole film. For example, Veselý's compilation omits the first few seconds of the second part, including the very first kiss, the exact segment which is so distorted in the original print; many others show only the first or only the second half. On the other hand, the format that comes closest to making the first kiss perceptible in its entirety—the original negative—was not meant for screening and was only made accessible with the digitization project.[54] The vintage print that was being screened at the turn of the nineteenth and twentieth centuries would be considered the most authentic by many; nevertheless, after being torn apart and assembled back together and suffering multiple distinctive scratches in the meantime, the first kiss is now significantly clouded. Restorative nostalgia would not be able to lean on the logic of "before and after" that is (or at least was for a long time) popular among many champions of digital restoration[55]—that is, two versions of a film presented side by side, with a degrading image before restoration on the left and a retouched, crystal-clear image after restoration on the right. Meanwhile, strictly reflective nostalgia would have to include all the versions at once and still not get ahold of what distinguishes the relationship between figurative and material spheres in the vintage print from the others.

Thus, if any kind of nostalgia persists, it needs to be conceived in relation to the crack-up. While we are watching the digitized vintage print and get to the punctured moment of a kiss, the archive affect (and effect) do not fade away; rather, they dissolve across two dimensions. What structures our longing is neither the film as a circulating artifact nor the film as a figurative event—it is the membrane that simultaneously reveals and discloses one at the expense of the other. This ambiguity allows us to make sense of the variety of factors that determine what we can or cannot feel nostalgically about. Furthermore,

---

[52] This compilation has been made available on the VOD platform dafilms.cz and consequently on YouTube. Bohumil Veselý, "Jan Kříženecký," *YouTube*, 2013, accessed December 31, 2022, https://www.youtube.com/watch?v=Rk2OrOXEmnM.

[53] See, for example, the episode *The First Czech with a Crank* (První Čech s klikou; Pavel Vantuch, 1993).

[54] See, for example, Olesen, "Film History in the Making," 143 or Paolo Cherchi Usai, David Francis, Alexander Horwath, and Michael Loebenstein, eds., *Film Curatorship: Archives, Museums, and the Digital Marketplace* (Wien: Synema – Gesellschaft für Film und Medien, 2008), 208–9.

[55] For the criticism of the "before/after" figure in digital restoration, see David Walsh, "There Is No Such Thing as Digital Restoration," in *Work/s in Progress: Digital Film Restoration Within Archives*, ed. Kerstin Parth, Oliver Hanley, and Thomas Ballhausen (Vienna: SYNEMA – Gesellschaft für Film und Medien, 2013), 32–3.

it can also help us realize how even the material elements that intruded upon the image ex-post can retroactively change the meanings and effects that the original event might or might not have entailed, to the extent that the logics of now/then, past/present, and before/after stop being referential. In order to find a different anchor that steps into the picture when these temporal coordinates stop functioning, we could ask whether the ambiguities and uncertainties should not be imbricated deeper within the archive effect itself.

The Powers of the False

The cinematic firsts are archival documents that bring us assurance yet often also confusion. We return to them to reaffirm that the history of Czech or other national cinema began at a specific time and place, thanks to a particular filmmaker who created a particular film object. Nonetheless, the gap in time, lack of convincing historical sources, and intense circulation and variation cause the archival evidence to be frequently not what it seems. For example, arguably the most canonical work of cinema's earliest period, *Workers Leaving the Lumière Factory in Lyon* (La Sortie de l'Usine Lumière à Lyon; 1895),[56] was only relatively recently found to exist in at least four versions, with the first one from March 1895 presumably being lost.[57] Some treasured milestones have been attributed to a wrong filmmaker or a wrong date of production (the case of *Footpads* and other films assigned to Robert W. Paul);[58] others have been revealed as staged (for example, Kříženecký's *Square of Purkyně in Královské Vinohrady/Purkyňovo náměstí na Králových Vinohradech*, one of the first three films presented at the Exhibition of Architecture and Engineering).[59] Another aspect that is often questioned

---

[56] Along with *The Arrival of a Train at La Ciotat* (L'Arrivée d'un train en gare de La Ciotat; 1896).
[57] Apparently, the subject was in such heavy demand that it had to be reshot on numerous occasions, as negatives became exhausted. See "FAQ—Movies," *Catalogue Lumière*, L'œuvre cinématographique des frères Lumière, accessed December 31, 2022, https://catalogue-lumiere.com/faq-movies/. This information is based on the prior research of Michelle Aubert, Jean-Claude Seguin et al. Michelle Aubert, and Jean-Claude Seguin, eds., *La production cinématographique des Frères Lumière* (Paris: BiFi, 1996), 214–15.
[58] Ian Christie, "Issues of Provenance and Attribution for the Canon: Bookending Robert Paul," in *Provenance and Early Cinema*, ed. Joanne Bernardi, Paolo Cherchi Usai, Tami Williams, and Joshua Yumibe (Bloomington: Indiana University Press, 2021), 70–9.
[59] The other two films were *Midsummer Pilgrimage in a Czechoslavic Village* (Svatojánská pouť v českoslovanské vesnici, 1898) and *March Past During Corpus Christi Feast in Hradčany* (Defilování vojska o Božím těle na Králových Hradčanech, 1898). Zdeněk Štábla, *Český kinematograf Jana Kříženeckého* (Praha: Československý filmový ústav,

is the films' representation of national themes, which may reproduce or even create prevailing stereotypes (for instance, the abundance of canals, windmills, cheese, tulip fields, and fishing villages in early Dutch films).[60] And last but not least, the pioneering status itself has been falsely or truthfully attributed to so many films that it has turned into a cliché, parodied by films such as *Forgotten Silver* (Peter Jackson and Costa Botes, 1995).

In this situation, any film historian, theorist, or archivist should embrace the fact that the archive effect, particularly when evoked by early cinematic works, will always be riddled with the "powers of the false." This phrase comes from Gilles Deleuze's *Cinema 2: The Time-Image* (originally published in 1985), signifying the capacity of film art to break down the dichotomy between truth and fiction and embrace fabulation, polyvocality, and contradiction to "make what has happened appear indeterminate and therefore question the legitimized and homogenized versions of events."[61] The aforementioned film *Forgotten Silver* unleashes the powers of the false to mock the fascination with cinematic firsts. It claims to have unearthed a body of film work by a fictional New Zealand filmmaker that proves New Zealanders were responsible for nearly all major innovations in cinema technology, from the invention of color and sound to the narrative structure of feature films.[62] Could we employ these powers of the false to challenge the first cinematic artifacts' archive effect, their claims for truth and temporal disparity?

Again, none other than Jaimie Baron comes to the rescue. In Chapter 2 of her book, she analyzes films that demonstrate "the ways in which the archive effect may be simulated or manipulated and explore the various reactions to these archival fabrications."[63] She claims that our reactions to fake documentaries such as *Forgotten Silver* "not only demonstrate our desire to believe that such revelatory documents can suddenly be discovered but also simultaneously reveal that found documents can be staged, producing a

---

1973), 71. The information is based on a letter that Josef František Pokorný's brother Vincenc sent to the National Technical Museum Prague on February 3, 1953. The film is considered lost.

[60] Sarah Dellmann, *Images of Dutchness: Popular Visual Culture, Early Cinema and the Emergence of a National Cliché, 1800–1914* (Amsterdam: Amsterdam University Press, 2019), 16–17.

[61] As Deleuze does not define the powers of the false in a precise way, I have taken a quote from Doro Wiese's book that builds on this concept. Doro Wiese, *The Powers of the False: Reading, Writing, Thinking beyond Truth and Fiction* (Evanston: Northwestern University Press, 2014), 34; Gilles Deleuze, *Cinema 2: The Time-Image* (Minneapolis: University of Minnesota Press, 2001), 126–55.

[62] For an analysis of *Forgotten Silver* and other "fake" documentaries, see Anderson, *Technologies of History*, 68–87.

[63] Baron, *The Archive Effect*, 12.

'false' archive effect and thereby subsequently undermining our faith in the archive effect as an index of the truth-value of documents about the past."[64] Such misuse can teach us to be more critical of the archive effect; however, for Baron, this skepticism is not always positive. In some cases, it may lead us to think more critically about our faith in audiovisual documents and exploit the multiple (even contradictory) meanings hidden within them. In others, it "may also lead us to doubt any found document's truth-value as well as its accepted meaning—especially when it may serve as evidence for something we wish to disbelieve or discount."[65] Thus, on the one hand, we have mockumentaries and essay films that employ the powers of the false for deconstructive purposes; on the other hand, there are "documentaries" that exploit the false archive effect to undermine established historical facts, including the Holocaust and Moon landing, and may promote paranoid or conspiratorial thinking.[66]

The strategies for inducing the false archive effect can be numerous: forging or doctoring audiovisual documents, decontextualization and recontextualization, physical damages, subversive music or voice-over commentary, staged re-enactments, analog or digital retouching, and so forth.[67] In the case of deconstructive found footage films that toy with the powers of the false, a critical juxtaposition is often at play to illustrate the multiplicity of truths and meanings and/or the mutual entanglement between different modes of representation.[68] However, there is one found footage/essay film that is particularly suitable for the context of early cinema (and pre-cinema), temporal disparity, and the first kiss—Thom Andersen's *Eadweard Muybridge, Zoopraxographer* (1975). Dedicated to the notorious pioneer of moving-image technology and one of the so-called precursors of cinema, the film offers a cinematic take on Muybridge's photographic

---

[64] Ibid., 50.
[65] Ibid.
[66] In her second monograph, Baron addresses the issue of misusing preexisting footage from a perspective of ethics, see Jaimie Baron, *Reuse, Misuse, Abuse: The Ethics of Audiovisual Appropriation in the Digital Era* (New Brunswick and Newark: Rutgers University Press, 2020).
[67] See also Alex W. Bordino, "Found Footage, False Archives, and Historiography in Oliver Stone's JFK," *The Journal of American Culture* 42, no. 2 (2019): 112–20.
[68] See the videographic exploration of Alfréd Radok's essay film *Distant Journey* (Daleká cesta; 1948) that me and Jiří Žák made for the National Film Archive, Prague: Jiří Anger and Jiří Žák, "Distant Journey through the Desktop," *[in]Transition: Journal of Videographic Film & Moving Image Studies* 8, no. 1 (2021), accessed December 31, 2022, http://mediacommons.org/intransition/distant-journey-through-desktop.

and chronophotographic experiments of the 1860s and 1870s.[69] Notably, the film ends with a poignant cinematic rendition of Muybridge's famous sequential photography, *The Kiss* (1872). We see a staged reproduction of the iconic scene, "falsified" by color, stop-motion technique, and re-enactment by contemporary actresses that, curiously enough, gets close to the jerky, flickering movement of the original. Due to the disposition of the Zoopraxiscope, each gesture was divided into successive but distinct phases, separated by inevitable moments of darkness.[70] Andersen foregrounds this discontinuity by cinematic means, simulating the interval between images by inserted black frames. Just as the two female figures are moving increasingly close to each other, the interval becomes shorter and shorter until it disappears right at the moment of the kiss. It is only by going against the grain of both modern cinema and its vision of a smooth, continuous movement between frames and Muybridge's sequential photography and its development of a single gesture that never truly materializes that the pregnant moment of the kiss can become visible. In other words, the false archive effect arises out of the Bergsonian "retrograde movement of the true"[71] that allows us to imagine what would happen if the Zoopraxiscope resolved its inherent contradictions and developed into cinema as we know it. Yet, perhaps more important than the result is the deconstructive process that shows us that even a pioneering cinematic moment that resonates in our memory is assembled from myriad micro-events scattered across the figurative and material dimensions of the images.

Thus far, the false archive effect has been attributed to found footage/appropriation films that produce it intentionally. What if the powers of the false arose *from below*, through the agency of the archival artifact itself? What happens when we realize that a well-known archival object is not what it has seemed to be, that its indexical value and temporal disparity may have always been dubious? Nowadays, every archival document uploaded on the internet already bears marks of past, present, and future appropriations,[72] and both

---

[69] For a general overview of the film, see Joseph Sgammato, "Naked Came the Stranger: Eadweard Muybridge, Zoopraxographer (Thom Andersen, 1975)," *Senses of Cinema* 20, no. 86 (2018), accessed December 31, 2022, http://sensesofcinema.com/2018/cteq/eadweard-muybridge-zoopraxographer-1975/.

[70] See, for example, Mary Ann Doane, *The Emergence of Cinematic Time: Modernity, Contingency, the Archive* (Cambridge: Harvard University Press, 2002), 199–205 or Eszter Polonyi, "Flicker: Thom Andersen Takes Muybridge to the Movies," in *Provenance and Early Cinema*, ed. Joanne Bernardi, Paolo Cherchi Usai, Tami Williams, and Joshua Yumibe (Bloomington: Indiana University Press, 2021), 287–304.

[71] Henri Bergson, *The Creative Mind: An Introduction to Metaphysics* (Mineola: Dover Publications, 2012), 11.

[72] See, for example, Russell, *Archiveology* and Baron, *Reuse, Misuse, Abuse*.

photochemical and digital deformations can alter the figurative content on their own merits. Under these circumstances, even a short, seemingly unimportant moment that lasts only a few seconds, such as the scratched kiss in *Assignation*, may disturb our belief in archival footage and broaden our notion of what constitutes the archive effect in the first place. The crack-up that manifests in the encounter between the first kiss and the vertical scratches has the potential to become such an accidental, unintentional power of the false, blurring the content to reveal a multitude of actors that need to be considered if we dare to label a specific filmic object as archival.

Scratch That Kiss

"It all started with a kiss." That is how Chuck Workman's *The First Hundred Years: A Celebration of American Movies* (1995) starts, and it is certainly not the only documentary on the history of cinema that begins in this fashion. Workman refers to the notorious film *The Kiss* (or *The May Irwin Kiss*) that William Heise made for Thomas Alva Edison in 1896. The film turned into a public sensation and sparked a huge debate on its supposed transgression of moral codes.[73] Even more important is its promise of visibility, stressed by the creators as well as period journalists. The film shows two actors, May Irwin and John Rice, kissing each other in a medium close-up shot, which only highlights its novelty and visceral impact.[74] A journalist writing on the film, for example, noted that the eighteen-second film's "six hundred different phases of a kiss leave little to the imagination."[75] Another report titled "Anatomy of a Kiss" stated: "For the first time in the history of the world it is possible to see what a kiss looks like . . . In the forty-two feet of kiss recorded by the kinetoscope every phase is shown with startling distinctness . . . The real kiss is a revelation. The idea of the kinetoscopic kiss has unlimited possibilities."[76] Although we have relatively little information

---

[73] Charles Musser, "The May Irwin Kiss: Performance and the Beginnings of Cinema," in *Visual Delights—Two: Exhibition and Reception*, ed. Vanessa Toulmin and Simon Popple (Eastleigh: John Libbey, 2005), 96–115. See also Gert Jan Harkema, "'The Very Act Itself, Even to the Smack': Early Cinema, Presence and Experience," in *New Perspectives on Early Cinema History*, ed. Mario Slugan and Daniël Biltereyst (London and New York: Bloomsbury Academic, 2022), 65–82.

[74] Jonathan Auerbach, *Body Shots: Early Cinema's Incarnations* (Berkeley: University of California Press, 2007), 73–5.

[75] Quoted in: Jordan Schonig, *The Shape of Motion: Cinema and the Aesthetics of Movement* (New York: Oxford University Press, 2021), 45.

[76] Quoted in: Linda Williams, *Screening Sex* (Durham and London: Duke University Press, 2008), 27.

on the period reception of *An Assignation in the Mill*,[77] the first kiss, framed in a tableau shot yet immediately followed by subsequent kisses between the characters, shares with *The May Irwin Kiss* (and other "first" cinematic kisses) the pioneering status and the sensation of perceiving an intimate and taboo event through the lens of a new medium.

What happens, then, when such a moment of plenitude gets scratched? By scratching, I do not mean the predictable marks that appear on every single worn-out film print—the vertical scratches signalizing the first kiss in *Assignation* distort the image content so gravely that the neuralgic point of early cinematic fascination almost ceases to exist. The scratched kiss recalls the techniques of scratching the film strip, ever-present in found footage filmmaking from the politically-informed work of Lettrists and Situationists to contemporary photochemical experiments with human and nonhuman materiality and viscerality by artists such as Vicky Smith, Johanna Vaude, or Péter Lichter.[78] Rather than merely evoking analog nostalgia,[79] the scratches as the powers of the false are at play to unleash different ways of looking at preexisting footage, unmasking the information discernible in the image as potentially more obscuring than revealing. Their uncompromising violence upon the image threatens the "ideology of the visible," the pretense that seeing a filmed reproduction of (present or past) reality equals recognizing and understanding that reality;[80] concerning the image content, our eyes betray us. The film's surface reveals that the archive effect depends on materiality just as much as on figuration and, crucially, that its bond to a specific time, space, and bodies is at best arbitrary and temporary.

Be that as it may, the scratched kiss in Kříženecký's film cannot be assessed by rules applicable to found footage scratch films—it relates to the (false) archive effect in its own unique way. I would hereby propose three functions of scratches that the weird shape exposes (Figures 4.5–4.8).

---

[77] For the reception of Kříženecký's films in their time and later accounts by his colleagues and companions, see Jaroslav Lopour, "Zatím jsme ubozí břídilové, a je těžké se s tím spřátelit!: Vzpomínky na začátky české filmové výroby do roku 1914," *Iluminace* 31, no. 4 (2019): 90–126.

[78] See, for example, Kim Knowles, *Experimental Film and Photochemical Practices* (Cham: Palgrave Macmillan, 2020). For more information on scratch film and scratch video, see Ingrid Guardiola Sánchez, "La imagen dialéctica en el audiovisual found footage: Un hiperarchivo de conceptos visuales" (PhD diss., Universidad Pompeu Fabra, 2015), 38–9; 389–96.

[79] As Thomas Levin notes: "The moment of the scratch is no longer the signal of malfunction but is instead the almost nostalgic trace of a bygone era of mechanical reproducibility." Thomas Y. Levin, "Indexicality Concrète: The Aesthetic Politics of Christian Marclay's Grammophonia," *Parkett* 56 (1999): 162.

[80] Jean-Louis Comolli, "Machines of the Visible," in *The Cinematic Apparatus*, ed. Teresa De Lauretis and Stephen Heath (New York: St. Martin's Press, 1980), 121–42.

1. Scratches as Indices

This function resonates with the electric horses in Chapter 2, only this time the indices derive their origin from the circulation of the film stock rather than the film's production process. They result from improper handling of the nitrate material (by filmmakers, projectionists, printers, archivists, or laboratory workers?) and/or from unexpected technological failure (for instance, by the film roll almost being ripped apart by the apparatus?). As Katherine Groo describes, "we have no way of knowing where, how, by whom, or by what they were formed," and thus they refuse the epistemologies that presuppose a causal link between how the elements of the image originated and how we perceive them.[81] In other words, unlike the static marks in *Spring Races*, the vertical scratches in *Assignation* bear no special relation to the kiss captured by the camera (other than distorting what remained of it ex-post)—their information value is limited to the

Figures 4.5–4.8 *An Assignation in the Mill* (Dostaveníčko ve mlýnici; 1898, source: nitrate print) © Národní filmový archiv.

---

[81] Groo, *Bad Film Histories*, 281.

assurance of the film's historicity and vulnerability to the ravages of time. And yet, the scratches are not entirely "hollowed-out signs," as Mary Ann Doane would say.[82] Although they do so accidentally, they happen to provide insight into the nature of their object. Appearing at the beginning of the second film roll, and for that reason perhaps more inclined toward damage, they emphasize the sutured character of the material that has been present all along. If the kiss were something that needed to occur separately from the unveiling of the poster, the scratches would indicate nothing but the fact that this separation in the figurative universe eventually found its way into the material universe. The emergent crack-up is a reminder that even elements that supposedly obscure, blur, or falsify the film's representation can make us perceive what was unique about the archival document in the first place.

2. Scratches as Cuts

This may sound overly speculative, but the vertical scratches create a way to make the otherwise invisible divide between the two scenes meaningful and resonant. As Charles Musser demonstrates, in the earliest days of cinema, editorial control was primarily held by the exhibitor, not the image-maker— "the process of assembling material into a coherent program was physically occurring in the course of exhibition."[83] In 1898,[84] a single shot or tableau was a defining unit of a film, and should a distinctive cinematic work consist of more than one tableau, the shots just mechanically followed one another. The exhibitor was responsible for juxtaposing individual shots and films within a screening program to create meaningful connections. Moreover, the dynamic between the segments was controlled by the operator—the way he or she moved the crank, slowly or quickly, forward or backward, structured the audience's attention as well as its affective engagement.[85] This was particularly handy with regard to kissing scenes—as Paolo Cherchi Usai says, when two lovers are hesitating before exchanging a kiss, "how long they will wait

---

[82] Mary Ann Doane, "The Indexical and the Concept of Medium Specificity," *Differences* 18, no. 1 (2007): 133.

[83] Charles Musser, "When Did Cinema Become Cinema? Technology, History, and the Moving Pictures," in *Technology and Film Scholarship: Experience, Study, Theory*, ed. Santiago Hidalgo (Amsterdam: Amsterdam University Press, 2018), 40.

[84] In this particular case, there was not much difference between the Czech lands and the rest of the world.

[85] Paolo Cherchi Usai, *Silent Cinema: A Guide to Study, Research and Curatorship* (London and New York: BFI – Bloomsbury Publishing, 2019), 181–5.

before embracing each other is entirely up to the projectionist."[86] The shift of attention that the vertical scratches enact allows us to imagine a retrograde thought experiment: What if we considered such physical interventions as forms of editing suited for an age when the cinematic exhibition was too volatile and the creative postproduction as we know it had yet to be invented? The punctured skin of the film we perceive when the characters approach each other and kiss for the first time turns the succession of shots into a meaning-making unit. It recalls the fact that the interval between two shots is never empty, always involving creative and material work, which, as the example of Thom Andersen's Muybridge documentary showed, also applies to a (seemingly uniform) gesture of kissing. Understood in this way, the crack-up might not only turn the scratches into meaning-making actors but also into media-reflexive gestures.

3. Scratches as Events

The split between two planes of existence highlighted by the vertical lines may also tell us a thing or two about the fundamental incompleteness of cinematic events. As indicated before, *An Assignation in the Mill* as a Czech cinema milestone evokes nostalgic sentiments yet also trauma. With the vertical scratches ripping the most soothing moment apart, such anxiety stems not only from our insecurity about whether the event initially happened just like we see it in hindsight but also from our fear that it might not have happened at all. The more pressure is put on the film to initiate Czech film history, the more accurate is Katherine Groo's Derrida-inspired formulation that "the event [. . .] escapes its reproduction and preservation in the archive. It rips a hole in history and leaves a void."[87] Regardless, this closing of the event is also a way of opening. The convenient localization of the scratches right at the divide in the vintage print can be read as a cipher for all the processes in the film that have never been—and will never be—fully realized. No matter how perfectly restored and digitized the original film strip was, the scar stands as a reminder that it will always be torn in two. No matter how majestic Šváb and his entourage look with the Czech Cinematograph poster, the introduction will always be interrupted way too soon. No matter how many kisses we see afterward, the actual first kiss in Czech cinema will never materialize. The only thing we can do with this absence is to embrace it and try to repeat the unrepeatable.

---

[86] Ibid., 315.
[87] Groo, *Bad Film Histories*, 95. See also Jacques Derrida, "Typewriter Ribbon: Limited Ink (2)," in *Without Alibi* (Redwood City: Stanford University Press, 2002), 135–6.

Coda: Never Happening, Always Repeating

In light of this triple function, the scratched kiss reveals that the archive effect does not necessarily depend on temporal disparity, strictly reflective or strictly restorative nostalgia, or appropriative intervention (without denying the value of these notions). The crack-up enacted between the first kiss and the film's fractured surface delineates the archival experience as always already pervaded with the powers of the false. It is not crucial where, how, by whom, or by what the rips emerged, nor whether any precise reproduction of the event had existed prior to such physical deformation. The very existence of the scratches changes the rules of the game, expressing nothing but the difficulty of expressing anything vis-à-vis the essential vulnerability of both filmic matter and cinematic firsts, thereby presenting a true "means without end," as Giorgio Agamben would say.[88]

The newly found openness of the first kiss in *An Assignation in the Mill* waits to be developed further. In a way, it addresses D. N. Rodowick's call for films that turn a potentially nostalgic or elegiac relation to past images into a creative destruction that "transforms the ontology of the image, unleashing new potentials within it, and new relations with it."[89] In 2022, the digitized vintage print was finally made available in the online space, which of course poses an opportunity for numerous ways of appropriation and ways of creating Baron's "intentional disparity" between the current perception of the footage and how it was created and received in its time.[90] The potential of the scratched kiss as "a moment that constantly passes and therefore does not pass"[91] can be unveiled in animated GIFs, compilations, experimental found footage films, or scholarly videographic essays. Since this chapter mentioned *Eadweard Muybridge, Zoopraxographer,* why not subject the scratched kiss between the two rolls to a similar deconstruction, adapted to digital technology? A stuttering movement that would make the characters' gestures as well as the scratches constantly appear and disappear, intermingle and diverge, to multiply the number of ways in which the archival document can differ from itself and yet still be understood and felt as archival. It is only through such experiments with the powers of the false that the milestones of (particularly the earliest) cinema can be reprogrammed to "give expression to a future image."[92]

---

[88] Giorgio Agamben, "Notes on Gesture," in *Means Without End: Notes on Politics* (Minneapolis and London: University of Minnesota Press, 2000), 49–62.
[89] D. N. Rodowick, *What Philosophy Wants from Images* (Chicago: University of Chicago Press, 2018), 22.
[90] Baron, *The Archive Effect,* 23.
[91] Rodowick, *What Philosophy Wants from Images,* 18.
[92] Ibid., 23.

5

Touching the Film Object with Surgical Gloves

Frankensteinian Frames and the Fragile Malleability of Cinematic Faces

July 1898. Another acting exercise staged and performed by Josef Šváb-Malostranský is being screened at the Exhibition. This time, nothing is left to the imagination. Šváb's face in a close-up shot mimics laughter and crying. However, despite the seemingly unambiguous intention to express two generic emotions through codified theatrical gestures, there is something strangely volatile about Šváb's facial expressions. Each transition from laughter to tears, from one phase of the gesture to the next, from a discernible face to a sutured mass of filmic matter, is burdened with unbearable weight. Is "touching" the film in video-editing software a way to decipher the expressions or to make them even more concealed? (Figures 5.1–5.4)

Laughter and Tears (Smích a pláč; 1898, source: nitrate print), one of the three joint ventures of Křiženecký and Šváb-Malostranský at the Exhibition of Architecture and Engineering,[1] stands out from the rest of the first Czech films for its (supposedly) all-revealing and self-explanatory character. This quality appears here somewhat prematurely, as a deviation from the tableauized spaces of period films.[2] It was certainly not the first cinematic work that involved a close-up of a face,[3] as Šváb later claimed.[4] Nonetheless, it came earlier than many pieces celebrated for a pioneering achievement in

---

[1] The other two are *An Assignation in the Mill* (Dostavenično ve mlýnici) and *Exhibition Sausage Seller and Bill-Poster* (Výstavní párkař a lepič plakátů).
[2] Scott Curtis, Philippe Gauthier, Tom Gunning, and Joshua Yumibe, eds., *The Image in Early Cinema: Form and Material* (Bloomington: Indiana University Press, 2018).
[3] See, for example, *Fred Ott's Sneeze* (William K. L. Dickson, 1894). According to Zdeněk Štábla, one German film, *From Seriousness to Laughter* (Vom Ernst zur Lachen; produced by Oskar Messter, 1897), was even based on a very similar theme. Zdeněk Štábla, *Český kinematograf Jana Křiženeckého* (Praha: Československý filmový ústav, 1973), 81.
[4] Josef Šváb-Malostranský, "Vzpomínka na prvá milování v Praze," *Rozpravy Aventina* 3, no. 18–19 (1928): 222.

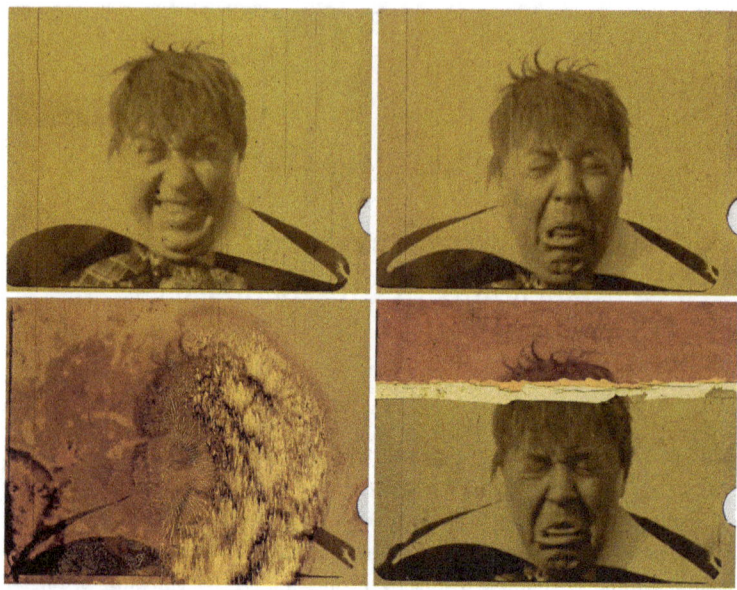

Figures 5.1–5.4 *Laughter and Tears* (Smích a pláč; 1898, source: nitrate print) © Národní filmový archiv.

this respect—three years earlier than *The Big Swallow* (James Williamson, 1901), five years earlier than *The Great Train Robbery* (Edwin S. Porter, 1903), fourteen years earlier than *The Musketeers of Pig Alley* (D. W. Griffith, 1912). More importantly, when viewed retrospectively, *Laughter and Tears* presents a utopian promise of a close-up as an end in itself, not as one of the many types of shots incorporated into the narrative system—a cinematic face as a self-sufficient unit that reveals the most basic emotions as well as affective micro-changes.

A film with such an explicit emphasis on affectivity is bound to elicit strong emotional responses and close engagement from the audience. However, once again, the film's physical characteristics trouble the issue. Out of the film materials from the 1890s in Kříženecký's estate, only a vintage print survived, bearing visible signs of mechanical damage and the now-familiar color palette (from yellow to orange to red). The landscape of Šváb's face must confront itself with minuscule rips, dots, and dust, as well as with colored textures—from orange lines to large red stains—that create landscapes of their own. In some of the frames, splices remain visible as marks of the film kept from falling apart only at the price of Šváb's head being covered with stitches and divided into zones of different colors and turning into a weird shape resembling Frankenstein's monster. The close-up, an emblem of absolute visibility, is revealed as a cracked surface prone to invasions from external actors of various origins. The most important thing is what happens between those poles—figurative and material spheres clash one more time, and it is not easy to tell whether the color blotches disrupt the close-up or whether the facial expressions rupture the inert pulsation of the film's skin. The crack-up operates on the border between two landscapes and, thanks to the film's theme, comes uncannily close to the association between crack-up and laughter (the verb *to crack up* literally means "to suddenly laugh a lot" or "to burst into laughter"). Could we take this explosive potential as an opportunity to explore the fragile boundaries between the spectator and the film object and their epistemological and aesthetic contexts?

What distinguishes the present examination of the crack-up in *Laughter and Tears* from the one investigated in, for example, *Grand Consecration of the Emperor Franz I Bridge* is precisely its relation to a formal feature and thematic content that draw the spectator into proximity. The close-up of Šváb's performance mobilizes what Anne Rutherford terms a "mimetic hook, bringing the spectator into contact with the image in a way that blurs the boundaries between self and other, viewer and [viewed], inside and outside of the image."[5] The level of physical deformation may alienate some spectators, yet it highlights how close to the image we really are and how this proximity does not always have to be revelatory and altogether pleasant. Additionally, the splices demonstrate not only the composite nature of the cinematic figure but also the touch's disturbing power to tear a film apart and assemble it back together. The film that we "touch" with our eyes touches us back, and not necessarily in the way we expect—to paraphrase Jean-Louis Chrétien, by no means does the touched have to respond in the same way as it is touched.[6] Approaching such a distorted film object, let alone connecting with it on an emotional level, seems perilous, even in the newly accessible digitized form.

In film and media studies, the potentialities and stakes of close encounters between films and spectatorial subjects have been covered by theories of "haptic visuality." This term has cemented a vital place in film and media studies over the last twenty-five years, mainly due to the legacy of Laura U. Marks, who appropriated it from art historian Alois Riegl or, more precisely, from Gilles Deleuze's and Félix Guattari's interpretation of Riegl's

---

[5] Anne Rutherford, *What Makes a Film Tick? Cinematic Affect, Materiality and Mimetic Innervation* (Berlin: Peter Lang, 2011), 30.
[6] Jean-Louis Chrétien, *The Call and the Response* (New York: Fordham University Press, 2004).

distinction between haptic and optic visuality.[7] The opening sentence of the entry on haptic visuality in *A Dictionary of Film Studies* states: "A sense of physical touching or being touched engendered by an organization of the film image in which its material presence is foregrounded and which evokes close engagement with surface detail and texture."[8] This notion proposes a film experience that invites us to contemplate the image itself rather than its place in the narrative flow, overcome the distance between us and the film object, and immerse ourselves in the sensations that moving images and sounds produce.[9] Haptic visuality derives its power from the surface textures of bodies and objects as much as from the skin of the film, leaving many opportunities for filmmakers to mix both and produce various weird shapes that actualize the crack-up for the spectator. Nevertheless, how does this concept stand face-to-face with dangerous film objects such as *Laughter and Tears*, whose haptic qualities cannot be attributed to artistic intention? Under what conditions does the cinematic face turn into an interface of the crack-up? What response does the Frankensteinian head invoke in a recipient who wants to analyze the film or even appropriate it for his or her own creative endeavor?

The attempts at touching and being touched by *Laughter and Tears* shall proceed in three rounds. The first one concerns itself with the epistemological dimension of haptic visuality in the digital space. It emphasizes the capacity of haptic visuality, with its attention toward details and accidents as well as intimate and idiosyncratic spectatorial experience, to inspire a self-reflexive film theory that can transform the analyzed film and the subject-object relations. At the same time, it mentions a few shortcomings of the haptic

---

[7] Laura U. Marks, *The Skin of the Film: Intercultural Cinema, Embodiment, and the Senses* (Durham: Duke University Press, 2000); Laura U. Marks, *Touch: Sensuous Theory and Multisensory Media* (Minneapolis: University of Minnesota Press, 2002); Alois Riegl, *Late Roman Art Industry* (Rome: Giorgio Bretschneider Editore, 1985); Gilles Deleuze and Félix Guattari, *A Thousand Plateaus: Capitalism and Schizophrenia* (Minneapolis: University of Minnesota Press, 1987). For more general philosophical and aesthetic accounts of hapticity, see Mark Paterson, *The Senses of Touch: Haptics, Affects and Technologies* (London: Routledge, 2007) or Mika Elo and Miika Luoto, eds., *Figures of Touch: Sense, Technics, Body* (Helsinki: The Academy of Fine Arts at the University of the Arts Helsinki, 2018).

[8] Annette Kuhn and Guy Westwell, *A Dictionary of Film Studies* (Oxford: Oxford University Press, 2012), 201.

[9] For more recent applications of haptic visuality in film studies, see, for example, Jennifer M. Barker, *The Tactile Eye: Touch and the Cinematic Experience* (Berkeley: University of California Press, 2009); Giuliana Bruno, *Surface: Matters of Aesthetic, Matter, and Media* (Chicago: The University of Chicago Press, 2014); Saige Walton, *Cinema's Baroque Flesh: Film, Phenomenology and the Art of Entanglement* (Amsterdam: Amsterdam University Press, 2016); Asbjørn Grønstad, Henrik Gustafsson, and Øyvind Vågnes, eds., *Gestures of Seeing in Film, Video and Drawing* (London and New York: Routledge, 2017).

approach that need to be adjusted when dealing with explosive artifacts such as *Laughter and Tears*. The second part demonstrates how the shift in subject-object relations is put into practice in videographic film studies. The haptic tendency in this discipline offers us tools for analysis that is affectively charged yet highly attentive to weird shapes of all kinds. Still, the subchapter also warns against mistaking videographic manipulation of the film object for possessing it. If we want to touch and be touched by films, we ought to target the elements that are already (however latently) present in them, and therefore find ways to prolong their crack-up. The final step is to investigate the specific configuration of the crack-up in selected frames of *Laughter and Tears*—those in which Šváb's head is stitched by a splice as Frankenstein's monster. By discerning two forms of the close-up—the figurative one and the material one—the analysis of the spliced frames portrays the cinematic face as a landscape consisting of manifold materialities and autoregulative processes and highlights how the two facial modalities can intertwine in surprising ways. The encompassing aim of this chapter is to reveal the haptic subject as someone who does not merely want to use the film object as a projection screen for his or her own fantasies and emotions but as someone who respectfully guides the tendencies hidden within the object's nuances and touches it with surgical gloves.

Approaching Films Haptically

Generally, a film critic or theorist is expected to maintain a certain level of distance, show that he or she can tame the luring of the apparatus, or at least project his or her fascination with the film into words and arrange them into a reasonable argument. However, haptic visuality gives the professional more leeway to let himself or herself become overwhelmed by the sheer affective power of the studied film object or phenomenon. Lauren Berlant echoes this sentiment when she reminds us that "the minute an object comes under analytical scrutiny, it bobs and weaves, becomes unstable, mysterious, and recalcitrant, seeming more like a fantasy than the palpable object it had seemed to be when the thinker/lover first risked engagement."[10] The critic is invited to an answer that does not arrive from an ex-post critical evaluation but resides in a time lag between the pathic stimulus that always comes too early to be processed and the response that always comes too late to be "completely at the height of experience"—something Bernhard Waldenfels

---

[10] Lauren Berlant, *Desire/Love* (Brooklyn: Punctum Books, 2012), 18.

terms "diastasis."[11] Any attempt to make sense of this experience in critical/theoretical writing must not escape this revelatory encounter; instead, the subject should champion, even fetishize, the fleeting and evanescent moments of the film and try to express the mysterious push-pull movement circulating between him or her and the object in similarly fleeting and evanescent words.

In one of her breakthrough studies, "Video Haptics and Erotics" (1998), Laura U. Marks suffuses her writing about the videotape *It Wasn't Love* (Sadie Benning, 1992) with tactile sensations right from the beginning. She describes her experience as "going on a journey into states of erotic being" that evokes "the longing for intimacy with another," "the painful and arousing awareness" of being "close yet distinct" to the author/protagonist, a loss of "sense of [her] own boundaries."[12] However, what triggers these intense sensations is a seemingly marginal moment—Benning slowly sucking her thumb, inches away from the unfocusable, low-resolution camera—that causes "the uncanny loss of proportion in which big things slip beyond the horizon of my awareness while small events are arenas for a universe of feeling."[13] It is this marginal detail that allows Marks to shape the future language of "haptic criticism," a manner of studying film that "keeps its surface rich and textured, so it can interact with things in unexpected ways. It has to be humble, willing to alter itself according to what it is in contact with."[14] More decisive than the detail's role in the film's formal structure or narrative action is the secret that it contains, something elusive yet piercing that establishes an encounter between the film/video object and the attuned film critic/scholar. The words stop being able to "lift off" the surface of the film object and the arresting fragment,[15] and instead of trying to possess it, they seek to express how indescribable, unanalyzable, or uninterpretable yet relentlessly seductive the fragment (and her attachment to it) really are.

Nonetheless, I would argue that the most fruitful moments of haptic criticism and any kind of scholarly analysis that stresses affective engagement with its objects do not lie in descriptions of bodily vibrations. More potential is enclosed in its self-reflexive, methodological dimension, in showcasing how this intense bond might unleash a minor perspective from which the film

---

[11] Bernhard Waldenfels, *Phenomenology of the Alien* (Evanston: Northwestern University Press, 2011); Bernhard Waldenfels, "The Role of the Lived-Body in Feeling," in *Rethinking Emotion*, ed. Rüdiger Campe and Julia Weber (Berlin and Boston: De Gruyter, 2014), 245–63.
[12] Laura U. Marks, "Video Haptics and Erotics," *Screen* 39, no. 4 (1998): 331.
[13] Ibid.
[14] Laura U. Marks, "Haptic Visuality: Touching with the Eyes," *Framework the Finnish Art Review*, no. 2 (2004): 79–82.
[15] Ibid.

object could appear in previously unseen contours. From Marks's account, we learn how she overcame the distance between her and the film and how these close encounters of the third kind often result from a minor, non-expressive detail, but we do not come to know much more about the detail itself. Is it something hidden within the image that is waiting to be discovered by an attentive beholder? Or is it something that comes into existence because of resonating with the spectator's subjective feelings, thoughts, and associations? If it is a mix of the two, how can this attachment to a peripheral detail lead to a compelling reimagination or even resignification of the respective film? Trying to touch the films of Jan Kříženecký, in the absence of any clear key to what is intentional or unintentional, what is dominant or marginal, what is accessible to the general audience and what only to "professionals" who devoted a significant amount of time to delve into the film objects, one cannot leave these questions aside.

Laughter and Tears seems to be a perfect case study in haptic visuality. The signs are all there: Šváb's face enlarged and abstracted from everything except for the spectator; sensations not only implied but literally enacted; marks of the nitrate stock's damages and distortions clearly visible; and many new options for manipulation with the image surface enabled by the digitization. The mysterious, almost mystical qualities ascribed to the close-up come to fruition through the visage bursting with emotions as well as the shattering filmic matter. Yet, it is precisely the easiness of such interpretation that should warn us against applying it too mechanically. One ought to remain wary of two pitfalls in particular—intentional fallacy and negative ontology—both inspired by Eugenie Brinkema's notorious critique of affect theory's shortcomings.[16]

First, unlike the arthouse and experimental films and videos Marks and her followers champion, the dissonance between the figurative and material dimensions in *Laughter and Tears* cannot be attributed to intentional design. Even though haptic criticism frequently cherishes film moments that are not necessarily results of authorial intent, there prevails an idea that haptic visuality is staged to provoke a mimetic response. For example, Marks's influential notion of film spectatorship presupposes a fusion between subject and object, a "concomitant loss of self in the presence of the other,"[17] in which the primary function of the aesthetic object is to produce sensations in the viewers and make us feel that the image and its manifold

---

[16] Eugenie Brinkema, *The Forms of the Affects* (London and Durham: Duke University Press, 2014).
[17] Marks, *Touch*, 20.

details exist "for us."[18] Spectators do not respond to literal emotional cues in the classical Hollywood sense, yet there is a certain presupposition of their attunement to the film object that denies the possibility of refusing its affective lure. In other words, an image is conceived as automatically stimulating Other that overwhelms the spectator without any opportunities for negotiation or oppositional reading and thus risks becoming a fetish. This intentional fallacy turns out to be doubly problematic for *Laughter and Tears*, as there is no clear causality between the film as originally schemed by Kříženecký and Šváb-Malostranský, the film as a circulating and decaying object, and the film as being watched in the digitized form. Rather than presupposing mutual embodiment between the viewer and the film image, *Laughter and Tears* offers a kind of distributed embodiment in which the individual actors operate according to their own rhythms, and any productive intersection between them depends on an imaginative (re)shaping of the crack-up by a critical spectator.

The second shortcoming echoes Eugenie Brinkema's criticism of affect theory's "negative ontology."[19] The encounter with the otherworldly moving image seems to "happen too quickly to have happened,"[20] to use the words of Brian Massumi, and therefore, the only perceptible effect is that of a rupture. The norms that are being disrupted can be multiple—classical figuration, mimetic representation, linear narration, central perspective, fixation on content, and so on—but the event of shattering the "ordinary" is almost always present. It is no wonder that haptic criticism, which is one of the products of the "affective turn" in film studies and other disciplines,[21] mostly does not offer proper instruments to analyze the specific details that invoke these extreme sensations. In the case of *Laughter and Tears*, speaking of the disruptive effects of the close-up would no longer be enough, as it now constitutes a standardized, all-too-recognizable form. The weird shape of a stitched Frankensteinian head presents something more than a "systemic excess"[22] or a symptom of decay. Although Šváb's disfigured face does not fit into our notion of discernible forms and figures, it recalls similar moments from our visual memory. Associations coming to mind may involve late

---

[18] Brinkema, *The Forms of the Affects*, 31–3.
[19] Ibid., 30–1.
[20] Brian Massumi, *Parables for the Virtual: Movement, Affect, Sensation* (Durham and London: Duke University Press, 2002), 30.
[21] Melissa Gregg and Gregory J. Seigworth, eds., *The Affect Theory Reader* (Durham: Duke University Press, 2010).
[22] Jiří Anger and Tomáš Jirsa, "We Never Took Deconstruction Seriously Enough (On Affects, Formalism, and Film Theory): An Interview with Eugenie Brinkema," *Iluminace* 31, no. 1 (2019): 67–8.

nineteenth-century photographs of heightened emotional expressions,[23] early twentieth-century animated screen portraits,[24] possessed figures from Francis Bacon's paintings, experimental found footage films such as *Decasia*, or, indeed, the now almost ordinary experience of seeing someone's face frozen and glitched in a Zoom window or deepfaked up to the point of unrecognizability.[25] Therefore, the experience of haptic visuality ought to be conceived positively, as overfull with meaning rather resistant to it,[26] and acknowledge that even though weird shapes may not always be the most obvious feature of moving images, they cannot be ignored.

How, then, can we touch a film object such as *Laughter and Tears* without falling into the double trap of intentional fallacy and negative ontology? According to Raymond Bellour, the problem lies in the "unattainability" of film:[27] if writing about cinema cannot quite put the finger on the unique assemblage of images and sounds into movement, describing how a single detail can reshape this multiplicity without intervening in the object itself becomes a doubly frustrating task. Now that digital technology has made film objects more accessible (albeit not necessarily attainable)[28] and susceptible to manipulation, haptic visuality can be expressed simultaneously in writing *about* film and writing *with* film, and thus endow the critic's touch with transformative powers. However, should this touching turn into retouching, that is, suturing out any disproportions between the film object and the subject's imagination, or disproportions within the object itself, the crack-up will cease to function, so moderation and respect ought to come first and foremost. Perhaps the noblest way of touching *Laughter and Tears*

---

[23] See, for instance, Georges Didi-Huberman, *Invention of Hysteria: Charcot and the Photographic Iconography of the Salpêtrière* (New York: MIT Press, 2003).

[24] Small, animated portraits constituted playful keepsakes or advertisements in the early twentieth century. They were evidence of ties between photography and cinema in both the popular imagination and scientific culture. Kim Timby, "'Cinema in a Single Photo': The Animated Screen Portrait of the 1910s," in *Between Still and Moving Images*, ed. Laurent Guido and Olivier Lugon (Bloomington: Indiana University Press, 2012), 97–111.

[25] Pietro Conte, "Mockumentality: From Hyperfaces to Deepfakes," *World Literature Studies* 11, no. 4 (2019): 11–25; Yvonne Zimmermann, "Videoconferencing and the Uncanny Encounter with Oneself: Self-Reflexivity as Self-Monitoring 2.0," in *Pandemic Media: Preliminary Notes Toward an Inventory*, ed. Philipp Dominik Keidl, Laliv Melamed, Vinzen Hediger, and Antonio Somaini (Lüneburg: Meson Press, 2020), 99–103.

[26] For inspiration, see Jordan Schonig's reading of the cinephiliac experience. Jordan Schonig, "The Haecceity Effect: On the Aesthetics of Cinephiliac Moments," *Screen* 61, no. 2 (2020): 256.

[27] Raymond Bellour, "The Unattainable Text," *Screen* 16. no. 3 (1975): 19–27.

[28] Raymond Bellour, "35 Years Later: Is the 'Text', Once Again, Unattainable?," in *Beyond the Essay Film*, ed. Julia Vassilieva and Deane Williams (Amsterdam: Amsterdam University Press, 2020), 33–48.

is approaching it one step at a time. In order to find specific forms of the affects, touch must be taken literally, extended to the individual frames that have their own ways of invoking affective responses. This time, looking at the films frame by frame[29] would not just serve to track the emergence of the crack-up as in Chapter 1 but contribute toward an active reshaping of the film experience from its most basic units. The following section attempts to provide tools to conceptualize how to walk this thin line.

The (Im)Possibility of Videographic Touching

In academic film theory, the idea of haptic intervention in its object of study already emerged in its golden age during the 1970s. Besides Raymond Bellour, who decided not to pursue the film object directly and rather thematized its fleetingness in self-reflexive writing,[30] Thierry Kuntzel went even further. The author of now-canonical articles of semiotic/psychoanalytic film theory— "The Film-Work" (1972) and "The Film-Work 2" (1975)—[31]confronted "the impossibility of recovering through description and analysis the essential meaning and nature of the film-experience,"[32] abandoned scholarly research, and turned to video art. We can already read in his early texts about "slowing or stopping [the film's] movement (continuity) to gauge the immobility (discontinuity) which sustains it, isolating visual or aural motifs, confronting and comparing them by means of reverse motion,"[33] under the guise of deconstructing the film as it is meant to be watched and revealing an underlying film-work that signifies its meanings. According to Kuntzel, it is the immediacy of analog video that actualizes this impulse, allowing us to touch the film object in a way that acknowledges its ongoing transformation and dialogue with individual and collective imagination. If the transposition of the film object from continuous movement into a complex, dynamic structure of interrelated building blocks substituted one system of meaning (linear) with another (structuralist), Kuntzel's "practical" research toned down the obsession with deciphering and experimented with what could

---

[29] Hannah Frank, *Frame by Frame: A Materialist Aesthetics of Animated Cartoons* (Berkeley: University of California Press, 2019).
[30] See, for example, Raymond Bellour, "Analysis in Flames," *Diacritics* 15, no. 1 (1985): 54–6.
[31] Thierry Kuntzel, "The Film-Work," *Enclitic* 2, no. 1 (1978): 38–61; Thierry Kuntzel, "The Film-Work 2," *Camera Obscura* 5, no. 2 (1980): 6–70.
[32] Hilary Radner and Alistair Fox, eds., *Raymond Bellour: Cinema and the Moving Image* (Edinburgh: Edinburgh University Press, 2018), 35.
[33] Kuntzel, "The Film-Work," 40–1.

emerge in-between movement and stasis, construction and deconstruction, the objective and the subjective. Ideally, the investigation should give birth to "another film," in which all sorts of images would unexpectedly mix, overlap, and transform each other as in a memory.[34]

With the advent of mass digitization in the late twentieth century, these dilemmas reemerged and resonated with interest in haptic visuality and the new cinephilia.[35] What Thomas Elsaesser described as "the instability of the images put in circulation, their adaptability even in their visual forms and shapes, their mutability of meaning"[36] provoked a strong temptation to reframe and reshape films, according to a logic that would unite the private idiosyncrasies of lifelong cinephiles with contemporary theoretical and historical concerns. These trends in film theory, as well as practical inspiration from experimental found footage filmmakers such as Ken Jacobs, Matthias Müller, Peter Tscherkassky, or Peggy Ahwesh, whose interventions in film objects married poetic and analytical ambitions,[37] had a significant impact on the birth of the "videographic essay" (also called "video essay" or "audiovisual essay") format and the discipline of "videographic film studies" (or at least on certain tendencies in this field).[38] This form of practical research provides much inspiration for haptic criticism—through its capacity to touch the film's images and sounds themselves and its ability to engage the body-in-film and the body-of-film at the same time. Its input is crucial for correcting the inclination of much written haptic criticism for either abstract musings

---

[34] Raymond Bellour, "Thierry Kuntzel and the Return of Writing," in *Between-the-Images*, ed. Raymond Bellour and Allyn Hardyck (Zurich: JRP/Ringier, 2012), 30–61.

[35] See Christian Keathley, *Cinephilia and History, or The Wind in the Trees* (Bloomington and Indianapolis: Indiana University Press, 2005) or Girish Shambu, *The New Cinephilia*, Expanded 2nd ed. (Montreal: caboose, 2020).

[36] Thomas Elsaesser, "Cinephilia or the Uses of Disenchantment," in *Cinephilia: Movies, Love and Memory*, ed. Marijke de Valck and Malte Hagener (Amsterdam: Amsterdam University Press, 2005), 38. See also Jessica McGoff, "Expresser, Agitator, Salve and Mirror: the Video Essay and Contemporary Cinephilia" (Master's Thesis, Amsterdam University, 2017).

[37] The relationship between experimental found footage and videographic film studies is covered, for example, in Manu Yáñez, "Thought, Action, and Imagination," *The Audiovisual Essay*, 2013, accessed December 31, 2022, http://reframe.sussex.ac.uk/audiovisualessay/frankfurt-papers/manu-yanez/; See also Jennifer Proctor, "Teaching Avant-Garde Practice as Videographic Research," *Screen* 60, no. 3 (2019): 466–74.

[38] These connections have been highlighted by Corey Creekmur, "How Does Film Feel? Toward Affective Videographic Criticism," *The Cine-Files*, no. 10 (2016), accessed December 31, 2022, http://www.thecine-files.com/how-does-film-feel2016/; Tiago Baptista, "Lessons in Looking: The Digital Audiovisual Essay" (PhD diss., Birkbeck, University of London, 2016), 142–69; Jiří Anger, "Dotýkat se nedosažitelného objektu: Haptická audiovizuální esej a antropotechnický interface," in *Operátoři (nových) médií*, ed. Tomáš Dvořák, Martin Charvát et al. (Praha: Nakladatelství Akademie múzických umění, 2022), 235–70.

on the elusiveness and transitivity of affect or subjectivist descriptions of bodily sensations. Eric Faden, one of the earliest videographic practitioners, sums it up nicely: "If I'm reading about the haptic or whatever, I may be tempted to throw my arms up in confusion. But the exciting challenge is to take the abstraction of the theory and make it concrete in the video form."[39] This context is essential for understanding how touching a film object (especially one that is already cracked) implies its appropriation and creative reimagination.

One of the pioneering video essayists, Catherine Grant, articulated these influences in a manifesto called *Touching the Film Object?* (2011).[40] The videographic essay is a remediation of Laura U. Marks's article "Haptic Visuality: Touching with the Eyes" (2004), letting its textual fragments find resonances with an iconic scene from Ingmar Bergman's *Persona* (1966). A bespectacled boy who tries to decipher a blurry image on a screen before he becomes a metaphor for the haptic critic. No matter how much he is striving to approach the unattainable object, the heroines' faces remain indiscernible. Due to Grant's use of the slow-motion effect and her refusal to show the end of the scene, the figures fail to lift off the grainy surface. Nevertheless, a close physical contact between the viewer and the film object has been established—one that does not promise resolution or meaning but binds them together in a state of mutual becoming. Whether this subtle transformation of a classic scene amounts to a coveted touch of the film object or bears witness to its impossibility is a question waiting to be addressed.

Grant's approach is not a lone anomaly. Since the videographic film studies began taking shape, many initial leading figures, such as Cristina Álvarez López, Adrian Martin, and Christian Keathley, and also later practitioners like Johannes Binotto, Ian Garwood, Barbara Zecchi, or Jessica McGoff, have been accentuating the intimate value of haptic contact with digital as well as photochemical film objects.[41] The practitioners often emphasize that

---

[39] Eric Faden, "In Dialogue: Eric Faden and Kevin B. Lee," in *The Videographic Essay: Practice and Pedagogy*, ed. Christian Keathley, Jason Mittell, and Catherine Grant (Scalar, 2019), accessed December 31, 2022, http://videographicessay.org/works/videographic-essay/in-dialogue-eric-faden-and-kevin-b-lee?path=contents.

[40] Catherine Grant, "Touching the Film Object? Notes on the 'Haptic'in Videographical Film Studies," *Filmanalytical*, August 29, 2011, accessed December 31, 2022, https://filmanalytical.blogspot.com/2011/08/touching-film-object-notes-on-haptic-in.html.

[41] Catherine Grant, "Déjà-Viewing?: Videographic Experiments in Intertextual Film Studies," *Mediascape: UCLA's Journal of Cinema and Media Studies* 7, no. 1 (2013), accessed December 31, 2022, http://www.tft.ucla.edu/mediascape/Winter2013_DejaViewing.html; Johannes Binotto, "In Lag of Knowledge," in *Practical Aesthetics*, ed. Bernd Herzogenrath (New York: Bloomsbury, 2020), 83–94; Ian Garwood, "From 'Video Essay' to 'Video Monograph'? Indy Vinyl as Academic Book," *NECSUS European Journal of Media Studies* 9, no. 1 (2020): 5–29. For a more theoretical account, see David

some phenomenal details of moving images and sounds become perceptible only by getting closer to their physical surface. In one recent videographic essay, *Videography 1978* (2021) by Cristina Álvarez López and Adrian Martin,[42] Martin excavates his forty-year-old memory of writing a book-length semiotic analysis of Otto Preminger's noir film *Angel Face* (1953) by touching various traces of the film at his home. As he describes, no matter how hard he tried at a close textual analysis in a Bellourian style,[43] the film eluded and escaped his grasp, and he never finished the book. By browsing through memory vignettes such as photograms, production stills, photo portraits of stars, and old notebooks, the essay portrays an alternative, ephemeral vision of the Hollywood classic, curiously linked to "the truth of gestures, atmospheres, moods" once championed in Jacques Rivette's review of the film[44] rather than the film's narrative and basic themes. However, as the videographic work argues, the fragments, particularly the photograms, also represent an alternative to the way we are watching and analyzing *Angel Face* with digital tools. In one scene, the film is imported into a video-editing program to highlight that some features of the photograms, notably the one that contains the last frame of one shot and the first frame of the next shot, are impossible to reproduce digitally. Haptic criticism therefore becomes a means by which an analyst may discover through a single detail the fundamental nonidentity of photochemical and digital frames, or, to use Martin's words, to "get close to the mystery of cinema on the edge of a cut." The videographic essay holds a cautious promise of answering Eugenie Brinkema's call to search for affect in formal and textual particularities instead of lengthy descriptions of embodied sensations,[45] albeit without abandoning the primacy of subjective film experience. Whether the main source of this affect lies in authorial subjectivity, specific material interventions, the inner workings of the ever-changing film object, or hidden algorithmic processes is up for debate.[46]

Colangelo, "Hitchcock, Film Studies, and New Media: The Impact of Technology on the Analysis of Film," in *Technology and Film Scholarship*, ed. Santiago Hidalgo (Amsterdam: Amsterdam University Press, 2018), 127–48.

[42] Cristina Álvarez López and Adrian Martin, "The Thinking Machine #48: Videography 1978," *Filmkrant*, April 26, 2021, accessed December 31, 2022, https://filmkrant.nl/video/the-thinking-machine-48-english/.

[43] Raymond Bellour, *The Analysis of Film* (Bloomington: Indiana University Press, 2000).

[44] Adrian Martin cites Rivette's review of *Angel Face* from *Cahiers du cinéma*.

[45] Brinkema, *The Forms of the Affects*. See also Girish Shambu, "On Video Essays, Cinephilia, and Affect," *Girish*, July 7, 2014, accessed December 31, 2022, https://girishshambu.net/2014/07/on-video-essays-cinephilia-and-affect.html.

[46] See, for example, Luka Arsenjuk, "To Speak, To Hold, To Live by the Image: Notes in the Margins of the New Videographic Tendency," in *The Essay Film: Dialogue, Politics,*

The hitherto described examples stress that haptic intervention is primarily about excavating the idiosyncratic, hidden, lost, and ideally also intimate. The transformation is meant to be subtle, actualizing what has, in a way, always been there. This approach toward found footage resonates with my general approach to the digitized films of Jan Křiženecký. The previous chapters indicated ways to further develop the specific deformations in individual film moments and extend the impulse of the weird shapes into a creation of new forms (assemblages of frames, GIFs, videographic exercises, and so on). Any haptic appropriation would come down to distinguishing and sculpting the crack-up rather than inventing it from scratch. Nonetheless, *Digital Křiženecký* requires more epistemological thinking on the part of the appropriator than the usual suspects of videographic film studies (Hollywood cinema, auteurist arthouse cinema, quality TV). Before one may say, "This is what I can do with the figures, objects, and places you all know," "This is the detail within your favorite film you failed to notice," or "This moment resonates with my deeply buried personal memories," he or she needs to deal with the fact that we do not know what the default state of the first Czech films is. Of course, *Persona* or *Angel Face* acquire a multitude of identities as digital files, being variously cropped, pixelated, and even colored, as one DVDRip of Bergman's film with a purplish layer I once possessed testifies. Still, in our memories and associations, they still gravitate toward visible and recognizable figures. From the other side of the spectrum, the films of Bill Morrison in the digital space partake in curious processes of hybridization, with nitrate rot and data corruption overlapping, yet we are trained to accept their materiality as inherent to the artistic intention. In the case of *Digital Křiženecký*, the weird shapes, however much their recognition may depend on my long-term engagement with the materials, are paradoxically the only things we can be sure of when we do not know the author's aim nor how the physical deformations got into the images. When looking at all the frames, only a minority of them does not include any deformations. Due to the existence of two transparent surfaces—the yellowish-orange veil and the contours of Šváb's head—even the ordinary dots, dust, and scratches become more visible, not to mention the assault presented by blotches and cuts in the more orange-to-red frames. When we decide to pursue *Laughter and Tears* haptically, we will not necessarily reveal hidden truths about the materials, but we will showcase the extent to which the crack-up depends on a combination between a subjective view *from below* and peripheral features of the object.

Utopia, ed. Elizabeth Papazian and Caroline Eades (London and New York: Wallflower Press, 2016), 275–99; Anger, "Dotýkat se nedosažitelného objektu." See also Chapter 6.

Paolo Cherchi Usai once said that a film archivist should treat the degrading film materials like a "physician who has accepted the inevitability of death even while he continues to fight for the patient's life."[47] To paraphrase him, a haptic critic confronted with the first Czech films also affirms his or her "patients'" (the dilapidated film objects') inescapable demise, yet constantly suspends the very act of death. In other words, he or she keeps the patients eternally stuck in a moment before death comes, similarly as in Jorge Luis Borges's short story "The Secret Miracle,"[48] in which the entire world freezes motionless while the main hero waits to be executed by the firing squad. The haptic critic forestalls the death of film artifacts in order to deny them any kind of resolution and reveal them in all their ambiguities. The weird shapes must forever remain caught in the loop between figuration and abstraction, photochemical and digital matter, stillness and movement, past and present. This is how the haptic critic may approach *Digital Křiženecký* without losing face—by "touching" the films with surgical gloves, carefully discerning the materials' inner tensions within the tiniest cinematic units, and playing them out frame by frame. To proceed to the specificities of the vintage print of *Laughter and Tears*, Šváb's Frankensteinian head is therefore investigated within the spliced frames. As a result, the face is reconceived as a double landscape—the figurative one and the material one—wherein the aesthetic integrity of the crack-up depends on how the haptic subject understands the Hippocratic oath.

The Cinematic Face as Frankenstein's Monster

The motifs relating haptic visuality to the close-up have been addressed from the earliest history of film theory. Jean Epstein, Béla Balázs, Walter Benjamin, or Karel Teige[49] embraced the close-up as an incentive for thinking and writing about film that is self-reflexive yet affectively engaged. Jordan

---

[47] Paolo Cherchi Usai, *The Death of Cinema: History, Cultural Memory, and the Digital Dark Age* (London: BFI, 2001), 105.
[48] Jorge Luis Borges, "The Secret Miracle," in *Ficciones* (New York: Grove Press, 1962), 143–50.
[49] See, for example, Béla Balázs, Erica Carter, ed., *Early Film Theory: Visible Man and The Spirit of Film* (New York and Oxford: Berghahn Books, 2010); Jean Epstein and Stuart Liebman, "Magnification and Other Writings," *October*, no. 3 (1977): 9–25; Walter Benjamin, "The Work of Art in the Age of Mechanical Reproduction," in *Illuminations*, ed. Hannah Arendt (London: Jonathan Cape, 1970), 219–53; Karel Teige, "K filmové avantgardě," in *Otázky divadla a filmu. III*, ed. Artur Závodský (Brno: Universita J.E. Purkyně, 1973), 303–28.

Schonig aptly describes how Epstein's essay "Magnification" (1921), one of the formative texts in this respect, begins "with a declaration of love for the close-up and a concession about the inadequacies of language to express that love," but "expresses it nevertheless."[50] Critics, theorists, and philosophers are allowed to use highly subjective, poetic, and even esoteric language and bestow upon the close-up abilities to reveal "the hidden life of little things"[51] or "entirely new structural formations of the subject."[52] Pinpointing what is specific about Šváb's face in *Laughter and Tears* warrants finding a gap between the familiar narratives that unite facial close-ups with transparency and revelation on the one hand and with opacity and masking on the other. Stating that it lies somewhere between the two, in what Noa Steimatsky terms "singular binding of concealment and disclosure,"[53] may be closest to the truth, yet without concretization, it could reek of relativism. Instead, one should ask questions: How can a face so dedicated to reproducing universal, all-recognizable emotions end up stuck in a state in which it is impossible to tell where the laughter ends and where the tears begin? How can a close-up shot scanned and rendered in 4K reveal more of the details that seemingly decompose the face from without than of the details hidden within the actor's face? How can the haptic subject mold the close-up to approach the crack-up that arises from these ambiguities without deflecting either of these four parts of the equation—emotional states, affective transitions, material details, figurative details—in favor of the other?

In addressing these questions, one idea is instructive: the close-up of Šváb's face is not the only close-up we can see. And I am not having in mind the (now firmly established) notion that the close-up shot is not exclusive to faces and can just as well reveal or mask hidden particularities of cinematic objects.[54] The inspiration comes from Kim Knowles—in the third chapter of her recent monograph, *Experimental Film and Photochemical Practices* (2020), she investigates "surface intervention as a form of cinematic close-

---

[50] Jordan Schonig, *The Shape of Motion: Cinema and the Aesthetics of Movement* (New York: Oxford University Press, 2021), 179.
[51] Béla Balázs, *Theory of the Film: Character and Growth of the New Art* (London: Dennis Dobson Ltd, 1952), 54.
[52] Benjamin, "The Work of Art in the Age of Mechanical Reproduction," 16.
[53] Noa Steimatsky, *The Face on Film* (New York: Oxford University Press, 2017), 20.
[54] See, for example, Gilles Deleuze, *Cinema 1: The Movement-Image* (London: The Athlone Press, 1986), 102–10; Francesco Casetti, "Objects on the Screen: Tools, Things, Events," in *Cinematographic Objects: Things and Operations*, ed. Volker Pantenburg (Berlin: August Verlag, 2015), 25–43; James Leo Cahill, *Zoological Surrealism: The Nonhuman Cinema of Jean Painlevé* (Minneapolis: University of Minnesota Press, 2019), 31–92. This idea was also exploited by experimental filmmakers such as Matthias Müller, Christoph Girardet, or Morgan Fisher.

up."⁵⁵ In the works of artists such as Vicky Smith or Charlotte Pryce, who manipulate directly with the film strip, "the close-up finds a new expressive dimension, tied not, as is traditionally the case, to the magnifying properties of the camera, but to the mechanical relationship between the film surface and the film projector."⁵⁶ Instead of exteriorizing the slightest changes in facial micro-physiognomy, what is revealed is the vibrant life of nonhuman agents, whose textures become more pronounced and make the traditional perspectival reference points fall away.⁵⁷ Regarding *Laughter and Tears*, someone who wants to touch the film object in a transformative way is definitely not as free—the world of micro-organisms that fills the Lumière film stock ravishes the figurative landscape whether he or she wants it or not, and the digitization made it even more complicated. While Vicky Smith at least dictates the initial terms of which parts of the image will be considered details and which will not, the appropriator of Kříženecký's film has no such possibility. He or she cannot even be so sure that the physical deformations resurfacing in the digital files are merely details, as they are so omnipresent. As noted earlier, the most haptic thing he or she can do is to caress the film frame by frame—both individually and as part of a mosaic—and search for images in which the magnifying properties of the camera and the film surface join forces in a most surprising way. As Bernhard Waldenfels notes, "pathos is surprise par excellence,"⁵⁸ and maybe the astonishment from the synergy of two close-ups, two roads toward the overlooked and peripheral, is the very thing that titillates the haptic imagination.

By scanning all the frames in a "haptic mosaic" (Figure 5.5), in which the mobile eye is allowed to roam over all the bricks that constitute the building of film,⁵⁹ one can distinguish four patterns. The first one (Figure 5.6) involves pictures in which the figurative contours of the face are not yet or no longer discernible. These come at the beginning and the end of the film strip, and for the current purpose, we abstract from them. The second, most frequent one (Figure 5.7) entails frames that show Šváb's face in relatively distinct outlines, covered by a yellow veil and disturbed by mechanical damages and dirt of a smaller order. Again, in the pursuit of the regime that puts the two forms of

---

⁵⁵ Kim Knowles, *Experimental Film and Photochemical Practices* (Cham: Palgrave Macmillan, 2020), 18.
⁵⁶ Ibid., 94.
⁵⁷ Ibid., 86.
⁵⁸ Waldenfels, "The Role of Lived Body in Feeling," 251.
⁵⁹ Roger Cardinal, "Pausing Over Peripheral Detail," *Framework* 30-31 (1986): 112–30; Catherine Grant and Amber Jacobs, "Persona Non Grata Sonata," *MAI: Feminism & Visual Culture* 1, no. 1 (2018), accessed December 31, 2022, http://maifeminism.com/persona-non-grata-sonata.

Figure 5.5 *Laughter and Tears* (Smích a pláč; 1898, source: nitrate print) © Národní filmový archiv.

the close-up together, besides providing context for the deformations, they are for now analytically disposable. The third one (Figures 5.8–5.9) consists of the actor's face being swallowed by large blobs of bacteria and fungi, with its double surface of the face and the yellowish-orange veil dissipating into hundreds of micro-organisms that open up tiny holes and branched paths of escape. This configuration succinctly demonstrates the fragility of the laughing/crying face and the whole mode of seeing that the close-up enacts. Nonetheless, it also resembles the logic of the color veil investigated in Chapter 1 to the extent that it does not require further elaboration.

As intriguing as the blobs are, perhaps the most original pattern is the fourth one (Figures 5.10–5.13). It includes images that are stitched together, usually involving two segments—the yellow one and the orange one—and producing, among other things, fascinating configurations in which Šváb's head appears to be torn (5.10, 5.11). The visible splice, as a physical joining of two separate pieces of film, liberates the images from mere representation and reconceives them within the cinematic process. It "becomes simultaneously the interruptive and the facilitator of a form of continuity,"[60] yet stages this continuity on the basest level of cinematic signification—the frame. In the spliced frames in *Laughter and Tears*, Josef Šváb-Malostranský is turning into a Frankenstein's monster, a head full of stitches that confuses us whether what we are seeing is still the well-known human actor or only his gestalt that was reassembled by technology into a different entity. His crying grimace freezes in a grotesque resignation to forces that shatter the dream of being captured on film to pieces. What remains is a divided surface where the individual parts no longer constitute the same plane of existence yet, curiously, do not disintegrate but still hold together. The close-up of the actor's face now presents a deindividualized head, reminiscent of Francis Bacon's tortured figures. As Gilles Deleuze said regarding Bacon's paintings, "For the face is a structured, spatial organization that conceals the head, whereas the head is dependent upon the body, even if it is the point of the body, its culmination. It is not that the head lacks spirit; but it is a spirit in bodily form, a corporeal and vital breath, an animal spirit."[61] Hence, by means of the splices, the explicit materiality of film starts to unveil the hidden materiality of the close-up—the face turns into a "piece of flesh,"[62] hardly discernible from the flesh of filmic matter. Nevertheless, what kind of intrusion does the alternative "Knowlesian" close-up in the form of a splice represent? How can something that sutures fragments that were disassembled or torn apart back

[60] Peter Gidal, *Materialist Film* (London and New York: Routledge, 2014), 108.
[61] Gilles Deleuze, *Francis Bacon: The Logic of Sensation* (London: Continuum, 2003), 20.
[62] Ibid., 25.

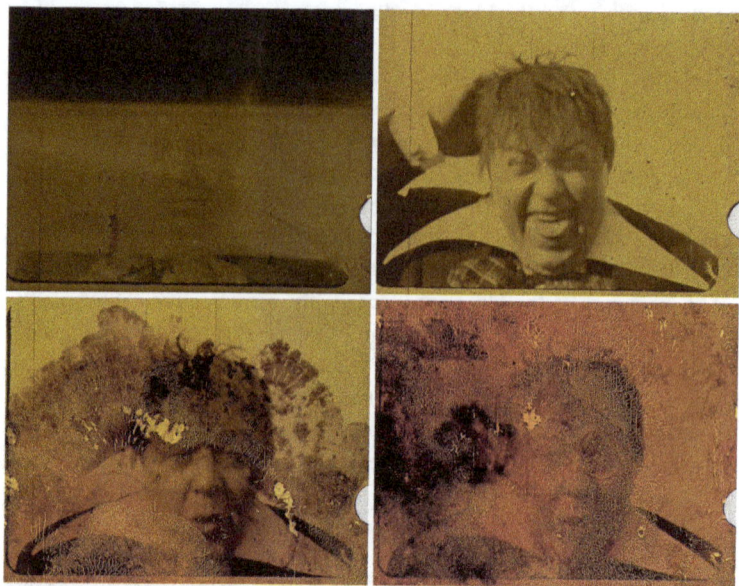

Figures 5.6–5.9 *Laughter and Tears* (Smích a pláč; 1898, source: nitrate print) © Národní filmový archiv.

into a seamless whole become a thing that exposes the weird shapes imposed by the crack-up as always on the brink of bursting out?

The facial close-up certainly has a history of inducing positive as well as negative emotions,[63] and James Whale's *Frankenstein* (1931) does not accomplish this ambiguity solely due to its emergence at the turn of the sound era. As Robert Spadoni comments, "the distorting and enervating effects of the early sound film close-up become the concrete attributes of one diegetic subject, regardless both of the distance between it and the camera and of the level of a viewer's medium awareness."[64] The inert, teflon-like head of the creature became a projection screen for the spectator's uncertainty about the human-machine assemblage that each close-up inevitably was, particularly

---

[63] For example, Yuri Tsivian describes expressions of shock and disgust at the graphic ugliness and gigantism of close-up faces in the reception of early Russian cinema. Yuri Tsivian, *Early Russian Cinema and Its Cultural Reception* (Chicago: University of Chicago Press, 1998), 154–6.

[64] Robert Spadoni, *Uncanny Bodies: The Coming of Film and the Origins of the Horror Genre* (Berkeley, Los Angeles, and London: University of California Press, 2007), 103.

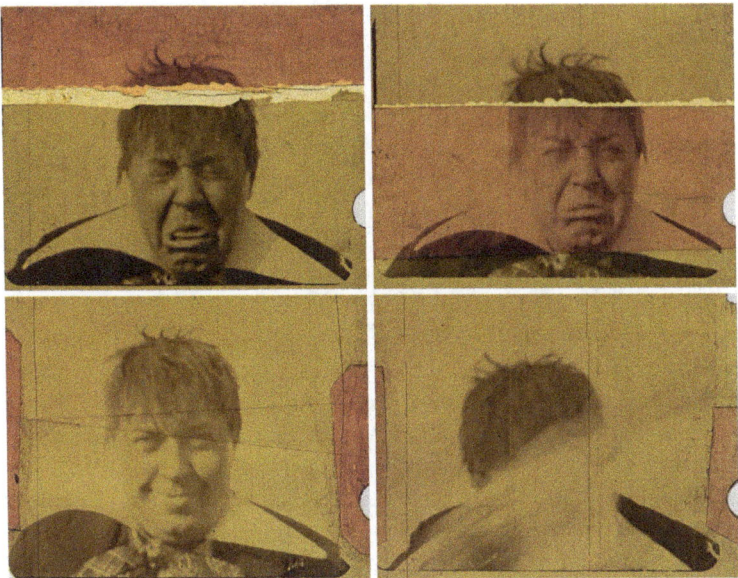

Figures 5.10–5.13 *Laughter and Tears* (Smích a pláč; 1898, source: nitrate print) © Národní filmový archiv.

in liminal periods of film history.[65] In this process, it was able to make the viewer more susceptible to the medium and at the same time pull him or her toward the image surface so that he or she could be convinced with his or her own haptic look how thick the filmic reality is. The monster's head can, then, be understood as a place where the two close-ups—that of the face and that of the medium/head—come together. However, the digitized *Laughter and Tears* allows us to touch the weird shape (and, by extension, also the crack-up) by making the two close-ups co-present yet visibly distinct. In *Frankenstein*, the medium was perceived as structuring context and dispositif, a cipher for the transition between silent and sound cinema; here, it changes into an intrusive cut that rearranges the surface without damaging or destroying its unity. The splice reminds us not only that the close-up is a strange space on the verge of the human and the technological, but that the very capability of its content and carrier to hold the image together in a recognizable configuration is always open for reassessment. Once a film frame gets torn apart, even the

---

[65] Shane Denson, *Postnaturalism: Frankenstein, Film, and the Anthropotechnical Interface* (Berlin: Transcript Verlag, 2014), 379–402.

best splice in the world cannot hide the fact that the film becomes something else. Nevertheless, as we do not know the origin of the splice, we cannot imagine the frame without it, and consequently, the splice is the only thing that stands as a close-up of the inevitable mutability and malleability of the frame. Remember Walter Murch's classic comparison of editing with surgery: "The 'patient' is pinned to the slab and: whack! Either/Or! This not That! In or Out! We chop up the poor film in a miniature guillotine then stick the dismembered pieces together like Dr Frankenstein's monster."[66] *Laughter and Tears* proves that this logic may apply not only to the classical montage but to the assemblage of the film's smallest units as well.

Someone who wants to shape the crack-up between the two close-ups would be advised not to satisfy himself or herself with dwelling on the splices' magic nor to replace the individual parts at will. Inspiration can come from a Frankensteinian film par excellence, Michael Fleming's experimental found footage film *Never Never Land* (2018). The work aims to deconstruct "our obsession with physical perfection, our domination and wanting to control everything"[67]—including our bodies and faces. For this reason, Fleming creates composite images that are stitched from two or more image fragments yet still look as if they complete each other. However, this correspondence is itself undermined by inserting or uncovering visible seams between the parts. The faces from family photo albums we used to know no longer exist as distinguished wholes; to make sense, they need to be reassembled, and, at the same time, they should not be camouflaged as originals and affirm their composite character. Thus, the close-up-in-film and the close-up-of-film are simultaneously put together yet kept apart, embracing the always-already-sutured character of the cinematic body. The surgical touch of Josef Šváb-Frankensteinský's face can follow in this film's steps.

Coda: The Perks of Touching the Untouchable

The reflection on the epistemological preconditions of touching fragmentary, distorted, and altogether weird film objects, such as the digitized nitrate print of *Laughter and Tears*, comes to an end. Its conclusions are provisional, but it should be clear that some of the implicit premises of haptic criticism—namely, intentional fallacy and negative ontology—will no longer suffice.

---

[66] Walter Murch, *In the Blink of an Eye: A Perspective on Film Editing* (Los Angeles: Silman James Press, 1992), 57.
[67] Michael Fleming, "Never Never Land," *Vimeo*, 2018, accessed December 31, 2022, https://vimeo.com/234667905.

First, as the existing clouds of rot, fungicidal paths, and Frankensteinian stitches emerged regardless of what was purposefully put into the images by the artist or any other human agent, Šváb's face is difficult to fetishize and thus cannot evoke the identification mechanisms that would ease us into thinking that we have been chosen by the film object. Second, the peculiar deformations encroaching upon Šváb's head impact the film so severely and so frequently that they cease to be peripheral and begin to strongly determine the meanings and effects of the film. A selection of stitched frames allowed us to discern specific configurations of the cinematic close-up—or, more precisely, two forms of the close-up (one figurative, one material). The clashes between these two modalities make for the most intensive variations of the crack-up that do not lead to rupture or destruction but create potent weird shapes, such as the stitched head of Frankensteinian proportions. Altogether, this investigation demonstrated how relative categories such as figuration and materiality, human and technological, continuity and discontinuity, or detail and whole can be, and how anyone who wants to intervene in the cracked-up film objects needs to do it with surgical caution.

If anyone wanted to pursue these principles in a videographic form, he or she has been offered inspiration, particularly from essays by Catherine Grant and the duo Cristina Álvarez López-Adrian Martin and experimental found footage films such as *Never Never Land*. Whether analog, digital, or hybrid, these works anticipated or directly approached the problem of shaping the unshapeable and embraced the specific distortions of their reference film objects for their hidden poetic and analytical potential. Still, to create a videographic work that marries haptic and self-reflexive impulses with scholarly analysis, it is necessary to develop a more structured, systematic approach. One that injects the idiosyncratic crack-up of the materials with theoretical notions pointing to something more general about the film medium in the digital interface and something that would be common for a larger family of archival films in the (post)digital space. How such an approach could look like and how it could be applied to *Digital Kříženecký* as a whole is outlined in the last chapter.

6

Shaping the Unshapeable?

Videographic Deformation and the First Frames of Czech Cinema

January 2022. The films of Jan Kříženecký have finally become available online. Watching the first Czech cinematic works for the first time in the online space, one wonders what really constitutes their "firstness." What if the real beginning of Czech cinema resides in images we often fail to grasp? The continuous movement of film, further smoothed by digital transfer, masks the individual building blocks out of which it is assembled, including the images that open every single film. This is why we need THE FIRST FRAMES OF CZECH CINEMA. (Figure 6.1)

Whenever we attempt to curate films from the very beginnings of cinema to contemporary spectators, multiple pressing questions always come to mind. Shall the ephemeral one-minute scenes be shown individually or as parts of larger wholes, sorted out according to thematic or chronological affinities? How do we successfully reproduce not only the films' content but also their inherent technological features or the distinctive quality of early cinematic experience? How is it possible to make the audience aware of the historical distance that the surviving archival artifacts covered without overwhelming it with extra information?[1] How can we navigate between the film materials' past, present, and future?

The DVD/Blu-ray collection *The Films of Jan Kříženecký*, published in late 2019 by the National Film Archive in Prague and curated by the author

---

[1] This topic was addressed poignantly by Elif Rongen-Kaynakçi during a discussion on curating early cinema: Jiří Anger, Jeanne Pommeau, Elif Rongen-Kaynakçi, Matěj Strnad, "A Season of Classic Films | Where, How and to Whom—The Challenges of Presenting Earliest Cinema," *Filmový přehled*, June 3, 2021, accessed December 31, 2022, https://www.filmovyprehled.cz/cs/kalendar/detail/a-season-of-classic-films-where-how-and-to-whom-the-challenges-of-presenting-earliest-cinema. Aslı Özgen and Elif Rongen-Kaynakçi, "The Transnational Archive as a Site of Disruption, Discrepancy, and Decomposition: The Complexities of Ottoman Film Heritage," *The Moving Image: The Journal of the Association of Moving Image Archivists* 21, no. 1–2 (2021): 77–99.

Figure 6.1 The first frames of all Kříženecký's films that were digitized from the original nitrate carriers (1898–1911, source: vintage prints and original negatives) © Národní filmový archiv.

of these lines,[2] strove to marry respectful cataloging and contextualization of the materials with reflecting the incompleteness of analog fragments and the necessary shifts that occur with the digitization process—in other words, it was an attempt at what Michael Loebenstein terms "presentation with seams."[3] Still, the edition was relatively tame when it came to deciphering the extent to which the digitized films' hybrid and fragmentary character shapes our experience of them. The unfamiliar and destabilizing elements, such as the yellowish-orange color or camera trembling, but also more common mechanical and chemical damages and ellipses, were documented and demonstrated by Jeanne Pommeau in a video featured in the DVD/Blu-ray extras.[4] Still, would it be possible to proceed from showing, analyzing, and contextualizing the film materials toward creating original interpretations (texts, videos, performances) of early cinematic artifacts as aesthetic, historical, and technological phenomena for the times we are living in? Now it is time to experiment with practical forms of presentation in which this potential shall be unleashed, in which the crack-up of *Digital Kříženecký* as a whole shall be showcased in a defamiliarizing yet still historically accurate fashion.

This chapter delimits one such experiment that goes beyond merely exhibiting and contextualizing the first Czech films and interprets them via original creative forms. Whereas previous chapters already alluded to this approach of performing research by means of the moving images and sounds themselves, Chapter 6 involves a full-fledged (albeit short) videographic essay that builds upon found footage and archival film practices as well as the evolving field of digital humanities.[5] A videographic essay titled *The First Frames of Czech Cinema* (Jiří Anger and Adéla Kudlová, 2021) plays with the paradoxes and contradictions of the earliest cinematic works. While we watch the *first* Czech films for the *first* time in a digital form, the very *first* images of

---

[2] Jiří Anger, ed., *Filmy Jana Kříženeckého/The Films of Jan Kříženecký*, DVD/Blu-ray (Praha: Národní filmový archiv, 2019).

[3] Paolo Cherchi Usai, David Francis, Alexander Horwath, and Michael Loebenstein, eds., *Film Curatorship: Archives, Museums, and the Digital Marketplace* (Wien: Synema – Gesellschaft für Film und Medien, 2008), 203.

[4] Jeanne Pommeau, "The Digitisation of Jan Kříženecký's Films," in *Filmy Jana Kříženeckého/The Films of Jan Kříženecký*, ed. Jiří Anger, DVD/Blu-ray Booklet (Praha: Národní filmový archiv, 2019), 31–5; Jeanne Pommeau, "The Digitisation of Kříženecký's Films" [videocommentary], in *Filmy Jana Kříženeckého/The Films of Jan Kříženecký*, ed. Jiří Anger, DVD/Blu-ray (Praha: Národní filmový archiv, 2019).

[5] Jason Mittell, "Videographic Criticism as a Digital Humanities Method," in *Debates in the Digital Humanities 2019*, ed. Matthew Gold and Lauren Klein (Minneapolis: University of Minnesota Press, 2019), accessed December 31, 2022, https://dhdebates.gc.cuny.edu/read/untitled-f2acf72c-a469-49d8-be35-67f9ac1e3a60/section/b6dea70a-9940-497e-b7c5-930126fbd180.

the works mostly stay overlooked. Thus, the essay gathers every single "first frame" of each digitized nitrate print and negative and assembles them into a compilation that reveals them in detail as well as part of a larger mosaic. On the one hand, the essay exploits the possibilities of digital technology to show the individual frames from multiple angles and bring obscure details to the fore; on the other, it is also a reflection of an early screening practice, when projectionists started the presentation with a still image that gradually evolved into a continuous movement. As I argue throughout the text, the videographic essay allows us to expose the first Czech film frames as malleable objects with photochemical as well as digital features.

To better approximate the aims and implications of the videographic essay, this study includes both the actual video and its written elaboration. The goal of this written accompaniment is to provide a methodological background for the videographic essay and analyze its theoretical implications. For this purpose, the following lines are dedicated first to a tendency in videographic film studies called "deformative criticism," which "strives to make the original work strange in some unexpected way, deforming it unconventionally to reveal aspects that are conventionally obscured in its normal version and discovering something new from it."[6] This approach resonates with the intention behind *The First Frames of Czech Cinema*, which involves breaking the films into archives of images and extracting the individual frames according to a parameter of being the first images in the respective films. In order to explain the relevance of this approach, its potentialities, as well as its limitations, must be addressed. The second part introduces the creative process behind *The First Frames of Czech Cinema*, explains the essay's subversive take on deformative criticism, and outlines the findings we obtain (or do not obtain) about the opening frames in their material and aesthetic ambiguity. In the spirit of *film theory from below*, the smallest units of film function as windows onto the possibility of making the crack-up resonate across the entire *Digital Kříženecký* corpus.

Breaking the Film Object

The hitherto undertaken examinations of Kříženecký's films have always involved deconstruction or breakage of the respective texts. Whether they were individual frames selected according to a pattern (*Spring Races* in Chapter 2, *Laughter and Tears* in Chapter 5), a succession of frames in

---

[6] Ibid.

which a pattern unfolded (*Grand Consecration* in Chapter 1, *Assignation* in Chapter 4), or an animated GIF that made a pattern discernible in movement (*Opening Ceremony* in Chapter 3), the forms that emerged were no longer pure instruments applied to find hidden meanings. By dissecting the digitized artifacts and gathering their individual units into configurations that make the crack-up visible and speculatively generative, the initial films transformed into new audiovisual objects in their own right. These new entities reveal motifs enclosed within the original artifacts, yet they also defamiliarize them, making them "stranger than strange."[7] Furthermore, the GIF and frames have the capacity to circulate partially independently of the originals and may enter new chains of production—for example, in the videographic exercises proposed in each chapter.

Still, would it be possible to turn this practice into a more systematic approach? What certain practitioners of videographic film studies term "deformative criticism"[8] allows us to imagine a situation in which, to quote Mark Sample, "the deformed work is the end, not the means to the end."[9] Inspired by a literary-theory manifesto "Deformance and Interpretation" (1999) by Lisa Samuels and Jerome McGann, deformative criticism does not ask "what does [the work of art] mean" but "how do we release or expose [its] possibilities of meaning?"[10] Rather than diving into the depths of a single film text, the approach aims to shift the rules of the game, distort the film and how we usually perceive it—whether in continuous flow or frame by frame—and transform it into a new aesthetic and scholarly object. Samuels and McGann paved the way by demonstrating what strategies such as reordering, isolating, altering, and adding can do to Wallace Stevens's poems.[11] However, deformative criticism also draws on the history of experimental filmmaking and found footage: for example, on the "cineseizures" by Martin Arnold that isolate, stretch, and loop moments

---

[7] The Audiovisual Essayist, "Making It Stranger than Strange," *YouTube*, 2020, accessed July 31, 2021, https://www.youtube.com/watch?v=pajDSY05zg0.
[8] One of the formative events for deformative criticism in videographic film studies was the 2017 Society for Cinema and Media Studies Workshop "Deformative Criticism and Digital Experimentation in Film and Media Studies." See Shane Denson, "Deformative Criticism at #SCMS17," *Medieinitiative*, February 16, 2017, accessed December 31, 2022, https://medieninitiative.wordpress.com/2017/02/16/deformative-criticism-at-scms17/.
[9] Mark Sample, "Notes Towards a Deformed Humanities," *Samplereality*, May 2, 2012, accessed December 31, 2022, https://samplereality.com/2012/05/02/notes-towards-a-deformed-humanities/.
[10] Lisa Samuels and Jerome McGann, "Deformance and Interpretation," *New Literary History* 30, no. 1 (1999): 28.
[11] Ibid., 37–45.

from classic Hollywood films to unearth latent psychoanalytic narratives within ordinary gestures and speeches.[12]

Videographic researchers such as Jason Mittell, Kevin L. Ferguson, or Alan O'Leary experiment with various kinds of software—both classic editing programs like Adobe Premiere or Final Cut and specialized image processing programs (ImageJ)[13]—to break their objects of study and "generate heretical and non-normative readings of media texts."[14] For example, Jason Mittell's project *Deformin' in the Rain* (2019–2020) subjects the classic musical *Singin' in the Rain* (1954) to more than twenty deformations, from traditional techniques like looping and slow motion through unusual spatial montage (scaled triptych, moving frame, and other tactics) to re-arranging all the shots ascending by length or presenting the sum of the film's frames as a barcode.[15] As the author stated previously, such processes of discovery and experimentation in themselves constitute research, enabling us to "break the seal that binds a film as a finished work" and see it from a myriad of possible and impossible angles.[16]

To make the outcome less predictable, the deformative approach is often also "parametric" or "algorithmic," whether in the narrow sense of operating according to a computerized step-based procedure or in the broader sense of subjecting a work to one or more generative constraints or parameters.[17] Samuels and McGann already mention "reading backward" as a critical method that "turns off the controls that organize the poetic system at some of its most general levels" and yields results we cannot predict in advance.[18] Similarly, many videographic practitioners deform films by succumbing them to a set of standardized procedures from which there can be no (or

---

[12] See Arnold's Cineseizure trilogy: *Pièce touchée* (1989), *Passage à l'acte* (1993), and *Alone. Life Wastes Andy Hardy* (1998). For an elaborate reflection of his works, see Akira Mizuta Lippit, *Ex-Cinema: From a Theory of Experimental Film and Video* (Berkeley and London: University of California Press, 2012), 56–72, 119–37.

[13] For more information about the creative use of ImageJ software, see, for example, Kevin L. Ferguson, "Slices of Cinema: Digital Transformation as Research Strategy," in *The Arclight Guidebook to Media History and the Digital Humanities*, ed. Charles R. Acland and Eric Hoyt (Sussex: REFRAME, 2016), 270–99 or Kevin L. Ferguson, "Digital Surrealism: Visualizing Walt Disney Animation Studios," *Digital Humanities Quarterly* 11, no. 1 (2017), accessed December 31, 2022, http://www.digitalhumanities.org/dhq/vol/11/1/000276/000276.html.

[14] Denson, "Deformative Criticism at #SCMS17."

[15] Jason Mittell, "Deformin' in the Rain: How (and Why) to Break a Classic Film," *Digital Humanities Quarterly* 15, no. 1 (2021), accessed December 31, 2022, http://www.digitalhumanities.org/dhq/vol/15/1/000521/000521.html.

[16] Mittell, "Videographic Film Criticism as a Digital Humanities Method."

[17] Alan O'Leary, "No Voiding Time. A Deformative Videoessay," *16:9*, September 30, 2019, accessed December 31, 2022, http://www.16-9.dk/2019/09/no-voiding-time/.

[18] Samuels and McGann, "Deformance and Interpretation," 36.

minimal) deviation and whose outcome should be down to chance, at least to the highest possible extent.[19] This is particularly the case of Mittell's various re-arrangements of *Singin' in the Rain*—for example, the exercise in which he re-organizes the entire film by ascending length of shots or a videographic version of Nicholas Rombes's "10/40/70" project, which juxtaposes three still frames from a feature film, from the arbitrary 10, 40, and 70 minute marks, and then analyzes what these images signify in terms of the fictional work and on their own.[20] The parametric approach presents a useful counterpoint to certain excesses of haptic criticism, especially to its preconception that the film object exists for us and can be manipulated at will to reflect our subjective experience. Its treatment of source materials as "archives of sounds and images"[21] is a way of accepting that the film object is never entirely what we want it to be and may potentially lead to serious questioning of what kind of object we are really "touching" in the software interface. What makes the supposedly unique configurations of the crack-up encountered in *Digital Kříženecký* thus far stand out among others? Could it be possible that these moments have been overrated because of my pre-selective intentional filter? Although I believe the answer is "no," the deformative/parametric approach I selected for *The First Frames of Czech Cinema* allows me to test whether there may be a crack-up that is less arbitrary and more distributed across the digitized body of work.

Be that as it may, deformative criticism naturally has its own pitfalls, sometimes reflected by videographic practitioners themselves,[22] that should be elaborated further. First and foremost, even if we decide to treat film as an archive of sounds and images, it does not mean such an archive is asymptomatic. The software we work with is still designed to keep us under the illusion of control, giving us (seemingly infinite but inherently limited) options to manipulate images and sounds without questioning the interface within which we are allowed to operate and which is tailored to visibility

---

[19] David Verdeure, "Deformative vs Performative," *Filmscalpel*, 2019, accessed December 31, 2022, https://www.filmscalpel.com/performative-vs-deformative/.

[20] Nicholas Rombes, *10/40/70: Constraint as Liberation in the Era of Digital Film Theory* (New York: Zero Books, 2014).

[21] Mittell, "Videographic Film Criticism as Digital Humanities Method."

[22] See, for example, Alan O'Leary "Workshop of Potential Scholarship: Manifesto for a Parametric Videographic Criticism," *NECSUS European Journal of Media Studies* 11, no. 1 (2021): 75–98. A more general debate on the shortcomings of the parametric approach also sparked between the attendants of videographic workshops at Middlebury College: Jason Mittell et al., "Becoming Videographic Critics: A Roundtable Conversation," in *The Videographic Essay: Practice and Pedagogy*, ed. Christian Keathley, Jason Mittell, and Catherine Grant (Scalar, 2019), accessed December 31, 2022, http://videographicessay .org/works/videographic-essay/becoming-videographic-critics-a-roundtable -conversation?path=contents.

and completeness.²³ The software interface gives us numerous options to combine and manipulate images and sounds, yet the available operations are pre-structured to enhance our power to possess films, making them as decipherable and effective as possible.²⁴ If we open the film in an ordinary media player such as VLC, our ability to manipulate images and sounds already presupposes that films are attainable objects adjusted to our needs of controlling time and ready at hand to deliver an audiovisual presence that masks the formatting processes active in the background (besides occasional glitches and buffers).²⁵ When we proceed toward working with films in video-editing software, our capacity to watch two or more images simultaneously, switching automatically between the viewing and editing windows, lures us into seeing all images as mutually connected, even if they are not (at least not necessarily). Furthermore, we are free to examine the individual images/frames in microscopic detail, yet the images themselves are always full of information. No matter how torn, decayed, or destroyed they are, they are the same rectangles filled with pixels—absence turns into presence.

Similarly, no matter how sophisticated the parameter is, its success in achieving surprising aesthetic or scholarly results is mostly determined by the way in which we select, arrange, and interpret the data. Whereas haptic criticism toys with mistaking the subjective for the (quasi)objective, deformative criticism risks confusing the objective with the (quasi)subjective. Importing our favorite film into Adobe Premiere and subjecting it to a finite number of universally available operations will not automatically yield ways of seeing it from unknown or even nonhuman perspectives. As our freedom in shaping moving images in programs such as Adobe Premiere, Final Cut, or iMovie is getting bigger and bigger, technologies grow more and more sophisticated methods to pre-structure our choices, maneuvering us into cleverly delimited ways of seeing. In the worst scenario, we get to perceive the film object not through the eyes of the program, but how the program wants us to perceive it—as a carefully designed and entirely replaceable consumer product lost in an endless play of clicks and pop-up windows. Thus, anyone who wants to exploit editing software's unique creative and scholarly potentialities must be wary of succumbing to a game in which, according

---

[23] Alexander Galloway, *The Interface Effect* (Cambridge: Polity, 2012); Neta Alexander and Arjun Appadurai, *Failure* (Cambridge: Polity, 2019); Jiří Anger and Kevin B. Lee, "Suture Goes Meta: Desktop Documentary and its Narrativization of Screen-Mediated Experience," *Quarterly Review of Film and Video* 40, no. 5 (2023): 595–622.
[24] For these reasons, Laura Mulvey speaks of a digital film spectator as "possessive spectator." Laura Mulvey, *Death 24x a Second: Stillness and the Moving Image* (London: Reaktion Books, 2006), 161–80.
[25] Shane Denson, *Discorrelated Images* (Durham: Duke University Press, 2020), 56–63.

to Vilém Flusser, "every virtuality, even the least probable, will be realized of necessity if the game is played for a sufficiently long time."[26] Rather than uncritically depending on machine creativity, we should think about the conditions under which we are breaking the film objects, about the complex interface between human intervention and technological automatism, and strive to defamiliarize not only how we see images but also how the software wants us to see them.

To inject the deformative with the performative,[27] the critic/theorist does not necessarily have to stage a convoluted critique of software ideology. A self-reflexive and performative gesture may lie in the selection of the source material itself or, more specifically, in choosing a film object that is, in a way, always already deformed, unsure whether it even qualifies as an object. Not a familiar Hollywood or arthouse film that needs an enlightened critic and high-end software to make it strange, nor an experimental found footage film that is already coded as intentionally defamiliarizing. *Digital Křiženecký* constitutes an entire corpus of such uncertain objects, even more so when we focus on the fact that their most basic building blocks—the individual frames—are the most unstable and undefinable elements. *The First Frames of Czech Cinema* seeks to become an exercise in deformative criticism, but one that puzzles the input as well as the output and does not let the algorithmic protocol have the final say on which perspective we should take.

Frames Caught Between Then and Now

As indicated earlier, *The First Frames of Czech Cinema* takes the form of a quasi-compilation that shows all the opening frames of the digitized nitrate prints and negatives (that is, those that carry at least a fragment of visual information, excluding the artificially added opening titles[28]) both individually and as parts of a larger mosaic. While watching the individual films, as soon as each of them starts playing, its opening frame appears, but only in a fleeting, almost imperceptible form—before we are able to process it, it disappears in an uncompromising 24 fps movement. Considering we aim for an imaginative return to the grassroots of cinema, the first frames

---

[26] Vilém Flusser, "Our Program," in *Post-History* (Minneapolis: Univocal Publishing, 2013), 22.
[27] Verdeure, "Deformative vs Performative."
[28] In the digitization process, only the frames that include at least partial visual information were scanned. The original prints and negatives with Křiženecký's films also contain blank frames at the beginning and end.

of the films, or at least what remained of them after all the years of decay, cannot be ignored. As they were the first images that were caught on camera and the first images that appeared during screening, waiting for the "sudden transformation from still image to moving illusion" that came as the cranking began,[29] they might be considered the actual cinematic firsts.

To make these images visible again, with all their complicated and often contradictory histories at play, the videographic essay should turn its attention toward the minor. In this sense, Hannah Frank's call for "studying a building not by walking its hallways or perusing its blueprints, but by examining each of its bricks"[30] can reach out to practical research as well. With the quantity of deformative operations we have at our disposal, we often forget about the nuances of the materials we want to deform. Although many videographic works pay attention to a single scene, the analytic or interpretive aim is usually related to its content, not to the material construction that shapes the individual image as a film object. Inspiration may come from videographic essays by Johannes Binotto, which are certainly not parametric/algorithmic in the vein of Mittell's or O'Leary's works but share a broader goal of dismantling the film object to make it strange.[31] Binotto demonstrates how "lingering on the small and particular" can counter the "habit of clicking and swiping through films, clips and images as swiftly as possible," which "follows completely the capitalist logic of quick and smooth consumption."[32] In a rhetoric partly recalling haptic criticism and the new cinephilia, he asks: "What multiplicity is there hidden in just one film moment, in just one audiovisual fragment, in one image, one sound?"[33] *The First Frames of Czech Cinema* pushes this idea in a more parametric direction, asking what if this singular fragment was not a specific image but any image that follows a specific protocol. This way, a game-changing detail may spring out of a whole corpus of visual elements without privileging one picture over the other.

---

[29] Tom Gunning, "An Aesthetic of Astonishment: Early Film and the (In)Credulous Spectator," in *Film Theory and Criticism*, ed. Leo Braudy and Marshall Cohen (New York and Oxford: Oxford University Press, 2009), 741.

[30] Hannah Frank, *Frame by Frame: A Materialist Aesthetics of Animated Cartoons* (Berkeley: University of California Press, 2019), 1.

[31] See, for example, Johannes Binotto, "Touching Sound," *Transferences*, February 2, 2018, accessed December 31, 2022, https://transferences.org/2018/02/02/touching-sound/; Johannes Binotto, "Trace," *Transferences*, 2020, accessed December 31, 2022, https://transferences.org/videoessays/performative-deformative-video-essays/trace/.

[32] Johannes Binotto, "Minor Instances, Major Consequences: Video Essay Workshop," *Transferences*, 2020, accessed December 31, 2022, https://transferences.org/lehre/video-essay-workshop/.

[33] Ibid.

The protocol for the essay was based on a now-firmly established fact that the earliest film projections were not all about movement. Tom Gunning's famous article "An Aesthetic of Astonishment: Early Film and the (In)Credulous Spectator" (1989) points out that "in the earliest Lumière exhibitions the films were initially presented as frozen unmoving images, projections of still photographs. Then, flaunting a mastery of visual showmanship, the projector began cranking and the images were made to move."[34] With the advent of mass digitization, the (re)found closeness between the still and the moving in cinema gained attention in academic circles[35] as well as the avant-garde (Matthias Müller, Christoph Girardet, Douglas Gordon, Karl Lemieux, and others), where this impulse already sprang to life in the 1960s and 1970s analog works by Peter Kubelka, Ernie Gehr, or Hollis Frampton.[36] Thomas Elsaesser considers the still image as cinema's "memento mori: reminding us that at the heart of the cinema are acts of intervention in the living tissue of time, that the cinema is 'death at work.'"[37] Therefore, showing the actual first frames of the first Czech films could be a way to demonstrate this repressed will to death at the very moment when the inert filmic matter starts to gain figurative contours. Our videographic experiment thereby examines the frame as a rupture in the cinematic movement, yet one that also initiates it and stirs it to life. In this way, the essay stages a complex dialectic between then and now: it utilizes the possibilities of digital technology to reflect on the transformation from stillness to movement to which early cinematic exhibitions owed part of their appeal.

The organization of the digitized films (28 files—15 nitrate prints, 13 original negatives) was based primarily on two criteria—the year of their production and thematic affinity. Frames 1–18 come from the pioneering films presented at the Exhibition of Architecture and Engineering in 1898: numbers 1–9 are from actualities that portrayed everyday life in Prague, 10–15 are from comedy scenes staged by Josef Šváb-Malostranský, and 16–18 stem from Kříženecký's obsession with Sokol athletic exercises. Frames 19–26 were extracted from other actualities from Prague life shot between 1901 and 1908, while the remaining two frames (27–28) present the monument

[34] Gunning, "An Aesthetic of Astonishment," 740.
[35] See, for example, Eivind Rossaak, ed., *Between Stillness and Motion: Film, Photography, Algorithms* (Amsterdam: Amsterdam University Press, 2010).
[36] The mutual inspiration between experimental filmmakers and new film historians is well-known. For an overview, see André Habib, "Finding Early Cinema in the Avant-garde: Research and Investigation," in *Provenance and Early Cinema*, ed. Joanne Bernardi, Paolo Cherchi Usai, Tami Williams, and Joshua Yumibe (Bloomington: Indiana University Press, 2021), 261–74.
[37] Thomas Elsaesser, "Stop/Motion," in *Between Stillness and Motion: Film, Photography, Algorithms*, ed. Eivind Rossaak (Amsterdam: Amsterdam University Press, 2010), 118.

of a famous Czech historian and politician, František Palacký—first as a foundation stone (1898), then as an almost complete sculpture (1911)[38]—and together represent a sort of longitudinal documentary that circumscribes both the creation of the monument and Kříženecký's creative career.[39]

The key question was how to present this assemblage of frames in a simple, not-too-intrusive form and simultaneously turn it into something more than an ordinary YouTube "supercut"[40] that would simply replace one form of determinism (frames as units lost in a continuous movement) with another (frames blindly following each other according to a preestablished linear pattern).[41] This is why we decided to show the frames in two forms at the same time—individually in detail and as building blocks of a larger mosaic. Each frame is first seen as an isolated image and "deformed" in various ways (rotating, flickering, zooming in and out, stretching and narrowing). Then, it is inserted into the background, where a mosaic of all the frames is being built. By combining "the sequential and the simultaneous modes of viewing,"[42] we present the first frames as irreducible to being erased or marginalized in favor of smooth and continuous flow as well as to being interchangeable units in a coherent whole. Paraphrasing Ian Bogost, the first frames "remind us that no matter how fluidly a system may operate, its members nevertheless remain utterly isolated, mutual aliens."[43] Of course,

---

[38] The camera was also present when the monument was formally unveiled on July 1, 1912, resulting in the film *Unveiling Ceremony of the Monument—July 1, 1912* (Slavnost odhalení pomníku 1. července 1912; Antonín Pech, 1912). The film includes material from the earlier fragment *František Palacký Monument Prior to Its Completion* (Pomník Františka Palackého před dokončením; 1911) that served as a source for the last frame (no. 28).

[39] The audiovisual essay does not involve three new compilations assembled from various (usually later-generation) materials and two recently found materials: *Escorting the Cradle of František Palacký from Hodslavice to the Prague Exhibition Grounds* (Přenesení kolébky Františka Palackého z Hodslavic na Výstaviště; 1898, source: nitrate print) and *Foundation Ceremony of the František Palacký Monument* (Slavnost odhalení pomníku Františka Palackého; 1898, source: original negative).

[40] Andy Baio, "Fanboy Supercuts, Obsessive Video Montages," *Waxy*, April 11, 2008, accessed December 31, 2022, https://waxy.org/2008/04/fanboy_supercuts_obsessive_video_montages/.

[41] Of course, there are many ways in which supercut can be employed in a more academically rigorous and/or aesthetically inventive manner. See, for example, Allison de Fren, "The Critical Supercut: A Scholarly Approach to a Fannish Practice," *The Cine-Files* 15 (2020), accessed December 31, 2022, http://www.thecine-files.com/the-critical-supercut-a-scholarly-approach-to-a-fannish-practice/; Max Tohline, "A Supercut of Supercuts: Aesthetics, Histories, Databases," *Open Screens* 4, no. 1 (2021), accessed December 31, 2022, https://www.openscreensjournal.com/article/id/6946/.

[42] Tingo Baptista, "Lessons in Looking: The Digital Audiovisual Essay," PhD diss. (Birkbeck, University of London, 2016), 160.

[43] Ian Bogost, *Alien Phenomenology, or What It's Like to Be a Thing* (Minneapolis: University of Minnesota Press, 2012), 40.

the intersection of the sequential and the simultaneous, the temporal and the spatial, is not without contradictions. On the one hand, the individual frames accumulate progressively faster so as to make the essay's rhythm and tempo more varied and consequential, which makes it more challenging for the viewer to appreciate each singular image. On the other hand, the mosaic that is being constructed out of the frames in the background allows the audience to get ahold of their similarities and differences, yet the more images appear, the smaller they look, and thus do not enable more nuanced comparison. Still, these contradictions were deemed necessary to account for the paradoxical existence of film as a medium, whose unresolved status between movement and stillness becomes even more apparent in the digital form (Figures 6.2–6.5).[44]

The videographic essay also includes a written quote by Hannah Frank as another layer that thickens the interplay between various modes of seeing. In the vein of many videographic works,[45] the text does not explain

Figures 6.2–6.5 *The First Frames of Czech Cinema* (Jiří Anger and Adéla Kudlová, 2021) © Národní filmový archiv.

---

[44] See, for example, Mulvey, *Death 24x a Second*.
[45] There is even a "sub-genre" of videographic film studies called the "videographic epigraph." "Videographic Epigraph," in *The Videographic Essay: Practice and Pedagogy*, ed. Christian Keathley, Jason Mittell, and Catherine Grant (Scalar, 2019), accessed

or mimic what is perceivable in the images but functions performatively as a distinctive meaning-making element. Frank's quote, more a manifesto for taking individual frames seriously than an analysis or interpretation of what is going on, is phased out into fragments and distributed in space, gradually revealing itself during the essay according to the rhythm of the images and turning the individual phrases into building blocks of their own kind, and eventually appearing in its whole at the end of the essay (Figure 6.5).

Finally, an experimental soundtrack by Jan Burian, which accompanies the digitized films of Jan Kříženecký on the DVD/Blu-ray release, was added and slightly modified to amplify the humming noise of the nitrate materials.

What can the essay teach us about the first frames of Kříženecký's films or, more generally, about the paradoxical existence of a digitized film frame? Even in cases where digitization remains as faithful to the original artifacts as possible, the new digital frames will inevitably diverge from their models in some respects, due to the material specificities of analog and digital media as well as to subtle intentional or unintentional shifts that occur during the intricate translation from grain to pixel.[46] The dilapidated images we see in the essay approximate the physical memory and patina of the originals, yet they also turn them into a snapshot, exempted from the life cycle of decaying nitrate prints and negatives and projected into a medium that allows for manipulating with the fragile frames as with any other visual data. *The First Frames of Czech Cinema* emphasizes this hybridity by "doubling" the traces of photochemical deformations in the digitized frames with further deformations of a digital kind. This approach takes aim at the often-presupposed neutrality and transparency of the digitization process, engaging digital manipulations in a way that makes the newly acquired malleability of the first Czech film frames directly perceptible. Also, the digital deformations (rotating, stretching, zooming, and so on) do not occlude the photochemical distortions but invent new perspectives from which we can grasp them. Again, the goal is to let the contradictions of the first frames of Czech cinema collide and reach productive encounters rather than resolve them in one way or another.

February 28, 2022, http://videographicessay.org/works/videographic-essay/videographic-epigraph.

[46] See Giovanna Fossati, *From Grain to Pixel: The Archival Life of Film in Transition*, 3rd Revised ed. (Amsterdam: Amsterdam University Press, 2018) or, more specifically, Serena Bellotti and Andrea Mariani, "The Digital Witness: Film Reconstruction and the Forensic Imagination in New Media Environments," *Cinergie – Il Cinema e le altre Arti* 20 (2021): 27–43; Patricia Ledesma Villon, "Indeterminable Frames: Exploring Digital Humanities Approaches and Applications for the Moving Image," *Cinergie – Il Cinema e le altre Arti* 20 (2021): 125–38.

The essay's shifting of perspectives also draws attention to the supposedly peripheral features of frames—the perforations. At the outset of cinema, perforations were often perceived as a "weakening" of film, something that makes films more vulnerable. The single pair of perforations Lumière brothers used was a compromise,[47] ensuring that the perforated film strip "would be less susceptible to tear or break from the impact, however minimal, of the claws" while still being able to advance steadily through the film gate.[48] As mentioned earlier, the films of Jan Kříženecký have only a single round hole on each side of the frame,[49] and thus they are significantly harder to project, restore, or even scan. Thanks to the videographic essay, we can see that the vintage Lumière perforations are not always present in their former state. Although the digitization report states that the not-yet standardized aspect ratio of the films was "adjusted in order to make the entire frame visible (even during moments of vertical instability) and also the perforation whenever it was possible,"[50] due to the limitations and divergences from current standard ratios, it was not always entirely viable. This is the reason why we usually see the perforation only at one edge of the frame in a semicircular form.

Furthermore, many of the digitized first frames (particularly those from the prints) are torn to such an extent that the circular holes are nowhere to be seen—some of them—13, 14, 18—now have no perforation, others—1, 2, 4, 10, 15—had at unknown time their parts replaced with later-generation film stock with four perforations. The latter group may be understood as a sign of restoration not done right but also as a document of how accidental or pragmatic physical interventions alter the archival object throughout the years. The single most intriguing case might be frame no. 5—taken from *Cyclists* (Cyklisté; 1898)—which preserves the Lumière half-circle yet also includes three other holes carved into the image as if the film was meant for standard projections. It is not clear whether they testify to mishandling by archivists or to damage undertaken in a machine designed for film stock with four perforations, but as an impossible archival artifact and as another weird shape, it belongs firmly to Groo's bad film histories (Figure 6.6).

Altogether, the videographic essay *The First Frames of Czech Cinema* presents the opening images as things with complex material histories that problematize even the few general notions we can state about the digitized

---

[47] For example, Étienne-Jules Marey used no perforations, while Thomas Alva Edison used four. Benoît Turquety, *Inventing Cinema: Machines, Gestures and Media History* (Amsterdam: Amsterdam University Press, 2019), 173.
[48] Ibid., 174.
[49] The only exception is *František Palacký Monument Prior to Its Completion* (frame no. 28), which was shot on a standard material with four rectangular perforations.
[50] Turquety, *Inventing Cinema*, 107.

Figure 6.6 *Cyclists* (Cyklisté; Jan Kříženecký, 1898, source: nitrate print) © Národní filmový archiv.

films of Jan Kříženecký. The deformative approach, albeit not followed dogmatically, allowed us to transform the corpus in a way that highlights its always incomplete, never fully self-coincident character. The crack-up that emerges shatters any illusion of transparency, fluidity, and compatibility in *Digital Kříženecký* yet also develops an idea that brings the materials together—no matter how polished the cinematic firsts are, the very first things we see of them are never what they seem to be.

Coda: Towards Videographic Archival Editions?

Both the videographic essay and its written accompaniment were meant to show that the curation of uncertain, disfigured, and fragmentary archival artifacts from the beginnings of cinema does not necessarily have to limit itself to filling the gaps; instead, it can embrace their lacunae as potentialities for aesthetic and educational actualization and estrangement. By critically employing tools of videographic criticism (or more specifically, the deformative/parametric approach), *The First Frames of Czech Cinema* attempts to stage various encounters between figuration and abstraction, analog and digital, stillness and movement, past and present that the digitization made visible in the first Czech films. By dissecting the opening frames, the essay accentuates the ambiguity of the films' firstness, entailing cherished historical status as well as inevitable fragility and vulnerability to doubts, and of their basic construction units, often overlooked yet self-sustainable and aesthetically potent. Further, the essay showed that the crack-up could manifest itself in all the films of Jan Kříženecký at once, within a single mosaic.

To point briefly toward the future, will there ever be a systematic videographic edition of archival films? Speaking of the first Czech films, the National Film Archive in Prague released an online collection of Kříženecký's films that built upon the original DVD/Blu-ray and brought in formats suitable for the online space, such as a map of all the places where Kříženecký shot his films, a timeline of his life, and a few videographic essays (including *The First Frames of Czech Cinema* in English and Czech).[51] Still, the videographic impulse is perhaps too one-sidedly oriented toward the films' materiality and ignorant of other issues such as the circulation of the materials in numerous compilations, documentaries, and TV shows or their larger historical context within the Austro-Hungarian Empire,[52] East-Central European region, or global cinema and culture at the turn of the nineteenth century as a whole. Generally, in marrying materialist concerns with issues of historicity and circulation lies a significant potential to make digital curation of marginal archival artifacts (and not just the earliest ones) more complex and, at the same time, more attractive to the audience.

---

[51] "Filmy Jana Kříženeckého," *Kontexty Filmového přehledu*, 2022, accessed December 31, 2022, https://www.filmovyprehled.cz/cs/kontexty/filmy-jana-krizeneckeho. Besides the two videographic essays included in the edition, see also Jan Kinzl and Max Stejskal, "Analog/Digitál: Trhliny v českém filmovém dědictví," *Film a doba on-line*, February 15, 2022, accessed December 31, 2022, https://filmadoba.eu/trhliny-v-ceskem-filmovem-dedictvi/. A longer videographic piece about the *Digital Kříženecký* project is currently being developed at the National Film Archive in Prague.

[52] For instance, the Hungarian National Film Archive (Nemzeti Filmintézet—Filmarchívum) has recently created a promotional audiovisual essay on a lost pioneering Hungarian film *The Dance* (A táncz; Béla Zsitkovszky, 1901). Enikő Löwensohn and Barnabás Weisz, "Birth of Hungarian Film—The Dance, 1901," *Nemzeti Filmintézet YouTube*, June 13, 2022, accessed December 31, 2022, https://www.youtube.com/watch?v=Zi8_eWwIxwU.

Conclusion

Digital Kříženecký Off the Scale?

After six chapters full of shattering weird shapes of various origins, functions, and aesthetic effects, the lingering question is whether the emphasis on the generative character of Fitzgerald's (and Deleuze's) crack-up has paid off. As a process by which the never-ending feud between figuration and materiality acquires (however provisional) shapes, the crack-up does not bring any assurance or resolution. In her article on the crack-up and the "event" as a signal of change and becoming that can be simultaneously creative and destructive, Fredrika Spindler asks directly: "How, then, are we to think the crack[-up] in order for it to become something else than destruction; how are we to think the event in order for it to not be necessarily fatal, and to transform instead into life?"[1] She mentions Deleuze's term "counter-actualization,"[2] which "allows the event to break loose from itself as it is incarnated."[3] In the closing paragraph of "Porcelain and Volcano," Deleuze argues that even though the transformative event must involve suffering and endure the crack-up being "inscribed in the flesh," this painful actualization must be doubled by a counter-actualization which "limits, moves, and transfigures it."[4] To counter-actualize the crack-up means to "give to the truth of the event the only chance of not being confused with its inevitable actualization" and "to give us the chance to go farther than we would have believed possible."[5]

Speaking of *Digital Kříženecký*, this coexistence of actualization with counter-actualization presents a conundrum that all the chapters had to tackle. The weird shapes had to be experienced and scrutinized for what they are, for the chaos and distortion that the yellowish-orange color, static marks, camera trembling, vertical scratches, and spliced frames bring into our notions of figuration and meaning. Their force rendered the

---

[1] Fredrika Spindler, "Event, Crack-up and Line of Flight—Deleuze Reading Fitzgerald," in *Rethinking Time: Essays on History, Memory, and Representation*, ed. Hans Ruin and Andrus Ers (Flemingberg: Södertörn University, 2011), 261.
[2] For an unknown reason, Spindler refers to the term as "counter-effectuation." Ibid.
[3] Ibid.
[4] Gilles Deleuze, "Porcelain and Volcano," in *The Logic of Sense* (London: The Athlone Press, 1990), 161.
[5] Ibid.

analytical endeavor more arbitrary and idiosyncratic, yet it also introduced significant freedom to materially and self-reflexively experiment with the films as malleable objects and respectfully intervene in their continuous transformation. This counter-actualization was directed toward extending the crack-up into the world and generating new forms of thinking *with* and *through* film and media objects, without ever forgetting that this thinking would not have sprung without its roots in the traces and gestures embedded within the individual frames and between them.

To be more specific, the book has showcased how specific weird shapes of the crack-up in *Digital Kříženecký* decenter and recenter established concepts of film theory *from below*. This gesture was developed throughout the chapters with four implicit motivations in mind: a shift of attention to details and accidents inspired by micro-history, an emphasis on material-technological properties guided by archival experience, a courage to confront theory with previously unimagined phenomena in the spirit of *theoria*, and an ability to think *with* and *through* the film object manifested by videographic practice. Altogether, this approach aimed to redefine the aesthetic, technological, and historical features of archival film in the (post)digital age and offer ways to expand its paradoxes and ambiguities. Various kinds of such extension or prolongation indicated throughout the manuscript hold the promise of counter-actualization of the crack-up, which is why the summary of the individual chapters below is oriented more toward the future.

In Chapter 1, the color veil in *Grand Consecration of the Emperor Franz I Bridge* disturbed the death of cinema debates by demonstrating how many possible deaths can be staged on a single image plane—the death of figures frozen in time and obscured by deformed shapes; the death instilled by historical decay (scratches, tears, splices); the death of the Lumière nitrate print embroiled in torn perforations and unstable movement; the death of the colors themselves, turning from bright yellow to rotting red; and, potentially, the death of digital compression and circulation. The color veil that brings these elements together while maintaining their diversity signals not only the inevitable death of cinema but also its extension into eternity. The newly found hybridity of Bill Morrison's *Decasia* and the following frame-by-frame approach inspired by Hannah Frank served as a wake-up call that we should not be inhibited by nostalgia and fetishism for the analog. Scholars and archivists should open the digital files in video-editing software, discern and isolate the places that seem most threatened by material evisceration, and seek to turn their death(s) into a colorful figuration of a future life force.

In Chapter 2, the electric horses showed multiple facets of indexicality that unfold when the profilmic reality becomes suffused with static electricity. The encounter between horse racers and marks of static electricity in *The*

First Day of the Spring Races of Prague reflects how even inconspicuous enactments of the crack-up through minuscule physical marks can question and enrich the age-old problem of cinema and its relation to reality. The quadruple logic of indexicality—expressed by the interrelated doubles of figuration and materiality, and trace and deixis—allowed us to approximate why elements tied to the film's production process, such as static marks, stand out from just any other indexical signs. The sharp, individuated white streaks targeted at the horses and jockeys affect the form and content of the images with such dynamism that they can be examined only when the figurative elements become a blur. The static marks thereby reveal electricity as an indexical force that disturbs the formation of a coherent diegetic reality, but also as a constitutive factor that co-determines the film's coming into being. Echoing Sami van Ingen's *Flame*, we could use the editing software as a divining rod that searches for places where it could generate the biggest amount of energy, the most developed crack-up.

In Chapter 3, the black wave on a trembling bridge in *Opening Ceremony of the Čech Bridge* encountered transduction, a principle involving both transversal distribution and regulative metastability, as a mechanism with significant aesthetic potential. The analysis in this chapter showed that transductive equilibrium could emerge accidentally, independent of artistic intervention or the ravages of time, through the autonomous creativity of a shaking camera. The only things necessary for revealing this phenomenon were a theoretically generative concept (transduction) and a slow observation of the details of the scene—pursued via the techniques of slow motion and looping inspired by the experimental films of Ken Jacobs, Al Razutis, and Siegfried A. Fruhauf—that regulate the margin of indeterminacy and allow the moment of transduction to endure. This shift opened up space for a sort of interventionist (but not mastering) scholarship, which should not be content with merely speaking or writing about analog and/or digital matter; instead, it should rather strive to translate the unique materiality of hybrid media art into a creative engagement with the moving images and sounds themselves. In the vein of Shane Denson's videographic manifesto, *The Algorithmic Nickelodeon*, this approach would consider deformations of the image/object and displacements of the analyst/subject simultaneously in order to imagine a form of audiovisual criticism for the digital age that would aim not only to analyze and interpret but also to reinvent our notion of subject-object relations.

In Chapter 4, the scratched kiss in *An Assignation in the Mill* delineated the archival experience as always already pervaded with the powers of the false. The vertical scratches emerging at the divide between the unveiling of the Czech Cinematograph poster and the "first kiss of Czech cinema" reveal that the archive effect does not necessarily depend on temporal disparity, reflective or restorative nostalgia, or appropriative intervention (without denying their value). It is not crucial where, how, by whom, or by what means the rips emerged, nor whether any precise documentation of the event existed prior to such physical deformation. The mere existence of the scratches changes the rules of the game, expressing nothing other than the difficulty of expressing anything vis-à-vis the essential vulnerability of both filmic matter and cinematic firsts. The potential of the scratched kiss as a moment that constantly passes and therefore does not pass can be unveiled similarly to Thom Andersen's *Eadweard Muybridge, Zoopraxographer*. A stuttering movement would make the characters' gestures as well as the scratches constantly appear and disappear, intermingle and diverge, thereby multiplying the number of ways in which the archival document can differ from itself and yet still be understood and felt as archival. It is only through such experiments with the powers of the false that the milestones of (particularly the earliest) cinema can be reprogrammed to give expression to a future image.

In Chapter 5, the stitched head of Josef Šváb-Malostranský in *Laughter and Tears* provoked a reflection on the epistemic preconditions of approaching fragmentary, distorted, and altogether weird film objects in an intimate yet analytically profound way. The principles of haptic visuality and haptic criticism help us conceive how to touch uncertain film objects and be touched by them, provided they revise their predilections to fetishization and Othering. First, Šváb's face, covered with Frankensteinian stitches, is not able to evoke the identification mechanisms that would ease us into thinking that we have been chosen by the film object, and thus it is difficult to fetishize. Second, the peculiar deformations encroaching upon Šváb's face are not necessarily cinephiliac details waiting to be discovered, as their impact on the film is so severe that they cease to be peripheral and threaten to take over the meanings and effects of the film. A selection of stitched frames allowed us to discern specific configurations of the cinematic close-up—a figurative one and a material one. The clashes between these two modalities do not lead to rupture or destruction but create cracked-up figures, such as the composite Frankensteinian images in Michael Fleming's *Never Never Land*. Altogether, this investigation demonstrated how relative categories such as transparency and opacity, human and technological, or the detail and the whole can be, and how anyone who wants to intervene in the cracked-up film objects must do so with surgical caution.

In Chapter 6, the videographic essay *The First Frames of Czech Cinema* presents the opening images of all of Kříženecký's digitized films as things with complex material histories that pertain to the past and present cinema at the same time. While the essay subjects the frames to multiple digital manipulations (flickering, rotating, zooming in and out, stretching and narrowing), paradoxically, it also returns us to the earliest cinematic projections, which often started with the opening images as still photographs. By combining sequential and simultaneous modes of viewing, the videographic work portrays the digitized first frames as irreducible to being erased or marginalized in favor of smooth and continuous flow as well as to being interchangeable blocks in a coherent whole. The crack-up embroiled within these 28 frames shatters any illusion of transparency, fluidity, and compatibility in *Digital Kříženecký* yet also develops an idea that brings the materials together—no matter how polished the cinematic firsts are, the very first things we see of them are never what they seem to be.

At present, my main preoccupation is how all these weird shapes of the crack-up in relatively marginal aesthetic objects can fare within the ceaseless flux of digital images. Is my focus on figurative and material details in early Czech films of any relevance in times when, to borrow words from the recent edited volume *Photography Off the Scale* (2021), "to see an image is by necessity to consider it as part of an extensive dataset or a database?"[6] Is the effort to play with electric horses and black waves not a futile diversion when we need to come to terms with billions of audiovisual data that are often not created by humans nor even meant to be seen by them? Are these individual material traces and gestures worthy of special attention when every single image can be "described according to thousands of separate dimensions?"[7] As resistant as they are to easy nostalgification, what can save the weird shapes in *Digital Kříženecký* from being disconnected from their context and assembled into algorithmically predesigned compilations and playlists of imperfect born-analog images and disturbing archival fragments?

The increasing datafication of the online space inevitably affects how we understand the theory and practice of found footage and archival film. Found footage as a mode of accumulating preexisting images into new arrangements dissolves into a highly automatized practice in which software makes the human appropriator seem more and more replaceable. Fascinating and thought-provoking found footage films are still being made, but now, when confronted with image overload and digital monoculture, the once

---

[6] Jussi Parikka and Tomáš Dvořák, "Introduction: On the Scale, Quantity and Measure of Images," in *Photography Off the Scale: Technologies and Theories of the Mass Image*, ed. Tomáš Dvořák and Jussi Parikka (Edinburgh: Edinburgh University Press, 2021), 4.

[7] Lev Manovich, "The Science of Culture? Social Computing, Digital Humanities and Cultural Analytics," *Journal of Cultural Analytics*, May 23, 2016, accessed December 31, 2022, https://culturalanalytics.org/article/11060.

subversive cultural role of the genre is being severely questioned by many.[8] The very principle of excavating previously unknown images or defamiliarizing images that are known too well has become both an impossibility and a cliché. Similarly, the amount of previously inaccessible archival footage in the digital sphere continues to grow, but the archives' loss of control over their presentation makes it harder and harder to discern what is "authentic" and what is not. All the upscaled, colorized, 4K, 60 fps early films emerging on YouTube within the last few years may seem scandalous to archivists and film historians, yet it appears highly probable that these enhanced archival films will be an entry point to early cinema for an overwhelming number of people. Despite the efforts of the National Film Archive (*Národní filmový archiv*) in Prague, *Digital Kříženecký* will not be immune to these processes and shifts. Still, it is worth curating the films' weird shapes as features that are always already new, and therefore at least provisionally resisting the temptation to make the films more "contemporary."

As pointed out in Chapter 6, videographic criticism offers a chance to reconcile the remnants of the archival impulse with the present (and near-future) digital condition and turn found footage into a form of curatorial and scholarly expression. The deformative/parametric approach is particularly useful for showing that digital humanities need not be merely quantitative, empirical, and oriented toward big data but can just as well be qualitative, poetic, and attuned to detail. This appeal is even more pressing in archival film theory and practice. While some archives and museums have experimented with videographic essays from time to time,[9] computer-driven archival research has been predominantly associated with the more quantitative strands of digital humanities.[10] Deformative experiments with *Digital Kříženecký* herald a more epistemological role for video-editing software, bringing the very integrity of the already highly unstable and fragmentary archival objects under intensive scrutiny. Not only do the computer-assisted tools allow us to better distinguish between different material traces and

---

[8] See, for example, Lars Henrik Gass, *Film and Art After Cinema* (Zagreb: Multimedijalni institut, 2019), 143–72.

[9] For an overview of how archival institutions toy with videographic practices, see Jiří Anger, "Shaping the Unshapeable? Videographic Curation of Early Czech Cinema," *Iluminace* 31, no. 1 (2022): 9–29.

[10] See Dimitrios Latsis and Grazia Ingravalle, "Guest Editors' Foreword: Digital Humanities and/in Film Archives," *The Moving Image: The Journal of the Association of Moving Image Archivists* 17, no. 2 (2017): xi–xv; Adelheid Heftberger, *Digital Humanities and Film Studies: Visualising Dziga Vertov's Work* (Berlin: Springer, 2019); Rossella Catanese, Adelheid Heftberger, and Christian Gosvig Olesen, "Introduction: Film Heritage and Digital Scholarship—Computer-Based Approaches to Film Archiving, Restoration and Philology," *Cinergie—Il Cinema e el altre Arti* 20 (2021): 2–6.

gestures in the artifacts, but they also enable us to create additional layers of deformation that unmask the variety of actors that co-constitute archival footage in the digital space. Perhaps such a transformation of video-editing programs into machines that dissect film objects into a multitude of weird shapes rather than a multitude of data is what can make the current regime of audiovisual abundance a bit more exciting.

Nevertheless, the impact of videographic criticism reaches beyond experimentation with video-editing software. It also bears the promise of a mode of writing that would be academic and, at the same time, perceptive of the conditions that establish any kind of film analysis or interpretation. The fact that film scholars encounter their research object within the variable space of software interfaces and pop-up windows inevitably transforms the terms of this research, and scholarly writing, even with all its centuries-old traditions and rules, should acknowledge this. The way I employed descriptions of videographic manipulations (frame by frame, GIF, slow motion, and so forth) throughout the text was intended not as a gimmick but as an attempt to establish these operations as crucial points of the research process, without which the individual forms of the crack-up would not have been quite as perceptible and theoretically intriguing. Videographic scholarship allows us to acknowledge that film is, first and foremost, a malleable object whose analysis and interpretation always partially involve participation in its continuous creation. The videographic attention toward details and accidents that can appear invisible while looking at the film objects from the perspective of big data or mass image, as well as its anchoring within the everyday experience with software interfaces and online landscapes, turns it into a perfect vehicle for connecting the singular and the universal, the old and the new, the scientific and the poetic, the expert and the fan.

Furthermore, videographic criticism addresses the dilemma of how to translate the crack-up and its weird shapes into theoretical writing. My deep conviction is that videographic essays not only help us think and write *with* and *through* moving images and sounds, but they may also inspire a shift in how film scholars use the written word. In his book *The End of Diversity in Art Historical Writing* (2020), James Elkins poignantly names the streamlining of academic writing in the humanities during the last few decades. In order to comply with the standards of scientific rigorosity and become more comprehensible, art history (and theory) lost much of its ambition to employ language for expressive value as well as reference, for form as well as content.[11] Conjecturally, I would say, it has also marginalized any preoccupation with

---

[11] James Elkins, *The End of Diversity in Art Historical Writing: North Atlantic Art History and Its Alternatives* (Berlin: de Gruyter, 2020), 205–7.

the nature of its objects of study and how we encounter them. As Elkins notes, it is doubly ironic that these trends are reproduced by art scholars versed in Deleuze, Barthes, Derrida, and other French poststructuralist thinkers, who always emphasized that writing is not just a tool of communication but a key factor of argumentation. To quote him directly: "we adhere to the discoveries of poststructuralism, but we write as if the only guides to writing were written by Cicero and Quintillian (the codifiers of qualities like 'plain,' 'clear,' and 'persuasive')."[12]

Thus, the videographic impulse was intended as a counter-actualization of the crack-up on the level of thinking just as well as on the level of writing. Although this book has not always followed Deleuze's words and concepts by heart, here his ethos shines brightly. *Film theory from below* must also write *from below*, find words that echo weird shapes of all kinds, rescue their remnants from the crack-up, and unleash them so that they stir our notions of what dealing with archival artifacts in the (post)digital space actually entails. Consider the present book a (half)modest attempt to translate this marriage of writing tools and thoughts into practice.

[12] Ibid., 206.

Bibliography

Agamben, Giorgio. "Notes on Gesture." In *Means Without End: Notes on Politics*, 49–62. Minneapolis and London: University of Minnesota Press, 2000.

Albera, Francois and Maria Tortajada, eds. *Cinema Beyond Film: Media Epistemology in the Modern Era*. Amsterdam: Amsterdam University Press, 2010.

Alloa, Emmanuel and Judith Michalet, "Differences in Becoming: Gilbert Simondon and Gilles Deleuze on Individuation." *Philosophy Today* 61, no. 3 (2017): 475–502.

Anderson, Steven F. *Technologies of History: Visual Media and the Eccentricity of the Past*. New Hampshire: Dartmouth College Press, 2011.

Andrew, Dudley. "Foreword to the 2004 Edition." In *What Is Cinema?* Vol. 1, edited by André Bazin, ix–xxiv. Berkeley: University of California Press, 2005.

Andrew, Dudley. *What Cinema Is! Bazin's Quest and Its Charge*. New York: Wiley-Blackwell, 2010.

Anger, Jiří, ed. *Filmy Jana Kříženeckého/The Films of Jan Kříženecký*. DVD/Blu-ray, Praha: Národní filmový archiv, 2019.

Anger, Jiří. "(Un)Frozen Expressions: Melodramatic Moment, Affective Interval, and the Transformative Powers of Experimental Cinema." *NECSUS European Journal of Media Studies* 8, no. 2 (2019): 25–47.

Anger, Jiří. "The Uncertain Oeuvre of a Czech Cinema Pioneer." *Revue Filmového přehledu*, January 27, 2020, accessed December 31, 2022, https://www.filmovyprehled.cz/en/revue/detail/the-uncertain-oeuvre-of-a-czech-cinema-pioneer.

Anger, Jiří. "Dotýkat se nedosažitelného objektu: Haptická audiovizuální esej a antropotechnický interface." In *Operátoři (nových) médií*, edited by Tomáš Dvořák, Martin Charvát et al., 235–70. Praha: Nakladatelství Akademie múzických umění, 2022.

Anger, Jiří. "Shaping the Unshapeable? Videographic Curation of Early Czech Cinema." *Iluminace* 31, no. 1 (2022): 9–29.

Anger, Jiří, ed. *Digitální Kříženecký: Nový život prvních českých filmů*. Praha: Národní filmový archiv, 2023.

Anger, Jiří, Jeanne Pommeau, Elif Rongen-Kaynakçi, and Matěj Strnad. "A Season of Classic Films | Where, How and to Whom—The Challenges of Presenting Earliest Cinema." June 3, 2021, accessed December 31, 2022, https://www.filmovyprehled.cz/cs/kalendar/detail/a-season-of-classic-films-where-how-and-to-whom-the-challenges-of-presenting-earliest-cinema.

Anger, Jiří and Jiří Žák, "Distant Journey Through the Desktop." *[in]Transition: Journal of Videographic Film & Moving Image Studies* 8, no. 1 (2021), accessed December 31, 2022, http://mediacommons.org/intransition/distant-journey-through-desktop.

Anger, Jiří and Kevin B. Lee, "Suture Goes Meta: Desktop Documentary and its Narrativization of Screen-Mediated Experience." *Quarterly Review of Film and Video* 40, no. 5 (2023): 595–622.

Anger, Jiří and Tomáš Jirsa, "We Never Took Deconstruction Seriously Enough (On Affects, Formalism, and Film Theory): An Interview with Eugenie Brinkema." *Iluminace* 31, no. 1 (2019): 65–85.

Arsenjuk, Luka. "On the Impossibility of Object Oriented Film Theory." *Discourse* 38, no. 2 (2016): 197–214.

Arsenjuk, Luka. "To Speak, To Hold, To Live by the Image: Notes in the Margins of the New Videographic Tendency." In *The Essay Film: Dialogue, Politics, Utopia*, edited by Elizabeth Papazian and Caroline Eades, 275–99. London and New York: Wallflower Press, 2016.

Arsenjuk, Luka. *Movement, Action, Image, Montage: Sergei Eisenstein and the Cinema in Crisis*. Minneapolis: Minnesota University Press, 2018.

Arthur, Paul. "Bodies, Language, and the Impeachment of Vision." In *A Line of Sight: American Avant-garde Film Since 1965*, 132–50. Minneapolis: University of Minnesota Press, 2005.

Assis, Paulo de. "Gilbert Simondon's 'Transduction' as Radical Immanence in Performance." *Performance Philosophy* 3, no. 3 (2017): 695–716.

Aubert, Michelle and Jean-Claude Seguin, eds. *La Production cinématographique des Frères Lumière*. Paris: BiFi, 1996.

Auerbach, Jonathan. *Body Shots: Early Cinema's Incarnations*. Berkeley: University of California Press, 2007.

Aumont, Jacques. "The Veiled Image: The Luminous Formless." In *Indefinite Visions: Cinema and the Attractions of Uncertainty*, edited by Martine Beugnet, Allan Cameron, and Arild Fetveit, 17–37. Edinburgh: Edinburgh University Press, 2017.

Bachmann, Alejandro. "The Trace of Walk That Has Taken Place—A Conversation with Peter Tscherkassky." *Found Footage Magazine* 4, no. 4 (2018): 27–33.

Baio, Andy. "Fanboy Supercuts, Obsessive Video Montages." *Waxy*, April 11, 2008, accessed December 31, 2022, https://waxy.org/2008/04/fanboy_supercuts_obsessive_video_montages/.

Balázs, Béla. *Theory of the Film: Character and Growth of the New Art*. London: Dennis Dobson Ltd, 1952.

Balázs, Béla and Erica Carter, ed. *Early Film Theory: Visible Man and The Spirit of Film*. New York and Oxford: Berghahn Books, 2010.

Ball, Christopher, Meghanne Barker, Elizabeth Edwards, Tomáš Kolich, W. J. T. Mitchell, Daniel Morgan, and Constantine V. Nakassis. "Opening Up the Indexicality of the Image, Again: A Virtual Roundtable." *Semiotic Review*, 2020, accessed December 31, 2022, https://semioticreview.com/ojs/index.php/sr/article/view/62.

Balzac, Honoré de. *The Wild Ass's Skin*. Oxford: Oxford University Press, 2012.

Baptista, Tiago. "Lessons in Looking: The Digital Audiovisual Essay." PhD diss., Birkbeck, University of London, 2016.
Barker, Jennifer M. *The Tactile Eye: Touch and the Cinematic Experience*. Berkeley: University of California Press, 2009.
Baron, Jaimie. *The Archive Effect: Found Footage and the Audiovisual Experience of History*. London: Routledge, 2014.
Baron, Jaimie. *Reuse, Misuse, Abuse: The Ethics of Audiovisual Appropriation in the Digital Era*. New Brunswick and Newark: Rutgers University Press, 2020.
Barrett, Estelle and Barbara Bolt, eds. *Carnal Knowledge: Towards a 'New Materialism' Through the Arts*. London and New York: I.B. Tauris, 2013.
Barthélémy, Jean-Hugues. *Life and Technology: An Inquiry Into and Beyond Simondon*. Lüneburg: Meson Press, 2015.
Barthes, Roland. "Diderot, Brecht, Eisenstein." In *Image, Music, Text*, 69–78. London: Fontana Press, 1977.
Barthes, Roland. *Camera Lucida: Reflections on Photography*. New York: Hill and Wang, 1982.
Barthes, Roland. *A Lover's Discourse: Fragments*. London: Vintage, 2002.
Batistová, Anna. "Poezie destrukce: Typologie, periodizace a reflexe destrukce filmových pohyblivých obrazů." *Iluminace* 17, no. 3 (2005): 27–46.
Baumbach, Nico. "Nature Caught in the Act: On the Transformation of an Idea of Art in Early Cinema." In *Cinematicity in Media History*, edited by Jeffrey Geiger and Karin Littau, 107–16. Edinburgh: Edinburgh University Press, 2013.
Bazin, André. "Le Kon-Tiki ou grandeur et servitudes du reportage filmé." *France Observateur*, April 30, 1952, 23–4.
Bazin, André. "Cinema and Exploration." In *What Is Cinema?* Vol. 1, 154–63. Berkeley: University of California Press, 2005.
Bazin, André. "Ontology of the Photographic Image." In *What Is Cinema?*, 3–12. Montreal: caboose, 2009.
Bellotti, Serena and Andrea Mariani. "The Digital Witness: Film Reconstruction and the Forensic Imagination in New Media Environments." *Cinergie - Il Cinema e le altre Arti* 20 (2021): 27–43.
Bellour, Raymond. "The Unattainable Text." *Screen* 16, no. 3 (1975): 19–27.
Bellour, Raymond. "Analysis in Flames." *Diacritics* 15, no. 1 (1985): 54–6.
Bellour, Raymond. "Thierry Kuntzel and the Return of Writing." In *Between-the-Images*, edited by Raymond Bellour and Allyn Hardyck, 30–61. Zurich: JRP/Ringier, 2012.
Bellour, Raymond. "35 Years Later: Is the "Text", Once Again, Unattainable?" In *Beyond the Essay Film*, edited by Julia Vassilieva and Deane Williams, 33–48. Amsterdam: Amsterdam University Press, 2020.
Benjamin, Walter. "The Work of Art in the Age of Mechanical Reproduction." In *Illuminations*, edited by Hannah Arendt, 219–53. London: Jonathan Cape, 1970.
Benjamin, Walter. "On the Image of Proust." In *Walter Benjamin: Selected Writings* Volume 2, 237–47. Cambridge: Belknap Press, 2005.
Bergson, Henri. *Matter and Memory*. New York: Zone Books, 1990.

Bergson, Henri. *The Creative Mind: An Introduction to Metaphysics*. Mineola: Dover Publications, 2012.

Berlant, Lauren. *Desire/Love*. Brooklyn: Punctum Books, 2012.

Berressem, Hanjo. "Local Color: Light in Faulkner." In *Media|Matter: The Materiality of Media|Matter as Medium*, edited by Bernd Herzogenrath, 69–95. New York: Bloomsbury Academic, 2015.

Bessy, Maurice and Lo Duca. *Louis Lumière inventeur*. Paris: Éditions Prisma, 1948.

Betancourt, Michael. "Dread Mechanics: The Sublime Terror of Bill Morrison's Decasia (2002)." *Bright Lights Film Journal*, January 14, 2015, accessed December 31, 2022, https://brightlightsfilm.com/dread-mechanics-the-sublime-terror-of-bill-morrisons-decasia-2002/.

Betancourt, Michael. *Glitch Art in Theory and Practice: Critical Failures and Post-Digital Aesthetics*. London: Routledge, 2017.

Beugnet, Martine, Allan Cameron, and Arild Fetveit, eds. *Indefinite Visions: Cinema and the Attractions of Uncertainty*. Edinburgh: Edinburgh University Press, 2017.

Beugnet, Martine and Richard Misek. "In Praise of Blur." *[in]Transition: Journal for Videographic Film & Moving Image Studies* 4, no. 2b (2017), accessed December 31, 2022, http://mediacommons.org/intransition/2017/07/11/praise-blur.

Binotto, Johannes. "Tributes—Pulse: A Requiem for the 20th Century: Death | Drive | Image." In *The Films of Bill Morrison: Aesthetics of the Archive*, edited by Bernd Herzogenrath, 241–51. Amsterdam: Amsterdam University Press, 2017.

Binotto, Johannes. "Touching Sound." *Transferences*, February 2, 2018, accessed December 31, 2022, https://transferences.org/2018/02/02/touching-sound/.

Binotto, Johannes. "In Lag of Knowledge: The Video Essay as Parapraxis." In *Practical Aesthetics*, edited by Bernd Herzogenrath, 83–94. New York: Bloomsbury, 2020.

Binotto, Johannes. "Minor Instances, Major Consequences: Video Essay Workshop." *Transferences*, 2020, accessed December 31, 2022, https://transferences.org/lehre/video-essay-workshop/.

Binotto, Johannes. "Trace." *Transferences*, 2020, accessed December 31, 2022, https://transferences.org/videoessays/performative-deformative-video-essays/trace/.

Bishop, Ryan, Kristoffer Gansing, Jussi Parikka, and Elvia Wilk. "Introduction." In *Across & Beyond: A Transmediale Reader on Post-digital Practices, Concepts, and Institutions*, edited by Ryan Bishop, Kristoffer Gansing, Jussi Parikka, and Elvia Wilk, 11–29. Berlin: Sternberg Press, 2017.

Blümlinger, Christa. "Lumière, the Train and the Avant-Garde." In *The Cinema of Attractions Reloaded*, edited by Wanda Strauven, 245–64. Amsterdam: Amsterdam University Press, 2006.

Blümlinger, Christa. *Kino aus zweiter Hand: Zur Ästhetik materieller Aneignung im Film und in der Medienkunst*. Berlin: Vorwerk 8, 2009.

Bogost, Ian. *Alien Phenomenology, or What It's Like to Be a Thing*. Minneapolis: University of Minnesota Press, 2012.
Bollmer, Grant. *Materialist Media Theory: An Introduction*. New York: Bloomsbury Academic, 2019.
Bordino, Alex W. "Found Footage, False Archives, and Historiography in Oliver Stone's JFK." *The Journal of American Culture* 42, no. 2 (2019): 112–20.
Bordwell, David, Janet Staiger, and Kristin Thompson. *The Classical Hollywood Cinema: Film Style & Mode of Production to 1960*. London: Routledge, 1998.
Borges, Jorge Luis. "The Secret Miracle." In *Ficciones*, 143–50. New York: Grove Press, 1962.
Boym, Svetlana. *The Future of Nostalgia*. New York: Basic Books, 2001.
Bozak, Nadia. *The Cinematic Footprint: Lights, Camera, Natural Resources*. New Brunswick: Rutgers University Press, 2010.
Branald, Adolf. *My od filmu*. Praha: Mladá fronta, 1988.
Brenez, Nicole. "'Is This the Precise Way That Worlds are Reborn?' The Films of Siegfried A. Fruhauf." In *Film Unframed: A History of Austrian Avant-Garde Cinema*, edited by Peter Tscherkassky, 276–85. Wien: SYNEMA - Gesellschaft für Film und Medien, 2012.
Brewer, John. "Microhistory and the Histories of Everyday Life." *Cultural and Social History* 7, no. 1 (2010): 87–109.
Brinkema, Eugenie. *The Forms of the Affects*. London and Durham: Duke University Press, 2014.
Bruno, Giuliana. *Surface: Matters of Aesthetic, Matter, and Media*. Chicago: The University of Chicago Press, 2014.
Cahill, James Leo. *Zoological Surrealism: The Nonhuman Cinema of Jean Painlevé*. Minneapolis: University of Minnesota Press, 2019.
Campanini, Sonia, Vinzenz Hediger, and Ines Bayer. "Minding the Materiality of Film: The Frankfurt Master's Program 'Film Culture: Archiving, Programming, Presentation.'" *Synoptique* 6, no. 1 (2018): 79–96.
Cardinal, Roger. "Pausing Over Peripheral Detail." *Framework* 30–31 (1986): 112–30.
Casetti, Francesco. "Objects on the Screen: Tools, Things, Events." In *Cinematographic Objects: Things and Operations*, edited by Volker Pantenburg, 25–43. Berlin: August Verlag, 2015.
Catanese, Rossella, Adelheid Heftberger, and Christian Gosvig Olesen. "Introduction: Film Heritage and Digital Scholarship—Computer-Based Approaches to Film Archiving, Restoration and Philology." *Cinergie - Il Cinema e el altre Arti* 20 (2021): 2–6.
Cavell, Stanley. *The World Viewed: Reflections on the Ontology of Film*. Cambridge, MA: Harvard University Press, 1971.
Chare, Nicholas and Liz Watkins, "The Matter of Film: Decasia and Lyrical Nitrate." In *Carnal Knowledge: Towards a 'New Materialism' Through the Arts*, edited by Estelle Barrett and Barbara Bolt, 75–87. London and New York: I.B. Tauris, 2013.

Chateau, Dominique and José Moure, eds. *Post-cinema: Cinema in the Post-art Era*. Amsterdam: Amsterdam University Press, 2020.
Cherchi Usai, Paolo. *Una passione inflammabile*. Turin: UTET, 1991.
Cherchi Usai, Paolo. *Silent Cinema: An Introduction*. London: BFI, 2000.
Cherchi Usai, Paolo. *The Death of Cinema: History, Cultural Memory, and the Digital Dark Age*. London: BFI, 2001.
Cherchi Usai, Paolo. "The Digital Future of Pre-digital Film Collections." *Journal of Film Preservation* 88 (2013): 9–16.
Cherchi Usai, Paolo. "The Lindgren Manifesto: The Film Curator of the Future." In *Work/s in Progress: Digital Film Restoration Within Archives*, edited by Kerstin Parth, Oliver Hanley, and Thomas Ballhausen, 28–9. Vienna: SYNEMA – Gesellschaft für Film und Medien, 2013.
Cherchi Usai, Paolo. *Silent Cinema: A Guide to Study, Research and Curatorship*. London and New York: BFI – Bloomsbury Publishing, 2019.
Cherchi Usai, Paolo, David Francis, Alexander Horwath, and Michael Loebenstein, eds. *Film Curatorship: Archives, Museums, and the Digital Marketplace*. Wien: Synema – Gesellschaft für Film und Medien, 2008.
Chrétien, Jean-Louis. *The Call and the Response*. New York: Fordham University Press, 2004.
Christie, Ian. "Issues of Provenance and Attribution for the Canon: Bookending Robert Paul." In *Provenance and Early Cinema*, edited by Joanne Bernardi, Paolo Cherchi Usai, Tami Williams, and Joshua Yumibe, 70–9. Bloomington: Indiana University Press, 2021.
Colangelo, David. "Hitchcock, Film Studies, and New Media: The Impact of Technology on the Analysis of Film." In *Technology and Film Scholarship*, edited by Santiago Hidalgo, 127–48. Amsterdam: Amsterdam University Press, 2018.
Combes, Muriel. *Gilbert Simondon and the Philosophy of the Transindividual*. Cambridge: MIT Press, 2012.
Comolli, Jean-Louis. "Machines of the Visible." In *The Cinematic Apparatus*, edited by Teresa De Lauretis and Stephen Heath, 121–42. New York: St. Martin's Press, 1980.
Conte, Pietro. "Mockumentality: From Hyperfaces to Deepfakes." *World Literature Studies* 11, no. 4 (2019): 11–25.
"Crack-up." *Cambridge Dictionary*, accessed December 31, 2022, https://dictionary.cambridge.org/dictionary/english/crack-up.
Creekmur, Corey. "How Does Film Feel? Toward Affective Videographic Criticism." *The Cine-Files*, no. 10 (2016), accessed December 31, 2022, http://www.thecine-files.com/how-does-film-feel2016/.
Cubitt, Sean. *Videography: Video Media as Art and Culture*. New York: St. Martin's Press, 1993.
Cubitt, Sean. "The Shadow." *MIRAJ Moving Image Research and Art Journal* 2, no. 2 (2013): 187–97.
Cuevas, Efrén. *Filming History from Below: Microhistorical Documentaries*. New York: Wallflower Press, 2022.

Culp, Andrew. *Dark Deleuze*. Minneapolis: University of Minnesota Press, 2016.

Curtis, Scott, Philippe Gauthier, Tom Gunning, and Joshua Yumibe, eds. *The Image in Early Cinema: Form and Material*. Bloomington: Indiana University Press, 2018.

De Bruyn, Dirk. "Recovering the Hidden Through Found-Footage Films." In *Carnal Knowledge: Towards a 'New Materialism' Through the Arts*, edited by Estelle Barrett and Barbara Bolt, 89–104. London and New York: I.B. Tauris, 2013.

Deleuze, Gilles. *Cinema 1: The Movement-Image*. London: The Athlone Press, 1986.

Deleuze, Gilles. "Porcelain and Volcano." In *The Logic of Sense*, 154–61. London: The Athlone Press, 1990.

Deleuze, Gilles. *The Logic of Sense*. London: The Athlone Press, 1990.

Deleuze, Gilles. "Zola and the Crack-Up." In *The Logic of Sense*, 321–33. London: The Athlone Press, 1990.

Deleuze, Gilles. *Cinema 2: The Time-Image*. Minneapolis: University of Minnesota Press, 2001.

Deleuze, Gilles. *Francis Bacon: The Logic of Sensation*. London: Continuum, 2003.

Deleuze, Gilles. *Foucault*. Minneapolis: University of Minnesota Press, 2006.

Deleuze, Gilles and Félix Guattari. *A Thousand Plateaus: Capitalism and Schizophrenia*. Minneapolis: University of Minnesota Press, 1987.

Dellmann, Sarah. *Images of Dutchness: Popular Visual Culture, Early Cinema and the Emergence of a National Cliché, 1800–1914*. Amsterdam: Amsterdam University Press, 2019.

Denson, Shane. *Postnaturalism: Frankenstein, Film, and the Anthropotechnical Interface*. Berlin: Transcript Verlag, 2014.

Denson, Shane. "Deformative Criticism at #SCMS17." *Medieninitiative*, February 16, 2017, accessed December 31, 2022, https://medieninitiative.wordpress.com/2017/02/16/deformative-criticism-at-scms17/.

Denson, Shane. "The Algorithmic Nickelodeon." *Medieninitiative*, June 22, 2019, accessed December 31, 2022, https://medieninitiative.wordpress.com/2019/06/22/the-algorithmic-nickelodeon/.

Denson, Shane. *Discorrelated Images*. Durham: Duke University Press, 2020.

Denson, Shane and Julia Leyda, eds. *Post-Cinema: Theorizing 21st-Century Film*. Sussex: REFRAME Books, 2016.

Derrida, Jacques. *Archive Fever: A Freudian Impression*. Chicago: The University of Chicago Press, 1996.

Derrida, Jacques. "Typewriter Ribbon: Limited Ink (2)." In *Without Alibi*, 71–160. Redwood City: Stanford University Press, 2002.

Didi-Huberman, Georges. *Invention of Hysteria: Charcot and the Photographic Iconography of the Salpêtrière*. New York: MIT Press, 2003.

Doane, Mary Ann. *The Emergence of Cinematic Time: Modernity, Contingency, the Archive*. Cambridge: Harvard University Press, 2002.

Doane, Mary Ann. "The Object of Theory." In *Rites of Realism: Essays on Corporeal Cinema*, edited by Ivone Margulies, 80–90. Durham: Duke University Press, 2003.

Doane, Mary Ann. "The Indexical and the Concept of Medium Specificity." *Differences* 18, no. 1 (2007): 128–52.

Eisenstein, Sergei. "Conspectus of Lectures on the Psychology of Art." In *The Eisenstein Collection*, edited by Richard Taylor, 231–48. Calcutta: Seagull Books, 2006.

Elcott, Noam M. *Artificial Darkness: An Obscure History of Modern Art and Media*. Chicago and London: University of Chicago Press, 2013.

Elder, R. Bruce. "Bart Testa: Back and Forth: Early Cinema and the Avant-Garde [book review]." *R. Bruce Elder*, 1992, accessed December 31, 2022, http://rbruceelder.com/documents/writing/bibliography/film/critical/1992_OnBartTestasBackAndForth.pdf.

Elkins, James. *The End of Diversity in Art Historical Writing: North Atlantic Art History and Its Alternatives*. Berlin: De Gruyter, 2020.

Elo, Mika and Miika Luoto, eds. Figures *of Touch: Sense, Technics, Body*. Helsinki: The Academy of Fine Arts at the University of the Arts Helsinki, 2018.

Elsaesser, Thomas. "Louis Lumière—The Cinema's First Virtualist?" In *Cinema Futures: Cain, Abel or Cable? The Screen Arts in the Digital Age*, edited by Thomas Elsaesser and Kay Hoffmann, 45–64. Amsterdam: Amsterdam University Press, 1989.

Elsaesser, Thomas. "Cinephilia or the Uses of Disenchantment." In *Cinephilia: Movies, Love and Memory*, edited by Marijke de Valck and Malte Hagener, 27–43. Amsterdam: Amsterdam University Press, 2005.

Elsaesser, Thomas. "Stop/Motion." In *Between Stillness and Motion: Film, Photography, Algorithms*, edited by Eivind Rossaak, 109–22. Amsterdam: Amsterdam University Press, 2010.

Enticknap, Leo. *Film Restoration: The Culture and Science of Audiovisual Heritage*. New York: Palgrave Macmillan, 2013.

Epstein, Jean and Stuart Liebman. "Magnification and Other Writings." *October* 3 (1977): 9–25.

Faden, Eric. "In Dialogue: Eric Faden and Kevin B. Lee." In *The Videographic Essay: Practice and Pedagogy*, edited by Christian Keathley, Jason Mittell, and Catherine Grant. Scalar, 2019, accessed December 31, 2022, http://videographicessay.org/works/videographic-essay/in-dialogue-eric-faden-and-kevin-b-lee?path=contents.

"FAQ—Movies." *Catalogue Lumière, L'œuvre cinématographique des frères Lumière*, accessed December 31, 2022, https://catalogue-lumiere.com/faq-movies/.

Farinelli, Gian Luca and Nicola Mazzanti, eds. *Il Cinema ritrovato: Teoria e metodologia del restauro cinematografico*. Bologna: Grafis, 1994.

Fay, Jennifer. *Inhospitable World: Cinema in the Time of the Anthropocene*. New York: Oxford University Press, 2018.

Ferguson, Kevin L. "Slices of Cinema: Digital Transformation as Research Strategy." In *The Arclight Guidebook to Media History and the Digital Humanities*, edited by Charles R. Acland and Eric Hoyt, 270–99. Sussex: REFRAME, 2016.

Ferguson, Kevin L. "Digital Surrealism: Visualizing Walt Disney Animation Studios." *Digital Humanities Quarterly* 11, no. 1 (2017), accessed December 31, 2022, http://www.digitalhumanities.org/dhq/vol/11/1/000276/000276.html.

Fetveit, Arild. "Death, Beauty, and Iconoclastic Nostalgia: Precarious Aesthetics and Lana Del Rey." *NECSUS European Journal of Media Studies* 4, no. 2 (2015): 187–207.

Fitzgerald, Francis Scott. "Pasting It Together." *Esquire*, 1936, accessed December 31, 2022, https://www.esquire.com/lifestyle/a4310/the-crack-up/.

Fitzgerald, Francis Scott. "The Crack-Up." *Esquire*, 1936, accessed December 31, 2022, https://www.esquire.com/lifestyle/a4310/the-crack-up/.

Fitzgerald, Francis Scott. *The Crack-Up*. New York: New Directions, 1945.

Fleming, Michael. "Never Never Land." *Vimeo*, 2018, accessed December 31, 2022, https://vimeo.com/234667905.

Flueckiger, Barbara. "Material Properties of Historical Film in the Digital Age." *NECSUS European Journal of Media Studies* 1, no. 2 (2012): 135–53.

Flueckiger, Barbara, Eva Hielscher, and Nadine Wietlisbach, eds. *Color Mania: The Material of Color in Photography and Film*. Baden: Lars Müllers Publishing, 2019.

Flusser, Vilém. "Our Program." In *Post-History*, 19–26. Minneapolis: Univocal Publishing, 2013.

Fort, Jeff. "André Bazin's Eternal Returns: An Ontological Revision." *Film-Philosophy* 25, no. 1 (2021): 42–61.

Fossati, Giovanna. "The Restoration of Beyond the Rocks." In *Work/s in Progress: Digital Film Restoration Within Archives*, edited by Kerstin Parth, Oliver Hanley, and Thomas Ballhausen, 111–20. Vienna: SYNEMA – Gesellschaft für Film und Medien, 2013.

Fossati, Giovanna. *From Grain to Pixel: The Archival Life of Film in Transition*, 3rd Revised ed. Amsterdam: Amsterdam University Press, 2018.

Frank, Hannah. *Frame by Frame: A Materialist Aesthetics of Animated Cartoons*. Berkeley: University of California Press, 2019.

Fren, Allison de. "The Critical Supercut: A Scholarly Approach to a Fannish Practice." *The Cine-Files* 15 (2020), accessed December 31, 2022, http://www.thecine-files.com/the-critical-supercut-a-scholarly-approach-to-a-fannish-practice/.

Freud, Sigmund. "'The Uncanny.'" In *Penguin Freud Library*, Vol. 14, 339–76. Harmondsworth: Penguin, 1991.

Friedberg, Anne. "The End of Cinema: Multimedia and Technological Change." In *Reinventing Film Studies*, edited by Christine Gledhill and Linda Williams, 438–52. London: Arnold, 2000.

Garwood, Ian. "From 'Video Essay' to 'Video Monograph'? Indy Vinyl as Academic Book." *NECSUS European Journal of Media Studies* 9, no. 1 (2020): 5–29.

Gass, Lars Henrik. *Film and Art After Cinema*. Zagreb: Multimedijalni institut, 2019.

Gaudreault, André and Philippe Marion. *The End of Cinema? A Medium in Crisis in the Digital Age*. New York: Columbia University Press, 2015.

Gaut, Berys. *A Philosophy of Cinematic Art*. New York and Cambridge: Cambridge University Press, 2010.

Gaycken, Oliver. "Through the Body with Laser Gun and Camera." In *Cinema of Exploration: Essays on an Adventurous Film Practice*, edited by James Leo Cahill and Luca Caminati, 40–56. New York and London: Routledge, 2020.

Gidal, Peter. *Materialist Film*. London and New York: Routledge, 2014.

Grant, Catherine. "Touching the Film Object? Notes on the 'Haptic' in Videographical Film Studies." *Filmanalytical*, August 29, 2011, accessed December 31, 2022, https://filmanalytical.blogspot.com/2011/08/touching-film-object-notes-on-haptic-in.html.

Grant, Catherine. "Déjà-Viewing?: Videographic Experiments in Intertextual Film Studies." *Mediascape: UCLA's Journal of Cinema and Media Studies* 7, no. 1 (2013), accessed December 31, 2022, http://www.tft.ucla.edu/mediascape/Winter2013_DejaViewing.html.

Grant, Catherine and Amber Jacobs, "Persona Non Grata Sonata." *MAI: Feminism & Visual Culture* 1, no. 1 (2018), accessed December 31, 2022, http://maifeminism.com/persona-non-grata-sonata.

Gregg, Melissa and Gregory J. Seigworth, eds. *The Affect Theory Reader*. Durham: Duke University Press, 2010.

Grønstad, Asbjørn. *Rethinking Art and Visual Culture: The Poetics of Opacity*. Cham: Palgrave Macmillan, 2020.

Grønstad, Asbjørn, Henrik Gustafsson, and Øyvind Vågnes, eds. *Gestures of Seeing in Film, Video and Drawing*. London and New York: Routledge, 2017.

Groo, Katherine. *Bad Film Histories: Ethnography and the Early Archive*. Minneapolis: University of Minnesota Press, 2019.

Groo, Katherine. "Let It Burn: Film Historiography in Flames." *Discourse* 41, no. 1 (2019): 3–36.

Groo, Katherine and Paul Flaig. "Historicity Begins with Decay and Ends with the Pretense of Immortality: An Interview with Paolo Cherchi Usai." In *New Silent Cinema*, edited by Katherine Groo and Paul Flaig, 53–62. London and New York: Routledge, 2015.

Grusin, Richard and Jocelyn Szczepaniak-Gillese, eds. *Ends of Cinema*. Minneapolis: University of Minnesota Press, 2020.

Guardiola Sánchez, Ingrid. "La imagen dialéctica en el audiovisual Found Footage: Un hiperarchivo de conceptos visuales." PhD diss., Universidad Pompeu Fabra, 2015.

Gunning, Tom. "Interview with Ken Jacobs." In *Films That Tell Time: A Ken Jacobs Retrospective*, 29–62. New York: American Museum of the Moving Image, 1989.

Gunning, Tom. "What's the Point of an Index? or, Faking Photographs." *Nordicom Review* 25, no. 1–2 (2004): 39–49.

Gunning, Tom. "Moving Away from the Index: Cinema and the Impression of Reality." *Differences* 18, no. 1 (2007): 29–52.

Gunning, Tom. "An Aesthetic of Astonishment: Early Film and the (In)Credulous Spectator." In *Film Theory and Criticism*, edited by Leo Braudy and Marshall Cohen, 736–50. New York and Oxford: Oxford University Press, 2009.

Habib, André. "Reel Changes: Post-mortem Cinephilia or the Resistance of Melancholia." In *Technology and Film Scholarship*, edited by Santiago Hidalgo, 79–100. Amsterdam: Amsterdam University Press, 2018.

Habib, André. "Finding Early Cinema in the Avant-garde: Research and Investigation." In *Provenance and Early Cinema*, edited by Joanne Bernardi, Paolo Cherchi Usai, Tami Williams, and Joshua Yumibe, 261–74. Bloomington: Indiana University Press, 2021.

Habib, André and Michel Marie, eds. *L'avenir de la mémoire. Patrimoine, restauration et réemploi cinématographiques*. Villeneuve d'Ascq: Presses Universitaires du Septentrion, 2013.

Harkema, Gert Jan. "'The Very Act Itself, Even to the Smack': Early Cinema, Presence and Experience." In *New Perspectives on Early Cinema History*, edited by Mario Slugan and Daniël Biltereyst, 65–82. London and New York: Bloomsbury Academic, 2022.

Heftberger, Adelheid. *Digital Humanities and Film Studies: Visualising Dziga Vertov's Work*. Berlin: Springer, 2019.

Hellerová, Franziska. "Proč se zabývat dějinami filmu? Několik poznámek k otázce, jak digitalizace mění náš obraz minulosti." *Iluminace* 27, no. 2 (2015): 41–56.

Herzogenrath, Bernd. "Aesthetics of the Archive: An Introduction." In *The Films of Bill Morrison: Aesthetics of the Archive*, edited by Bernd Herzogenrath, 11–29. Amsterdam: Amsterdam University Press, 2017.

Herzogenrath, Bernd. "Decasia. The Matter | Image: Film is also a Thing." In *The Films of Bill Morrison: Aesthetics of the Archive*, edited by Bernd Herzogenrath, 84–96. Amsterdam: Amsterdam University Press, 2017.

Herzogenrath, Bernd, ed. *The Films of Bill Morrison: Aesthetics of the Archive*. Amsterdam: Amsterdam University Press, 2017.

Herzogenrath, Bernd. "Toward a Practical Aesthetics: Thinking With." In *Practical Aesthetics*, edited by Bernd Herzogenrath, 1–24. London and New York: Bloomsbury Publishing, 2020.

Higgins, Scott. "The Silent Screen, 1895–1927: Editing." In *Editing and Special/Visual Effects*, edited by Charlie Keil and Kristen Whissel, 22–36. New Brunswick: Rutgers University Press, 2016.

Hilsabeck, Burke. "The 'Is' in *What Is Cinema?*: On André Bazin and Stanley Cavell." *Cinema Journal* 55, no. 2 (2016): 25–42.

Hoolboom, Mike. "Three Decades of Rage: An Interview with Al Razutis." In *Al Razutis Iconoclast*, edited by Mike Hoolboom, 55–72. 2009, accessed December 31, 2022, http://mikehoolboom.com/thenewsite/docs/601.pdf.

Jacobs, Ken. "Perfect Film." *Light Cone*, accessed December 31, 2022, https://lightcone.org/en/film-4154-perfect-film.

Jirsa, Tomáš. "For the Affective Aesthetics of Contemporary Music Video." *Music, Sound, and the Moving Image* 13, no. 2 (2019): 187–208.

Jirsa, Tomáš. *Disformations: Affects, Media, Literature*. New York: Bloomsbury Academic, 2021.

Johnson, Ryan J. *Deleuze, A Stoic*. Edinburgh: Edinburgh University Press, 2020.

Johnston, Nessa. "Sounding Decay in the Digital Age: 'Audio-Visions' of *Decasia* (2002) and *Lyrical Nitrate* (1991)." In *The Music and Sound of Experimental Film*, edited by Holly Rogers and Jeremy Barham, 219–32. New York: Oxford University Press, 2017.

Joret, Blandine. *Studying Film with André Bazin*. Amsterdam: Amsterdam University Press, 2019.

Keathley, Christian. *Cinephilia and History, or The Wind in the Trees*. Bloomington and Indianapolis: Indiana University Press, 2005.

Keathley, Christian Jason Mittell and Catherine Grant, eds. *The Videographic Essay: Criticism in Sound and Image*. Montreal: caboose, 2019.

Keathley, Christian, Jason Mittell, and Catherine Grant, eds. *The Videographic Essay: Practice and Pedagogy*. Scalar, 2019, accessed December 31, 2022, http://videographicessay.org/works/videographic-essay/index.

Kim, Jihoon. *Between Film, Video, and the Digital: Hybrid Moving Images in the Post-Media Age*. New York: Bloomsbury Academic, 2018.

Kinzl, Jan and Max Stejskal. "Analog/Digitál: Trhliny v českém filmovém dědictví." *Film a doba on-line*, February 15, 2022, accessed December 31, 2022, https://filmadoba.eu/trhliny-v-ceskem-filmovem-dedictvi/.

Kliment, Petr and Jeanne Pommeau, "The Presentation of Kříženecký's Cinematograph" [videocommentary]. In *Filmy Jana Kříženeckého/The Films of Jan Kříženecký*, edited by Jiří Anger. DVD/Blu-ray. Praha: Národní filmový archiv, 2019.

Knowles, Kim. *Experimental Film and Photochemical Practices*. Cham: Palgrave Macmillan, 2020.

Kracauer, Siegfried. *Theory of Film: The Redemption of Physical Reality*. Princeton: Princeton University Press, 1997.

Kuhn, Annette and Guy Westwell, *A Dictionary of Film Studies*. Oxford: Oxford University Press, 2012.

Kuntzel, Thierry. "The Film-Work." *Enclitic* 2, no. 1 (1978): 38–61.

Kuntzel, Thierry. "The Film-Work 2." *Camera Obscura* 5, no. 2 (1980): 6–70.

Landy, Marcia. *Cinema & Counter-History*. Bloomington and Indianapolis: Indiana University Press, 2015.

Latsis, Dimitrios and Grazia Ingravalle. "Guest Editors' Foreword: Digital Humanities and/in Film Archives." *The Moving Image: The Journal of the Association of Moving Image Archivists* 17, no. 2 (2017): xi–xv.

Leeder, Murray. *The Modern Supernatural and the Beginnings of Cinema*. Cham: Palgrave Macmillan, 2017.
Le Grice, Malcolm. *Experimental Cinema in the Digital Age*. London: BFI, 2001.
Levin, Thomas Y. "Indexicality Concrète: The Aesthetic Politics of Christian Marclay's Grammophonia." *Parkett* 56 (1999): 162–9.
Levine, Matthew. "A Poetic Archeology of Cinema: The Films of Bill Morrison." *Found Footage Magazine* 1, no. 1 (2015): 6–15.
Leyda, Jay. *Films Beget Films: A Study of the Compilation Film*. New York: Hill and Wang, 1964.
Lindeperg, Sylvie and Ania Szczepanska. *Who Owns the Images?* Lüneburg: Meson Press, 2021.
Lippit, Akira Mizuta. *Ex-Cinema: From a Theory of Experimental Film and Video*. Berkeley and London: University of California Press, 2012.
Loné, Eric. "Lumière." In Harold Brown, *Physical Characteristics of Early Films as Aids to Identification*, edited by Camille Blot-Wellens, 165–8. Brussels: FIAF, 2020.
López, Cristina Álvarez and Adrian Martin. "The Thinking Machine #48: Videography 1978." *Filmkrant*, April 26, 2021, accessed December 31, 2022, https://filmkrant.nl/video/the-thinking-machine-48-english/.
Lopour, Jaroslav. "Zatím jsme ubozí břídilové, a je těžké se s tím spřátelit! Vzpomínky na začátky české filmové výroby do roku 1914." *Iluminace* 31, no. 4 (2019): 90–126.
Löwensohn, Enikő and Barnabás Weisz. "Birth of Hungarian film—The Dance, 1901." *Nemzeti Filmintézet YouTube*, June 13, 2022, accessed December 31, 2022, https://www.youtube.com/watch?v=Zi8_eWwIxwU.
Lumière, Louis and Antoine Lumière. *Notice sur le Cinématographe*. Lyon: Société anonyme des plaques et papiers photographiques A. Lumière et ses fils, 1897.
Lyotard, Jean-Francois. *Discourse, Figure*. Minneapolis: University of Minnesota Press, 2011.
Lyotard, Jean-Francois. "Acinema." In *Acinemas: Lyotard's Philosophy of Film*, edited by Graham Jones and Ashley Woodward, 33–42. Edinburgh: Edinburgh University Press, 2017.
Macdonald, Iain. *Hybrid Practices in Moving Image Design: Methods of Heritage and Digital Production in Motion Graphics*. New York: Springer International Publishing, 2016.
Mackenzie, Adrian. *Transductions: Bodies and Machines at Speed*. London: Continuum, 2002.
Mackenzie, Adrian. "Transduction: Invention, Innovation and Collective Life." Unpublished manuscript, 2003, accessed December 31, 2022, http://www.lancs.ac.uk/staff/mackenza/papers/transduction.pdf.
Mackenzie, Scott and Janine Marchessault, eds. *Process Cinema: Handmade Film in the Digital Age*. Montreal: McGill-Queen's University Press, 2019.
Mannoni, Laurent. "Les Appareils cinématographiques Lumière." *1895*, 82 (2017): 52–85.

Manoff, Marlene, "Theories of the Archive from Across the Disciplines." *Portal: Libraries and the Academy* 4, no. 1 (2004): 9–25.
Manovich, Lev. *The Language of New Media*. Cambridge: MIT Press, 2002.
Manovich, Lev. *Software Takes Command*. New York: Bloomsbury Academic, 2013.
Manovich, Lev. "The Science of Culture? Social Computing, Digital Humanities and Cultural Analytics." *Journal of Cultural Analytics*, May 23, 2016, accessed December 31, 2022, https://culturalanalytics.org/article/11060.
Marks, Laura U. "Video Haptics and Erotics." *Screen* 39, no. 4 (1998): 331–48.
Marks, Laura U. *The Skin of the Film: Intercultural Cinema, Embodiment, and the Senses*. Durham: Duke University Press, 2000.
Marks, Laura U. *Touch: Sensuous Theory and Multisensory Media*. Minneapolis: University of Minnesota Press, 2002.
Marks, Laura U. "Haptic Visuality: Touching with the Eyes." *Framework the Finnish Art Review*, no. 2 (2004): 79–82.
Marks, Laura U. "Thinking Like a Carpet: Embodied Perception and Individuation in Algorithmic Media." *Acta Universitatis Sapientiae, Film and Media Studies* 7, no. 1 (2013): 7–20.
Marks, Laura U. "Let's Deal with the Carbon Footprint of Streaming Media." *Afterimage* 47, no. 2 (2020): 46–52.
Massumi, Brian. *Parables for the Virtual: Movement, Affect, Sensation*. Durham and London: Duke University Press, 2002.
Matuszewski, Boleslas. "A New Source of History." *Film History* 7, no. 3 (1995): 322–324.
McGoff, Jessica. "Expresser, Agitator, Salve and Mirror: The Video Essay and. Contemporary Cinephilia." Master's Thesis, Amsterdam University, 2017.
Meden, Jurij. *Scratches and Glitches: Observations on Preserving and Exhibiting Cinema in the Early 21st Century*. New York: Columbia University Press, 2021.
Merkin, Noa. "Little Patch of Yellow: On the Detail in Film." PhD diss., University of Chicago, 2020.
Metahaven, *Digital Tarkovsky*. Moscow: Strelka Institute, 2018.
Mihailova, Mihaela, Jen Bircher, Robert Bird, Mariana Johnson, Ian Bryce Jones, Ryan Pierson, Alla Gadassik, and Tim Palmer. "Teaching (Like) Hannah Frank (1984–2017): A Tribute." *The Moving Image: The Journal of the Association of Moving Image Archivists* 18, no. 1 (2018): 84–92.
Mittell, Jason, et al. "Becoming Videographic Critics: A Roundtable Conversation." In *The Videographic Essay: Practice and Pedagogy*, edited by Christian Keathley, Jason Mittell and Catherine Grant. Scalar, 2019, accessed December 31, 2022, http://videographicessay.org/works/videographic-essay/becoming-videographic-critics-a-roundtable-conversation?path=contents.
Mittell, Jason. "Videographic Criticism as a Digital Humanities Method." In *Debates in the Digital Humanities 2019*, edited by Matthew Gold and Lauren Klein. Minneapolis: University of Minnesota Press, 2019, accessed December 31, 2022, https://dhdebates.gc.cuny.edu/read/untitled-f2acf72c-a469-49d8-be35-67f9ac1e3a60/section/b6dea70a-9940-497e-b7c5-930126fbd180.

Mittell, Jason. "Deformin' in the Rain: How (and Why) to Break a Classic Film." *Digital Humanities Quarterly* 15, no. 1 (2021), accessed December 31, 2022, http://www.digitalhumanities.org/dhq/vol/15/1/000521/000521.html.

Morgan, Daniel. "Rethinking Bazin: Ontology and Realist Aesthetics." *Critical Inquiry* 32, no. 3 (2006): 443–81.

Mulvey, Laura. *Death 24x a Second: Stillness and the Moving Image*. London: Reaktion Books, 2006.

Murch, Walter. *In the Blink of an Eye: A Perspective on Film Editing*. Los Angeles: Silman James Press, 1992.

Musser, Charles. "The May Irwin Kiss: Performance and the Beginnings of Cinema." In *Visual Delights—Two: Exhibition and Reception*, edited by Vanessa Toulmin and Simon Popple, 96–115. Eastleigh: John Libbey, 2005.

Musser, Charles. "A Cinema of Contemplation, a Cinema of Discernment: Spectatorship, Intertextuality and Attractions in the 1890s." In *The Cinema of Attractions, Reloaded*, edited by Wanda Strauven, 159–80. Amsterdam: Amsterdam University Press, 2006.

Musser, Charles. "When Did Cinema Become Cinema? Technology, History, and the Moving Pictures." In *Technology and Film Scholarship: Experience, Study, Theory*, edited by Santiago Hidalgo, 33–50. Amsterdam: Amsterdam University Press, 2018.

Negarestani, Reza. "Drafting the Inhuman: Conjectures on Capitalism and Organic Necrocracy." In *The Speculative Turn: Continental Materialism and Realism*, edited by Levi R. Bryant, Nick Srnicek and Graham Harman, 182–201. Melbourne: Re.Press, 2011.

Niemeyer, Katharina, ed. *Media and Nostalgia: Yearning for the Past, Present and Future*. Basingstoke and New York: Palgrave Macmillan, 2014.

Noordegraaf, Julia. "The Analog Film Projector in Marijke van Warmerdam's Digitized Film Installations." In *Exposing the Film Apparatus: The Film Archive as a Research Laboratory*, edited by Giovanna Fossati and Annie van den Oever, 211–22. Amsterdam: Amsterdam University Press, 2016.

Noys, Benjamin. *The Persistence of the Negative: A Critique of Contemporary Continental Theory*. Edinburgh: Edinburgh University Press, 2010.

O'Leary, Alan. "No Voiding Time. A Deformative Videoessay." *16:9*, September 30, 2019, accessed December 31, 2022, http://www.16-9.dk/2019/09/no-voiding-time/.

O'Leary, Alan. "Workshop of Potential Scholarship: Manifesto for a Parametric Videographic Criticism." *NECSUS European Journal of Media Studies* 11, no. 1 (2021): 75–98.

Olesen, C. G. "Film History in the Making." PhD diss., Amsterdam University, 2017.

Pantenburg, Volker. "Videographic Film Studies." In *Handbuch Filmanalyse*, edited by Malte Hagener and Volker Pantenburg. Berlin: Springer, 2020.

Parikka, Jussi. *A Geology of Media*. Minneapolis: University of Minnesota Press, 2015.

Parikka, Jussi and Tomáš Dvořák. "Introduction: On the Scale, Quantity and Measure of Images." In *Photography Off the Scale: Technologies and Theories of the Mass Image*, edited by Tomáš Dvořák and Jussi Parikka, 1–21. Edinburgh: Edinburgh University Press, 2021.

Parth, Kerstin, Oliver Hanley, and Thomas Ballhausen, eds. *Work/s in Progress: Digital Film Restoration Within Archives*. Vienna: SYNEMA – Gesellschaft für Film und Medien, 2013.

Passafiume, Tania, et al. "Instructions: A Visual Glossary of Six Stages of Nitrate Film Base Deterioration." *Library and Archives Canada*, accessed December 31, 2022, https://www.bac-lac.gc.ca/eng/about-us/publications/electronic-books/Pages/visual-glossary-nitrate-deterioration.aspx.

Paterson, Mark. *The Senses of Touch: Haptics, Affects and Technologies*. London: Routledge, 2007.

Peirce, Charles Sanders. *Collected Papers of Charles Sanders Peirce*, Vol. 4. Cambridge: Harvard University Press, 1933.

Peirce, Charles Sanders. *The Essential Peirce: Selected Philosophical Writings*, Vol. 1, edited by Nathan Houser and Christian Kloesel. Bloomington: Indiana University Press, 1992.

Peterson, Jennifer Lynn. "Rough Seas: The Blue Waters of Early Nonfiction Film." In *The Colour Fantastic: Chromatic Worlds of Silent Cinema*, Giovanna Fossati et al., 75–93. Amsterdam: Amsterdam University Press, 2018.

Peterson, Jennifer Lynn. "Cinema, Nature, and Endangerment." In *Ends of Cinema*, edited by Richard Grusin and Jocelyn Szczepaniak-Gillese, 53–78. Minneapolis: University of Minnesota Press, 2020.

Pierson, Ryan. *Figure and Force in Animation Aesthetics*. New York: Oxford University Press, 2019.

Pierson, Ryan, ed. "In Focus: Drawing on the Margins: Animation in Film and Media." *Journal of Cinema and Media Studies* 61, no. 1 (2021): 142–84.

Pocock, Antonia. "Figurative." *The University of Chicago, Theories of Media Keywords Glossary*, accessed December 31, 2022, http://csmt.uchicago.edu/glossary2004/figurative.htm.

Polonyi, Eszter. "Flicker: Thom Andersen Takes Muybridge to the Movies." In *Provenance and Early Cinema*, edited by Joanne Bernardi, Paolo Cherchi Usai, Tami Williams, and Joshua Yumibe, 287–304. Bloomington: Indiana University Press, 2021.

Pommeau, Jeanne. "The Digitisation of Křiženecký's Films" [videocommentary]. In *Filmy Jana Křiženeckého/The Films of Jan Křiženecký*, edited by Jiří Anger. DVD/Blu-ray. Praha: Národní filmový archiv, 2019.

Pommeau, Jeanne. "The Digitisation of Jan Křiženecký's Films." In *Filmy Jana Křiženeckého/The Films of Jan Křiženecký*, edited by Jiří Anger, 31–5. DVD/Blu-ray Booklet. Praha: Národní filmový archiv, 2019.

Pommeau, Jeanne. "Le mystère des couleurs des pellicules du Cinématographe Lumière." Conference paper, Domitor 2020, November 17, 2020, accessed December 31, 2022, https://domitor2020.org/en-ca/le-mystere-des-couleurs-des-pellicules-du-cinematographe-lumiere/.

Pommeau, Jeanne. "Studie ve žluté: Hypotézy o přítomnosti zapomenutých barev v lumièrovských filmových pásech." In *Digitální Kříženecký: Nový život prvních českých filmů*, edited by Jiří Anger, 76–107. Praha: Národní filmový archiv, 2023.

Pommeau, Jeanne and Jiří Anger, "The Digitization of Jan Kříženecký's Films." *Iluminace* 31, no. 1 (2019): 104–7.

Powers, John. "A DIY Come-On: A History of Optical Printing in Avant-Garde Cinema." *Cinema Journal* 57, no. 4 (2018): 71–95.

Proctor, Jennifer. "Teaching Avant-Garde Practice as Videographic Research." *Screen* 60, no. 3 (2019): 466–74.

Radner, Hilary and Alistair Fox, eds. *Raymond Bellour: Cinema and the Moving Image*. Edinburgh: Edinburgh University Press, 2018.

Ranciére, Jacques. *Aisthesis: Scenes from the Aesthetic Regime of Art*. London and New York: Verso, 2013.

Revel, Jacques. "Micro-analyse et Construction du Social." In *Jeux d'echelles: La micro-analyse à la expérience*, edited by Jacques Revel, 15–36. Paris: Seuil/Gallimard, 1996.

Reynolds, Simon. *Retromania: Pop Culture's Addiction to Its Own Past*. London: Faber & Faber, 2010.

Riegl, Alois. *Late Roman Art Industry*. Rome: Giorgio Bretschneider Editore, 1985.

Rithdee, Kong. "Corona and the Death of Cinema (again)." *Bangkok Post*, March 30, 2020, accessed July 31, 2021, https://www.bangkokpost.com/life/social-and-lifestyle/1889185/corona-and-the-death-of-cinema-again-.

Rodowick, D. N. *The Crisis of Political Modernism: Criticism and Ideology in Contemporary Film Theory*. Berkeley: University of California Press, 1995.

Rodowick, D. N. *Reading for the Figural, or, Philosophy after the New Media*. Durham and London: Duke University Press, 2001.

Rodowick, D. N. *The Virtual Life of Film*. Harvard: Harvard University Press, 2007.

Rodowick, D. N. *What Philosophy Wants from Images*. Chicago: University of Chicago Press, 2018.

Rombes, Nicholas. *10/40/70: Constraint as Liberation in the Era of Digital Film Theory*. New York: Zero Books, 2014.

Rossaak, Eivind, ed. *Between Stillness and Motion: Film, Photography, Algorithms*. Amsterdam: Amsterdam University Press, 2010.

Rozenkrantz, Jonathan. *Videographic Cinema: An Archaeology of Electronic Images and Imaginaries*. London and New York: Bloomsbury Academic, 2020.

Ruiz, Raúl. "Folklore." In *Poéticas del cine*, 417–35. Santiago: Ediciones Universidad Diego Portales, 2013.

Russell, Catherine. *Archiveology: Walter Benjamin and Archival Film Practices*. Durham: Duke University Press, 2018.

Rutherford, Anne. *What Makes a Film Tick? Cinematic Affect, Materiality and Mimetic Innervation*. Berlin: Peter Lang, 2011.

Sample, Mark. "Notes Towards a Deformed Humanities." *Samplereality*, May 2, 2012, accessed December 31, 2022, https://samplereality.com/2012/05/02/notes-towards-a-deformed-humanities/.

Samuels, Lisa and Jerome McGann, "Deformance and Interpretation." *New Literary History* 30, no. 1 (1999): 25–56.

Sayers, Nicola. *The Promise of Nostalgia: Reminiscence, Longing and Hope in Contemporary American Culture*. London: Routledge, 2020.

Schaff, Rachel. "The Photochemical Conditions of the Frame." *Cinéma & Cie* 16, no. 26–27 (2016): 55–64.

Schneider, Jaron. "Stop Upscaling and Colorizing Photos and Videos, Historians Say." *Petapixel*, October 5, 2020, accessed December 31, 2022, https://petapixel.com/2020/10/05/stop-upscaling-and-colorizing-photos-and-videos-historians-say/?fbclid=IwAR0iy9BJTpRpX3PWuejmbdvTHbp8X5KppEceTw1NTJZRlRBV-M7SumqxQJk.

Schonig, Jordan. "The Haecceity Effect: On the Aesthetics of Cinephiliac Moments." *Screen* 61, no. 2 (2020): 255–71.

Schonig, Jordan. *The Shape of Motion: Cinema and the Aesthetics of Movement*. New York: Oxford University Press, 2021.

Schrey, Dominik. *Analoge Nostalgie in der digitalen Medienkultur*. Berlin: Kulturverlag Kadmos, 2017.

Sgammato, Joseph. "Naked Came the Stranger: *Eadweard Muybridge, Zoopraxographer* (Thom Andersen, 1975)." *Senses of Cinema* 20, no. 86 (2018), accessed December 31, 2022, http://sensesofcinema.com/2018/cteq/eadweard-muybridge-zoopraxographer-1975/.

Shambu, Girish. "On Video Essays, Cinephilia, and Affect." *Girish*, July 7, 2014, accessed July 31, 2021, https://girishshambu.net/2014/07/on-video-essays-cinephilia-and-affect.html.

Shambu, Girish. *The New Cinephilia*. Expanded 2nd ed. Montreal: caboose, 2020.

Shaviro, Steven. *The Cinematic Body*. Minneapolis: University of Minnesota Press, 1993.

Sheehan, Rebecca A. *American Avant-Garde Cinema's Philosophy of the In-Between*. New York: Oxford University Press, 2020.

Shiryaev, Denis. "21 Old Films from 1895 to 1902 Colorized and Upscaled in 60 fps, with Sound." *YouTube*, 2021, accessed December 31, 2022, https://www.youtube.com/watch?v=YZuP41ALx_Q.

"Silent Movie GIFs." *Twitter*, accessed December 31, 2022, https://twitter.com/silentmoviegifs.

Simondon, Gilbert. "The Position of the Problem of Ontogenesis." *Parrhesia* 7 (2009): 4–16.

Simondon, Gilbert. *On the Mode of Existence of Technical Objects*. Minneapolis: Univocal Publishing, 2017.

Simondon, Gilbert. *Individuation in Light of Notions of Form and Information*. Minneapolis: University of Minnesota Press, 2020.

Sitney, P. Adams. *Visionary Film: The American Avant-Garde, 1943–2000*. New York: Oxford University Press, 2002.

Sjöberg, Patrik. *The World in Pieces: A Study of Compilation Film.* Stockholm: Aura, 2001.
Skoller, Jeffrey. *Shadows, Specters, Shards: Making History in Avant-Garde Film.* Minneapolis: University of Minnesota Press, 2005.
Smejkal, Zdeněk. "Rané práce Karla Smrže o dějinách českého filmu." In *Otázky divadla a filmu*, edited by Artur Závodský, 265–80. Brno: Universita J.E. Purkyně, 1970.
Smither, Roger and Catherine A. Surowiec, eds. *This Film Is Dangerous: A Celebration of Nitrate Film.* London: FIAF, 2002.
Sobchack, Vivian. ""Cutting to the Quick": Techne, Physis, and Poiesis and the Attractions of Slow Motion." In *The Cinema of Attractions Reloaded*, edited by Wanda Strauven, 337–51. Amsterdam: Amsterdam University Press, 2006.
"Sorry for a Lag in Posting…" *The Biograph Project Facebook*, April 2, 2020, accessed December 31, 2022, https://www.facebook.com/filmpreservatio nsociety/videos/621649468415755/.
Spadoni, Robert. *Uncanny Bodies: The Coming of Film and the Origins of the Horror Genre.* Berkeley, Los Angeles, and London: University of California Press, 2007.
Sperb, Jason. *Flickers of Film: Nostalgia in the Time of Digital Cinema.* New Brunswick: Rutgers University Press, 2016.
Spindler, Fredrika. "Event, Crack-up and Line of Flight—Deleuze Reading Fitzgerald." In *Rethinking Time: Essays on History, Memory, and Representation*, edited by Hans Ruin and Andrus Ers, 257–65. Flemingberg: Södertörn University, 2011.
Štábla, Zdeněk. *Český kinematograf Jana Kříženeckého.* Praha: Československý filmový ústav, 1973.
"Static Mark." *Glossary of the National Film and Sound Archive of Australia*, accessed December 31, 2022, https://www.nfsa.gov.au/preservation/ preservation-glossary/static-mark.
Steimatsky, Noa. *The Face on Film.* New York: Oxford University Press, 2017.
Stevens, Kyle. "Introduction: The Very Thought of Theory." In *The Oxford Handbook of Film Theory*, edited by Kyle Stevens, 1–12. New York: Oxford University Press, 2022.
Stoler, Ann Laura. "Colonial Archives and the Arts of Governance." *Archival Science* 2, no. 1–2 (2002): 87–109.
Šváb-Malostranský, Josef. "Dopis Josefa Švába-Malostranského Janu Kříženeckému a Josefu Pokornému z 30. dubna 1898." Archiv Národního technického muzea, Sbírka vzpomínek a rukopisů k dějinám techniky a průmyslu, inv. č. 338.
Šváb-Malostranský, Josef. "Vzpomínka na prvá milování v Praze." *Rozpravy Aventina* 3, no. 18–19 (1928): 222–3.
Svatoňová, Kateřina. "Kříženecký's Films in the Context of Industrial Exhibitions" [videocommentary]. In *Filmy Jana Kříženeckého/The Films of Jan Kříženecký*, edited by Jiří Anger. DVD/Blu-ray. Praha: Národní filmový archiv, 2019.

Swender, Rebecca. "Claiming the Found: Archive Footage and Documentary Practice." *The Velvet Light Trap* 64 (2009): 3–10.
Tavernier, Bertrand and Thierry Frémaux, eds. *Lumière ! Le cinématographe 1895–1905*. DVD/Blu-ray. Lyon: Institut Lumière, 2015.
Teige, Karel. "K filmové avantgardě." In *Otázky divadla a filmu. III*, edited by Artur Závodský, 303–28. Brno: Universita J.E. Purkyně, 1973.
Testa, Bart. *Back and Forth: Early Cinema and the Avant-Garde*. Toronto: Art Gallery of Ontario, 1992.
Thacker, Eugene. *After Life*. Chicago and London: The University of Chicago Press, 2010.
Thacker, Eugene. *In the Dust of This Planet: Horror of Philosophy*, Vol. 1. Winchester: Zero Books, 2011.
Thacker, Eugene. *Starry Speculative Corpse: Horror of Philosophy*, Vol. 2. Winchester: Zero Books, 2015.
Thacker, Eugene. *Tentacles Longer Than Night: Horror of Philosophy*, Vol. 3. Winchester: Zero Books, 2015.
The Audiovisual Essayist. "Making It Stranger than Strange." *YouTube*, 2020, accessed December 31, 2022, https://www.youtube.com/watch?v=pajDSY05zg0.
Timby, Kim. ""Cinema in a Single Photo": The Animated Screen Portrait of the 1910s." In *Between Still and Moving Images*, edited by Laurent Guido and Olivier Lugon, 97–111. Bloomington: Indiana University Press, 2012.
Timeline of Historical Film Colors. accessed December 31, 2022, https://filmcolors.org/.
Tohline, Max. "A Supercut of Supercuts: Aesthetics, Histories, Databases." *Open Screens* 4, no. 1 (2021), accessed December 31, 2022, https://www.openscreensjournal.com/article/id/6946/.
Trnka, Jan. "Provenance filmových materiálů: Původ a životaběh negativů a kopií s kinematografickými díly Jana Kříženeckého." In *Digitální Kříženecký: Nový život prvních českých filmů*, edited by Jiří Anger, 108–43. Praha: Národní filmový archiv, 2023.
Tryon, Chuck. *Reinventing Cinema: Movies in the Age of Media Convergence*. New Brunswick: Rutgers University Press, 2009.
Tsivian, Yuri. *Early Cinema in Russia and Its Cultural Reception*. Chicago: University of Chicago Press, 1998.
Turquety, Benoît. "Why Additive? Problems of Color and Epistemological Networks in Early (Film) Technology." In *The Colour Fantastic: Chromatic Worlds of Silent Cinema*, Giovanna Fossati et al., 109–24. Amsterdam: Amsterdam University Press, 2018.
Turquety, Benoît. "Lumière ! Le Cinématographe 1895–1905. Les Films Lumière présentés par Bertrand Tavernier et Thierry Frémaux." *1895*, 78 (2016): 209–14.
Turquety, Benoît. *Inventing Cinema: Machines, Gestures and Media History*. Amsterdam: Amsterdam University Press, 2019.

Turquety, Benoît. *Medium, Format, Configuration: The Displacements of Film.* Lüneburg: Meson Press, 2019.

Turquety, Benoît. "Not Corrected or Otherwise Manipulated: Digitizing the Films of Jan Kříženecký." *Iluminace* 32, no. 4 (2020): 124–30.

Ustarroz, César, ed. "Special on Bill Morrison." *Found Footage Magazine*, no. 1 (2015).

Ustarroz, César, ed. "Special on Yervant Gianikian and Angela Ricci Lucchi." *Found Footage Magazine*, no. 3 (2017).

Ustarroz, César, ed. "Special on Peter Tscherkassky." *Found Footage Magazine*, no. 4 (2018).

Verdeure, David. "Deformative vs Performative." *Filmscalpel*, 2019, accessed December 31, 2022, https://www.filmscalpel.com/performative-vs-deformative/.

Veselý, Bohumil. "Jan Kříženecký." *YouTube*, 2013, accessed December 31, 2022, https://www.youtube.com/watch?v=Rk2OrOXEmnM.

"Videographic Epigraph." In *The Videographic Essay: Practice and Pedagogy*, edited by Christian Keathley, Jason Mittell, and Catherine Grant. Scalar, 2019, accessed December 31, 2022, http://videographicessay.org/works/videographic-essay/videographic-epigraph.

Villon, Patricia Ledesma. "Indeterminable Frames: Exploring Digital Humanities Approaches and Applications for the Moving Image." *Cinergie – Il Cinema e le altre Arti* 20 (2021): 125–38.

Waldenfels, Bernhard. *Phenomenology of the Alien.* Evanston: Northwestern University Press, 2011.

Waldenfels, Bernhard. "The Role of the Lived-Body in Feeling." In *Rethinking Emotion*, edited by Rüdiger Campe and Julia Weber, 246–63. Berlin and Boston: De Gruyter, 2014.

Walsh, David. "There Is No Such Thing as Digital Restoration." In *Work/s in Progress: Digital Film Restoration Within Archives*, edited by Kerstin Parth, Oliver Hanley and Thomas Ballhausen, 30–42. Vienna: SYNEMA – Gesellschaft für Film und Medien, 2013.

Walton, Saige. *Cinema's Baroque Flesh: Film, Phenomenology and the Art of Entanglement.* Amsterdam: Amsterdam University Press, 2016.

Wees, William. *Recycled Images: The Art and Politics of Found Footage Films.* New York: Anthology Film Archives, 1993.

Wiese, Doro. *The Powers of the False: Reading, Writing, Thinking Beyond Truth and Fiction.* Evanston: Northwestern University Press, 2014.

Willemen, Paul. "Through the Glass Darkly: Cinephilia Reconsidered." In *Looks and Frictions: Essays in Cultural Studies and Film Theory*, 223–58. Bloomington: Indiana University Press, 1994.

Williams, Linda. *Screening Sex.* Durham and London: Duke University Press, 2008.

Wollen, Peter. "Ontology and Materialism in Film." In *Readings and Writings: Semiotic Counter-Strategies*, 189–207. London: Verso, 1982.

Yáñez, Manu. "Thought, Action, and Imagination." *The Audiovisual Essay*, 2013, accessed December 31, 2022, http://reframe.sussex.ac.uk/audiovisualessay/frankfurt--papers/manu--yanez/.

Yetter, Sean. "The IMAX of the 1890s | HOW TO SEE the First Movies." *The Museum of Modern Art*, 2019, accessed July 31, 2021, https://www.youtube.com/watch?v=BBNwiPgknn8&feature=youtu.be.

Yue, Genevieve. *Girl Head: Feminism and Film Materiality*. New York: Fordham University Press, 2021.

Zimmermann, Yvonne. "Videoconferencing and the Uncanny Encounter with Oneself: Self-Reflexivity as Self-Monitoring 2.0." In *Pandemic Media: Preliminary Notes Toward an Inventory*, edited by Philipp Dominik Keidl, Laliv Melamed, Vinzenz Hediger, and Antonio Somaini, 99–103. Lüneburg: Meson Press, 2020.

Žukauskaitė, Audronė. "Deleuze, Simondon, and Beckett: From Being to Becoming." In *The Dark Precursor: Deleuze and Artistic Research*, edited by Paulo de Assis and Paulo Guidici, 272–8. Leuven: Leuven University Press, 2017.

Filmography

(nostalgia) (Hollis Frampton, 1971)
50 Years of Cinema (50 let kinematografie; František Sádek, 1946)
Alone. Life Wastes Andy Hardy (Martin Arnold, 1998)
An Assignation in the Mill (Dostaveníčko ve mlýnici; Jan Kříženecký, 1898)
Angel Face (Otto Preminger, 1953)
Automobile Accident (Accident d'automobile; Auguste Lumière and Louis Lumière, operator unknown, 1903–1905)
Barbie (Greta Gerwig, 2023)
Between the Nile and the Congo (Tusschen Nijl en Congo; Paul Julien, c. 1930)
Boat Leaving the Port (Barque sortant du port; Auguste Lumière and Louis Lumière, operator Louis Lumière, 1895)
Chemical Intervention in (Film) History (Jürgen Reble, 2019)
Coach Transport (Kočárová doprava; Jan Kříženecký, 1898)
Concorde Square (Obelisks and Fountains) (Place de la Concorde (obélisque et fontaines); Auguste Lumière and Louis Lumière, operator unknown, 1897)
Cowboy and "Indian" Film (Raphael Montañez Ortiz, 1958)
Crack, Brutal, Grief (R. Bruce Elder, 2000)
Cyclists (Cyklisté; Jan Kříženecký, 1898)
Decasia: The State of Decay (Bill Morrison, 2002)
Deformin' in the Rain (Jason Mittell, 2019–2020)
Eadweard Muybridge, Zoopraxographer (Thom Andersen, 1975)
Escorting the Cradle of František Palacký from Hodslavice to the Prague Exhibition Grounds (Přenesení kolébky Františka Palackého z Hodslavic na Výstaviště; Jan Kříženecký, 1898)
Exercises with Indian Clubs by the Sokol of Malá Strana (Cvičení s kužely Sokolů malostranských; Jan Kříženecký, 1898)
Exhibition Sausage Seller and Bill-Poster (Výstavní párkař a lepič plakátů; Jan Kříženecký, 1898)
Fallen Asleep When Young (Silja; Teuvo Tulio, 1937)
Flame (Polte; Sami van Ingen, 2018)
Forgotten Silver (Peter Jackson and Costa Botes, 1995)
Footpads (Unknown [allegedly Robert W. Paul], 189?)
Foundation Ceremony of the František Palacký Monument (Slavnost odhalení pomníku Františka Palackého; Jan Kříženecký, 1898)
Frankenstein (James Whale, 1931)
František Palacký Monument Prior to Its Completion (Pomník Františka Palackého před dokončením; Jan Kříženecký, 1911)
Fred Ott's Sneeze (William K. L. Dickson, 1894)
From Seriousness to Laughter (Vom Ernst zur Lachen; produced by Oskar Messter, 1897)

Grand Consecration of the Emperor Franz I Bridge (Slavnostní vysvěcení mostu císaře Františka I.; Jan Kříženecký, 1901)
History of Czechoslovak Cinema, Part I (Dějiny československé kinematografie I; Vojtěch Količ, 1967)
How It Started (Jak to začalo; Květa Lehovcová, 1968)
In Search of Lost Time (Hledání ztraceného času; Pavel Vantuch, 1991–2012)
Indochina: Children Gathering Rice Scattered by Western Women (Enfants annamites ramassant des sapèques devant la Pagode des Dames; Auguste Lumière and Louis Lumière, operator Gabriel Veyre, 1900)
It Wasn't Love (Sadie Benning, 1992)
Jan Kříženecký (Bohumil Veselý, 1968)
Jan Kříženecký (Vojtěch Trapl, 1983)
keep that dream burning (Rainer Kohlberger, 2017)
Kon-Tiki (Thor Heyerdahl, 1950)
La sortie (Siegfried A. Fruhauf, 1999)
Laughter and Tears (Smích a pláč; Jan Kříženecký, 1898)
Lumière! (Lumière! L'aventure commence; Thierry Frémaux, 2016)
Lumière's Train, Arriving at the Station (Al Razutis, 1979)
Lyrical Nitrate (Lyrisch Nitraat; Peter Delpeut, 1991)
March Past During Corpus Christi Feast in Hradčany (Defilování vojska o Božím těle na Královských Hradčanech; Jan Kříženecký, 1898)
Midsummer Pilgrimage in a Czechoslavic Village (Svatojanská pouť v českoslovanské vesnici; Jan Kříženecký, 1898)
Never Never Land (Michael Fleming, 2018)
Night and Fog (Nuit et brouillard; Alain Resnais, 1955)
Old Town Firemen (Staroměstští hasiči; Jan Kříženecký, 1898)
Opening Ceremony of the Čech Bridge (Slavnost otevření nového Čechova mostu; Jan Kříženecký, 1908)
Passage à l'acte (Martin Arnold, 1993)
Passio (Paolo Cherchi Usai, 2006)
Persona (Ingmar Bergman, 1966)
Pièce touchée (Martin Arnold, 1989)
Psycho (Alfred Hitchcock, 1960)
Queen Victoria's Last Visit to Ireland (Unknown, 1900)
Rubber (Quentin Dupieux, 2010)
Sallie Gardner at the Gallop (Eadweard Muybridge, 1878)
Satan's Railway Ride (Satanova jízda po železnici; Jan Kříženecký, 1906)
Singin' in the Rain (Stanley Donen, 1954)
Square of Purkyně in Královské Vinohrady (Purkyňovo náměstí na Královských Vinohradech; Jan Kříženecký, 1898, lost)
Thank You, Mr. Kříženecký (Díky, pane Kříženecký; Oleg Reif, 1978)
The Algorithmic Nickelodeon (Shane Denson, 2019)
The Arrival of a Train at La Ciotat (L'Arrivée d'un train en gare de La Ciotat; Auguste Lumière and Louis Lumière, operator Louis Lumière, 1896)

The Bey of Tunis and His Entourage Descend the Steps of the Bardo (Le bey de Tunis et les personnages de sa suite descendant l'escalier du Bardo; Auguste Lumière and Louis Lumière, operator Alexandre Promio, 1903)
The Big Swallow (James Williamson, 1901)
The First Day of the Spring Races of Prague (První den jarních dostihů pražských; Jan Kříženecký, 1908)
The First Frames of Czech Cinema (Jiří Anger and Adéla Kudlová, 2021)
The First Hundred Years: A Celebration of American Movies (Chuck Workman, 1995)
The Great Train Robbery (Edwin S. Porter, 1903)
The Kiss (Eadweard Muybridge, 1872)
The May Irwin Kiss (William Heise, 1896)
The Musketeers of Pig Alley (D. W. Griffith, 1912)
The Philosophy of Horror: A Symphony of Film Theory (Péter Lichter and Bori Máté, 2020)
The Stolen Jewels (D. W. Griffith, 1908)
Tom, Tom, the Piper's Son (Ken Jacobs, 1969)
Touching Sound (Johannes Binotto, 2018)
Touching the Film Object? (Catherine Grant, 2011)
Trace (Johannes Binotto, 2020)
Transparences (Trasparenze; Yervant Gianikian and Angela Ricci Lucchi, 1998)
Unveiling Ceremony of the Monument—July 1, 1912 (Slavnost odhalení pomníku 1. července 1912; Antonín Pech, 1912)
Vertigo (Alfred Hitchcock, 1958)
Videography 1978 (Cristina Álvarez López and Adrian Martin, 2021)
Westminster Bridge (Pont de Westminster; Auguste Lumière and Louis Lumière, operator unknown, 1896)
When Photographs Came to Life (Když oživly fotografie; Ivo Novák, 1958)
Workers Leaving the Lumière Factory in Lyon (La Sortie de l'Usine Lumière à Lyon; Auguste Lumière and Louis Lumière, operator Louis Lumière, 1895)

Supplements

The First Frames of Czech Cinema

Videographic essay
Created by: Jiří Anger and Adéla Kudlová
Music: Jan Burian
Length: 04:19
Date of production: 2021
Production: National Film Archive (Národní filmový archiv)
© Národní filmový archiv, 2021

Index

abstraction   7, 8, 10, 19, 24, 25, 28, 34, 44, 50–2, 55, 69, 79, 85, 86, 89, 95, 98, 105, 141, 142, 145, 170
accident   5, 10, 11, 13–15, 21–4, 51, 55, 65–7, 76, 85, 87, 90, 95, 102, 110, 125, 128, 134, 169, 174, 175, 179
actuality   11, 27, 31, 65, 83, 96
aesthetics   3, 5, 6, 9–16, 21, 27–8, 31, 34–7, 44, 46, 49–52, 54, 57, 59–60, 62, 65, 67, 70, 84–6, 90–3, 95, 102–3, 108, 133, 137, 140, 145, 157–9, 162, 165, 170–1, 173–5, 177
affect   1, 8, 11–12, 13 n.34, 18, 35, 110, 117–20, 128, 132, 135–8, 140, 142, 143, 145–6
affect theory   1, 12, 13 n.34, 137–8
algorithm   16, 103, 143, 160, 163, 164, 175, 177
Algorithmic Nickelodeon, The (Denson)   103, 175
Álvarez López, Cristina and Martin, Adrian   142–3, 153
analog   15–16, 21, 37 n.17, 43, 44, 46–7, 61, 70, 86, 92, 123, 126, 140, 153, 157, 165, 168, 170, 174, 175, 177, *see also* photochemical film
Andersen, Thom   28, 123–4, 129, 176
Andrew, Dudley   63
appropriation   43, 46, 52, 62, 94, 112, 114, 123 n.66, 124, 130, 142, 144
archival film   2, 5, 6, 15, 16, 21, 23, 26, 28, 35, 43, 45, 48, 67, 86, 110, 153, 157, 171, 174, 177–8
    archival artifact   24, 35, 107, 108, 112, 124, 155, 169–71, 180

archival document   109–12, 117, 121, 124, 128, 130, 176
archival footage   2, 14, 20, 21, 46–7, 50, 94, 111, 112, 125, 178–9
archival turn   110
archive effect   26, 28, 108, 110, 112, 114, 116–17, 121–6, 130, 176, *see also* Baron, Jaimie
    archive affect   117, 118, 120
    false archive effect   110, 123–4, 126
Arnold, Martin   159, 160 n.12
Arsenjuk, Luka   77, 79 n.58, 143 n.46
Assignation in the Mill, An (Kříženecký)   4, 26, 28, 36, 105–10, 112, 115–17, 119, 125–30, 131 n.1, 159, 175
Aumont, Jacques   79
Austro-Hungarian Empire   2, 6, 171

Bacon, Francis   17, 139, 149
bad film histories   9 n.19, 115, 169, *see also* Groo, Katherine
Balzac, Honoré de   113
Baron, Jaimie   19 n.54, 28, 69 n.32, 110, 112–14, 116–19, 122–3, 130
Barthes, Roland   11–12, 17 n.45, 73, 113
Bataille, Georges   73
Bazin, André   35, 38–41, 47, 52, 63–5, 73, 77
Bellour, Raymond   57 n.82, 139, 140, 141 n.34, 143
Bergson, Henri   21, 124
Berlant, Lauren   135
Betancourt, Michael   47 n.54, 48–9
Between the Nile and the Congo (Julien)   67

Big Swallow, The (Williamson) 96, 132
Binotto, Johannes 58, 109 n.10, 142, 164
blur 2, 7, 18, 29, 32, 44, 45, 51, 55, 68, 69, 77–9, 94, 98, 100, 103, 125, 128, 133, 142, 175
Bogost, Ian 166
Borges, Jorge Luis 145
Boym, Svetlana 116 n.39, 117–18
Bozak, Nadia 73, 81 n.61
Branald, Adolf 96
Brinkema, Eugenie 8, 13, 13 n.34, 18, 137–8, 143

camera instability 5, 26, 27, 31 n.3, 83, 91, 92, 94, 96, 97
  camera trembling 3 n.7, 16, 45, 83 n.1, 86, 92, 108, 109, 114, 157, 173
  vertical and horizontal 27, 83, 85, 95–8, 100–1
Cherchi Usai, Paolo 15–16, 37 n.17, 38 n.17, 40–4, 47 n.53, 92, 93 n.32, 99 n.56, 128, 145
Chrétien, Jean-Louis 133
cinematic first 28, 110, 121–2, 130, 164, 170, 176, 177, *see also* early Czech cinema/first Czech films
Cinématographe 24, 26, 27, 37 n.15, 68, 71–3, 76, 83–5, 94, 97, *see also* camera instability; Lumière brothers
Cinématographe-type 3, 84
circulation 13, 21, 35, 43–5, 48, 62, 106, 108, 109, 111, 114, 119–21, 127, 138, 141, 159, 171, 174
close-up 8, 28, 101, 125, 131–3, 135, 137, 138, 145–7, 149–53, 176
  cinematic face 28, 131–2, 134, 135, 145

compilation 29, 36, 106, 108 n.7, 111 n.15, 119–20, 130, 158, 163, 166 n.39, 171, 177
  supercut 166
compression 15, 16, 37, 44, 45, 48, 54, 70, 174
contingency 11, 12, 18, 25, 39, 73, 75–6, 78, 113
counter-actualization 173–4, 180, *see also* Deleuze, Gilles
crack-up 1, 10, 18, 22–9, 34–5, 42, 44, 46, 50–2, 56–7, 61, 62, 67–8, 71, 76, 79–81, 83–4, 86, 87, 90, 91, 93, 98, 99, 102, 108–10, 112, 116, 120, 125, 128–30, 133–5, 138–40, 144–6, 150–3, 157–9, 161, 170, 171, 173–7, 179–80, *see also* Deleuze, Gilles; Fitzgerald, Francis Scott
  as paradox 24–5
  as persistence 23–4
  as surface 25–6
Cubitt, Sean 48, 98
Cuevas, Efrén 5, 110 n.13
curation 2, 20, 40, 43 n.44, 101, 155, 170–1, 178
Cyclists (Kříženecký) 169–70
Czech Cinematograph 28, 105–7, 112, 129, 175
Czech lands 6, 74, 128 n.84

death of cinema 8, 15, 16 n.39, 26, 27, 35, 37, 40–1, 44, 46, 47, 56–7, 174, *see also* Cherchi Usai, Paolo
death drive 16, 27, 36, 41, 50, 51, 55
Decasia: The State of Decay (Morrison) 20–1, 28, 46–52, 54, 57, 69, 118–19, 139, 174
decay 12, 14, 20, 21, 28, 33, 34, 36–7, 39–50, 52, 54, 63, 68–9, 72, 81, 108–10, 117–19, 138, 162, 164, 168, 174

degradation   14, 16, 33, 35, 42, 43, 45, 54, 86, 108, 114
defect   10, 21, 24, 71, 83, 92
deformation   2, 3, 5, 14–17, 19, 20, 27–9, 34–6, 40, 43, 45–6, 49, 56, 62, 72, 77, 81, 89, 92, 103, 109–10, 114, 115, 118–19, 125, 130, 133, 144, 147, 149, 153, 155, 160, 164, 168, 175, 176, 179
deformative criticism   158–63, 170, 178, *see also* videographic criticism
   parametric approach   160–1, 164, 170, 178
Deformin' in the Rain (Mittell)   160
deixis   27, 66–70, 77, 80, 175, *see also* indexicality
Deleuze, Gilles   8, 17, 22–5, 52, 57, 69 n.30, 79, 87, 122, 133, 146 n.54, 149, 173, 180
Denson, Shane   7 n.15, 91, 92 n.25, 101, 103, 159 n.8, 175
detail   2, 6, 7, 10–15, 18, 24, 26, 28, 29, 52, 65, 66, 70, 74, 87, 96, 100, 134, 136–9, 143–4, 146–7, 153, 158, 162, 164, 166, 174–9
Diderot, Denis   65, 113 n.27
digital   3, 5–7, 9, 14–16, 19–21, 29, 31, 33, 35, 37–8, 40, 41, 43–9, 52, 54–8, 60–2, 70, 72, 74–6, 78, 80–1, 86, 93, 97, 103, 114, 117–18, 120, 123, 125, 130, 134, 139, 142–5, *see also* digitization
   digital age   7, 9, 61
   digital space   7, 9, 15, 29, 134, 144, 153, 179, 180
   (post)digital   6, 7, 9, 61, 153, 174, 180
   digital humanities   157, 178
Digital Kříženecký   5–1, 13–16, 18, 21, 23–4, 26, 29, 31, 33, 36, 42, 45, 46, 49, 57, 61, 70, 110, 118, 144, 145, 153, 157, 158, 161, 163, 170, 173–4, 177–8, *see also* Kříženecký, Jan
digitization   2–3, 5, 9, 15–16, 21, 27, 29, 31 n.3, 36, 43, 45, 47, 48, 57, 59–62, 68, 70, 72–4, 79, 80, 83–5, 96–7, 107, 111, 112, 115, 117, 120, 129, 130, 133, 137, 138, 141, 144, 147, 151, 152, 156–9, 161, 163, 165, 168–70, 176–7
   digital preservation   17, 35
   digital restoration   3, 43, 62, 72, 93, 117, 120
   nonintrusive/noninterventionist approach   3, 61, 63, 69, 84, 118
disfiguration   9, 14, 40, 46, 138, 170
distributed embodiment   91, 95, 101–2, 138, *see also* Denson, Shane; transduction
Doane, Mary Ann   11 n.24, 16 n.39, 66–7, 75 n.50, 128
DVD/Blu-ray   2, 72 n.40, 155, 157, 168, 171

Eadweard Muybridge, Zoopraxographer (Andersen)   28, 123–4, 130, 176
early cinema   2, 3, 6, 10–11, 29, 46, 61 n.5, 71, 75, 77, 85, 92–4, 96, 99, 101 n.60, 62, 103, 105, 107, 110, 112–15, 118, 119, 121–3, 125, 126, 128, 130–2, 150 n.63, 155, 157–8, 165, 171, 176–8
early Czech cinema/first Czech films   2, 3, 5–7, 21, 36, 105, 106 n.3, 119, 131, 144, 145, 155, 157, 165, 170–1
editing   14, 29, 46, 48, 58, 61, 76, 77, 81, 103, 112, 128–9, 131, 143, 152, 160, 162, 174, 175, 178–9, *see also* video-editing software
Eisenstein, Sergei   79, 113 n.27

Elder, R. Bruce 47 n.53, 94
electricity 5, 14, 16, 26, 27, 45, 59–63, 68, 70–3, 76–7, 79–81, 109, 114, 127, 174–5, *see also* static electricity
Elkins, James 179–80
Elsaesser, Thomas 96 n.44, 141, 165
epistemology 9, 10, 26, 109–11, 127, 133, 134, 144, 152
event 5, 11 n.29, 15, 17, 18, 23, 28, 34, 39, 59–61, 63, 65, 67–70, 74, 76, 77, 80, 95, 105, 108–10, 112, 113, 116, 119–22, 124, 126, 129, 130, 136, 138, 173, 176
Exhibition of Architecture and Engineering 105–6, 121, 131, 165
experimental cinema 6, 9, 10, 14, 19, 21, 22, 24, 28, 35, 51, 57, 58, 85–6, 88, 92, 93, 95, 101, 102, 126 n.78, 130, 137, 139, 141, 146, 152, 156, 163, 165 n.36, 175, *see also* found footage

Faden, Eric 142
fetishism 25, 58, 136, 138, 153, 174, 176
figuration 6, 10, 11, 13–15, 17–28, 34–6, 41, 42, 44–58, 62, 66–70, 74–7, 80, 83–90, 92–8, 100, 102, 108–10, 114, 116–20, 124–6, 128, 133, 135, 137, 138, 145–7, 153, 165, 170, 173–7, *see also* between figuration and materiality
  figurative content 14–15, 17–19, 22, 24, 34–6, 42, 47, 51, 57, 59, 68, 74, 76, 77, 93, 108, 110, 118, 125
  figurative sphere/dimension 10, 14, 17, 19, 21, 24, 25, 26, 27, 34, 41, 50, 56–7, 67, 76, 77, 84, 86, 88, 90, 97, 102, 117, 120, 124, 128, 133, 137, 145, 147 (*see also* material sphere/dimension)
  figure 5, 13, 15, 17–21, 24, 31, 34, 39, 42, 44, 49–52, 54, 55, 57, 61, 62, 65, 66, 68, 69, 73, 74, 77, 79, 83–5, 90–1, 95, 96, 98, 100–2, 124, 133, 138–9, 142, 144, 149, 174, 176
  between figuration and materiality 6, 10, 14–15, 19, 21–8, 34–5, 42, 44, 45, 52–3, 55–7, 67–9, 75–7, 80, 83–4, 86–90, 92–8, 100, 102, 108–10, 114, 116, 117, 120, 124, 126, 128, 133, 135, 137, 145, 146, 153, 173, 175–7, *see also* crack-up
film history 19, 21, 37 n.17, 40–1, 57, 95, 109, 110, 151
film medium 3, 8, 9, 15, 19, 24, 38, 62, 64, 153
film object 2, 6, 9, 28, 29, 121, 131, 133–43, 145, 147, 152–3, 158, 161–4, 174, 176, 179
film technology 21, 35, 60, 61, 73, 85, 86, 92, 107
film theory 1–2, 5, 6, 8–11, 21, 26, 37 n.17, 39, 77, 78, 86, 87, 134, 140, 141, 145, 158, 174, 178, 180, *see also* film theory from below
film theory from below 1, 2, 5–10, 15, 23, 25, 26, 29, 36, 51, 70, 87, 110, 116, 124, 144, 174, 180
  theory as archival experience 6–7, 174
  theory as micro-perspective 5–6, 174
  theory as theoria 8–9, 174
  theory as videographic practice 9–10, 174
film-philosophy 1, 8

First Day of the Spring Races of Prague, The (Křiženecký) 4, 24, 26, 27, 59–60, 62–6, 68–70, 74–81, 84, 109, 127, 158, 175
First Frames of Czech Cinema, The (Anger and Kudlová) 29, 155, 157–8, 161, 163–4, 167–71, 176, *see also* videographic criticism
first kiss, the 28, 105, 115, 119–20, 123, 125, 126, 129, 130, 175, *see also* scratched kiss
Fitzgerald, Francis Scott 1, 10, 22–4, 173
Flame (van Ingen) 28, 81, 175
Fleming, Michael 19, 28, 152, 176
flicker 97, 114, 115, 118, 124, 166, 177
Flusser, Vilém 163
Forgotten Silver (Jackson) 122
form 12–13, 15, 18, 20, 50, 54, 72, 74, 76, 79, 89–90, 96, 100, 138, 140, 144, 149, 179, *see also* figuration, figure
affective formalism 18 (*see also* Brinkema, Eugenie)
motion forms 18 (*see also* Schonig, Jordan)
found footage 6, 9, 15, 19–23, 26, 28, 35, 45, 46, 47 n.53, 50, 57, 69, 81, 84–6, 88, 91–3, 95, 101, 102, 108, 109 n.10, 110, 111, 114, 123, 124, 126, 130, 139, 141, 144, 152, 153, 157, 159, 163, 177–8, *see also* experimental cinema
fragment 16, 20, 22, 29, 36, 49, 69, 76, 83, 102, 108, 118, 136, 142, 143, 149, 152, 157, 163, 164, 168, 170, 176–8
frame 2, 7–10, 13, 17, 26–9, 31, 33–5, 48, 51–6, 61, 64, 66–70, 74–5, 77–8, 80–1, 88, 92, 93 n.34, 94–8, 101, 109, 113, 117, 119, 124, 131, 132, 135, 140, 143–5, 147, 149, 151–3, 155–71, 173, 174, 177, 179
frame by frame 9, 10, 29, 35, 48, 51, 53, 55, 70, 77, 88, 92, 95, 140, 145, 147, 159, 174, 179 (*see also* Frank, Hannah)
between the frames 88, 92, 95–6, 98
frame rate 7, 99, *see also* projection
24 frames per second 7, 31 n.1, 51, 163
Francis, David 93
Frank, Hannah 13 n.38, 18, 51 n.73, 74, 55, 164, 167–8, 174
Frankenstein (Whale) 101, 150
Frankenstein's monster 3, 14, 17, 28, 91, 101, 131, 134, 135, 138, 145, 149–53, 176
Frankensteinian frame 131 (*see also* spliced frames)
Frankensteinian head 134, 138, 145 (*see also* stitched head)
Frémaux, Thierry 72, 93
Fruhauf, Siegfried A. 28, 101, 102, 175
fuzz 60, 64, 68, *see also* Cinématographe

Gaudreault, André 16 n.39, 37, 41
gesture 6, 9, 13, 22, 26, 28, 57, 66, 68, 70, 76, 79, 80, 112, 113, 124, 129–31, 143, 160, 163, 174, 176, 177, 179
GIF 3, 10, 13, 21, 83, 98, 101, 130, 144, 159, 179
glitch 15, 20, 49, 139, 162
grain 43 n.44, 45, 46, 54, 59, 107, 115, 119 n.49, 142, 168
Grand Consecration of the Emperor Franz I Bridge (Křiženecký) 4, 15, 21, 26, 27, 31–2, 34–6, 39, 42–6, 50–7,

59, 62, 80, 84, 109, 114, 133, 159, 174
Grant, Catherine 9 n.21, 142, 147 n.59, 153
Grønstad, Asbjørn 78–9, 134 n.9
Groo, Katherine 9 n.19, 16, 38 n.17, 40 n.32, 45, 57, 66 n.21, 67–8, 115, 119, 127, 129, 169
Gunning, Tom 38 n.20, 70, 99 n.54, 131 n.2, 164 n.29, 165

haptic visuality 8, 26, 28, 133–5, 137, 139, 141, 142, 145, 176, *see also* Marks, Laura U.
haptic criticism 136–8, 140–5, 152, 161, 162, 164, 176
haptic mosaic 147
touching the film object 28, 131, 137, 140–3, 145, 147, 152, 161, 176
Herzogenrath, Bernd 9 n.20, 16 n.39, 21 n.58, 41, 47 n.54, 49, 58 n.84, 69 n.31, 109 n.10, 142 n.41
historicity 7, 9, 14, 66, 67, 109–10, 112, 118, 128, 171
history from below 5–6, *see also* Cuevas, Efrén
horror 25, 46, 49–50, 52, 56, 62
hybridity 16, 19, 35, 43–6, 48, 51, 57, 62, 90, 91, 96, 100, 101, 103, 116, 144, 153, 157, 168, 174, 175
dialectic of medium hybridity and specificity 16, 44, 90
hybrid moving images 16, 44–5, 46, 62 (*see also* Kim, Jihoon)

incomplete 9, 31, 129, 157, 170
indexicality 8, 14, 15, 26, 27, 35, 38–41, 47, 53, 59, 61–71, 73–5, 77, 80–1, 111, 123, 124, 174–5
hollowed-out signs 67, 128 (*see also* Doane, Mary Ann)

quadruple logic of indexicality 27, 59, 68, 69, 80, 81, 175
trace vs. deixis 27, 66, 68, 70, 80, 175
Ingen, Sami van 28, 81, 175
intentional disparity 19 n.54, 130, *see also* archive effect
intentional fallacy 137–8, 139, 152, *see also* haptic visuality
intentionality 2, 3, 10–13, 15, 20, 21, 27, 35, 46, 51, 52, 54, 85, 86, 88, 92, 95, 98, 108, 124–5, 130, 131, 134, 137–9, 144, 152, 158, 161, 163, 168
It Wasn't Love (Benning) 136

Jacobs, Ken 19, 21, 94, 95, 99 n.54, 100, 102, 141, 175
Joret, Blandine 39

keep that dream burning (Kohlberger) 58
Kim, Jihoon 16, 38, 44–6, 90, 96
Knowles, Kim 20 n.55, 38 n.17, 126 n.78, 146, 149
Kohlberger, Rainer 58
Kon-Tiki (Heyerdahl) 39–40
Kříženecký, Jan 2–4, 7, 8, 10, 15, 16, 26, 28, 31, 33–4, 36 n.11, 37, 39–41, 43, 45, 48, 51, 52, 56, 59–60, 62, 63, 65, 66, 68–70, 73–5, 77, 81, 83–5, 95, 96 n.46, 102, 106 n.3, 107, 116, 120, 121, 126, 131, 132, 137, 138, 144, 147, 155–6, 158, 163 n.28, 165–6, 168–71, 176, *see also* Digital Kříženecký; early Czech cinema/first Czech films
Kuntzel, Thierry 140

later-generation print 36, 107, 119
Laughter and Tears (Kříženecký) 4, 8, 26, 28, 131–5, 137–9, 144–53, 158, 176

Loebenstein, Michael   157
loop   28, 29, 101, 102, 145, 159, 160, 175
Lumière brothers   3, 7, 10, 11, 13, 14, 16, 26–9, 33–4, 36 n.12, 37, 44, 57, 60, 68, 70–5, 77, 80, 83–6, 93, 94, 96 n.45, 97, 97 n.52, 101, 103, 115, 121, 121 n.57, 147, 165, 169, 174
Lumière's Train, Arriving at the Station (Razutis)   28, 94

Mackenzie, Adrian   86, 88 n.11, 89–90
Manoff, Marlene   110–11
Marion, Philippe   16 n.39, 37, 41
Marks, Laura U.   12 n.33, 73 n.47, 116, 133–4, 136–7, 142
Massumi, Brian   138
materiality   3, 5–7, 9, 10, 13–17, 19–28, 33–8, 62, 66–70, 75–7, 79–80, 83–8, 90–8, 100, 102–3, 107–10, 112–14, 116–18, 120, 121, 124, 126, 128, 129, 133–5, 137, 143–6, 149, 153, 158, 164, 168–71, 173–8, *see also* between figuration and materiality; figurative sphere/dimension
  filmic matter   15, 20, 24, 25, 35, 41, 44, 47, 49, 50, 52, 57, 62, 66, 67, 77, 86, 118, 130, 131, 137, 149, 165, 176
  material carrier   14, 34, 49, 54, 57, 113, 117
  material sphere/dimension   14, 19, 21, 24–7, 34, 40, 66, 86, 88, 90, 102, 117, 120, 124, 128, 133, 137, 145
Matuszewski, Bolesław   61, 111
McGann, Jerome   159, 160
Meden, Jurij   7
Merkin, Noa   11 n.27, 13, 18

Mittell, Jason   9 n.21, 157 n.5, 160–1, 164
Model Image, *see also* Cherchi Usai, Paolo
Morgan, Daniel   62 n.7, 64–5
Morrison, Bill   16 n.39, 19–21, 28, 37 n.17, 41 n.36, 46–9, 58 n.84, 69, 81, 118–19, 144, 174
mummy complex   36, 38–41, 47, 64, *see also* Bazin, André
Muybridge, Eadweard   28, 75–6, 123–4, 129, 130, 176

National Film Archive (Národní filmový archiv) in Prague   2, 3, 40, 43, 57, 123 n.68, 155, 171, 178
negative ontology   137–9, 152, *see also* haptic visuality
Never Never Land (Fleming)   28, 152, 153, 176
new cinephilia   12, 139 n.26, 141, 164
new materialism   20
nitrate negative   3, 4, 29, 43, 59–61, 71, 74, 75, 78, 79, 83, 84, 96, 97 n.49, 99, 107, 117, 120, 121 n.57, 156, 158, 163, 165, 168
  original negative   3, 4, 29, 59–60, 74, 75, 78, 79, 83, 84, 96, 97 n.49, 99, 107, 117, 120, 156, 163 n.28, 165
nitrate print   3, 4, 7, 14, 15, 27, 29, 31–4, 36, 41–8, 53, 55–7, 59, 72, 74 n.49, 93, 97, 105–8, 112, 114–20, 126, 127, 129–32, 145, 148, 150–2, 156, 163, 165, 166 n.39, 168–70, 174
  vintage print   33, 36, 48, 59, 74 n.49, 107, 117, 120, 129, 130, 132, 145, 166, 169
nonhuman   14–16, 35, 41, 57, 59, 65, 78, 91, 98, 126, 147, 162

nostalgia 110, 116–18, 120, 126, 130, 174, 176
 reflective nostalgia 117–18, 119, 120, 130, 176 (*see also* Boym, Svetlana)
 restorative nostalgia 117–18, 119, 120, 130, 176 (*see also* Boym, Svetlana)

Olesen, C. G. 111, 178 n.10
ontology 15, 16, 22, 26, 27, 35, 38–43, 44 n.47, 46, 50, 56, 57, 63, 77, 86, 88, 94, 130, 137–9, 152
 ontology of the photographic image 15, 38–40, 41, 63–4 (*see also* Bazin, André)
Opening Ceremony of the Čech Bridge (Křiženecký) 3 n.7, 4, 21, 24, 26, 27, 83–4, 86–90, 92, 94–102, 109, 159, 175

Peirce, Charles Sanders 66–7
perforation 7, 31, 36, 44, 45, 54, 60 n.3, 64, 68, 70, 93 n.34, 97, 107, 115, 169, 174
philosophy of technology 86, *see also* Simondon, Gilbert
photochemical film 6, 15, 19, 21, 29, 35, 37–9, 43–5, 47–8, 56, 62, 70, 102, 118, 125, 126, 142–3, 145, 146, 158, 168, *see also* analog
photography 11, 15, 27, 33, 38–40, 47, 48, 59, 61–6, 68, 70, 75, 76, 81, 96, 123–4, 139, 165, 177
 photography off the scale 177
Pierson, Ryan 18–19, 51 n.73
pixel 16, 43 n.44, 46, 54, 55, 81, 144
 pixelation 54, 55, 144
Planchon, Victor 33
Pommeau, Jeanne 2 n.5, 3, 32–3, 68 n.28, 96, 157

powers of the false 28, 110, 121–4, 126, 130, 175–6, *see also* Deleuze, Gilles
practical research 9, 140–1, 164, *see also* videographic criticism
 thinking with 9, 174 (*see also* Herzogenrath, Bernd)
projection 7, 29, 31 n.1, 94, 115, 127, 129, 158, 165, 169, 177, *see also* frame rate
punctum 11, 73, *see also* Barthes, Roland

Ranciére, Jacques 76
Razutis, Al 19, 28, 94–5, 100, 102, 175
reality 10, 27, 38–41, 47–50, 59–71, 73–4, 76–80, *see also* indexicality
 profilmic reality 62, 68, 74, 76, 79, 96, 174
 realism 63–5, 77
repetition 29, 57, 88, 101, 110, 129, 130, *see also* GIF; loop
representation 2, 6, 11–14, 17, 20, 32, 34, 38, 39, 42, 49, 57, 62, 65, 66, 68, 74, 76–7, 79, 80, 83, 93, 94, 98, 109, 111, 113, 115, 122, 123, 128, 138, 143, 149
resolution 31, 45, 49, 78, 83, 118, 136
 4K 3, 16, 45, 79, 80, 118, 146, 178
 high-resolution 31, 45, 49, 83
 low-resolution 78, 136
retouching 3, 7, 10, 34, 45, 59, 61, 70, 72, 81, 108, 111, 114, 120, 123, 139, *see also* digitization
Rodowick, D. N. 16 n.39, 17 n.45, 26 n.73, 39 n.25, 130
Rombes, Nicholas 161
Rosen, Philip 64
ruin 14, 15, 35, 36, 52, 72, 117, 118, 119 n.49
Rutherford, Anne 133

Samuels, Lisa 159, 160
Schonig, Jordan 11 n.25, 18, 125 n.75, 139 n.26, 146
Simondon, Gilbert 8, 25, 27, 86–91, 102
Sitney, P. Adams 94
slow motion 20, 29, 49, 81, 92 n.25, 98–100, 102, 142, 160, 179
slow observation 88, 92, 102, 175
Sobchack, Vivian 99–100
Sortie, La (Fruhauf) 28, 101
speculation 2, 5, 8–10, 18, 23, 51, 53, 55, 75, 88, 128, 159
Spindler, Fredrika 173
splice 2, 5, 8, 14, 17, 26, 28, 31, 44, 112, 132, 133, 135, 145, 149, 151–2, 173, 174
  spliced frames 2, 26, 135, 145, 149, 173
stabilization 31 n.3, 45, 84–5, 93, *see also* camera instability; digitization
static electricity 5, 14, 16, 27, 45, 59, 61, 70–2, 76–7, 80, 114, 174, *see also* electric horses
  lightning bolts 2, 13, 24, 27, 59, 61, 63, 70–2, 74–7, 79, 81, 84
  static marks 5, 26, 27, 45, 59–65, 67, 68, 70–5, 77, 80–1, 108, 109, 127, 173–5
Stevens, Kyle 8
stillness 29, 145, 158, 164, 165, 167, 170
subject-object relations 103, 134–5, 175
surface 5, 14, 16, 21, 22, 25, 33–4, 40, 41, 46, 49, 50, 52–6, 67, 68, 81, 115, 126, 130, 133, 134, 136, 137, 142–4, 146–7, 149, 151
surgical gloves 28, 131, 135, 145
Šváb-Malostranský, Josef 17, 28, 105–7, 112, 116–17, 129, 131–3, 135, 137–8, 144–7, 149, 152–3, 165, 176

temporal disparity 19 n.54, 112–16, 119, 122–4, 130, 176, *see also* archive effect
temporality 13, 16, 18, 20, 24, 36, 38, 39, 47 n.55, 48, 66, 69, 86, 90, 112–16, 119, 121–4, 130, 167, 176
  aging 14, 21, 33, 42, 64, 68, 115 (*see also* decay)
  ravages of time 3, 21, 34, 38, 55, 64, 102, 108, 128, 175
Thacker, Eugene 25, 50, 55 n.80, 100
tinting and toning 32–3, 51, 53, 54
Tom, Tom, the Piper's Son (Jacobs) 94
Touching the Film Object? (Grant) 142
trace 9, 13, 22, 27, 28, 34, 35, 40, 41, 46, 66–70, 76, 77, 79, 80, 143, 168, 174, 175, 177, 178, *see also* indexicality
transduction 25–7, 83, 87–92, 95–103, *see also* Simondon, Gilbert
  equilibrium 25, 28, 83, 86–7, 90, 91, 94, 95, 99–102, 175
  individuation 87, 89, 91, 101
  margin of indeterminacy 91, 92, 95, 100, 102, 175
  metastability 87, 88, 90, 102, 175
Tscherkassky, Peter 19, 20 n.56, 85, 141
Tsivian, Yuri 10 n.22, 85 n.5, 150 n.63
Turquety, Benoît 10 n.23, 34 n.9, 70 n.33, 72 n.44, 73, 85 n.6, 86 n.7, 92–3, 169 n.47

vertical scratches 26, 28, 108, 125–9, 173, 175
video-editing software 29, 46, 58, 77, 81, 131, 162, 174, 175, 178–9
  Adobe Premiere 160, 162
  ImageJ 160

videographic criticism   9, 29, 103, 130, 135, 140–4, 153, 155, 157–61, 164, 165, 167, 169–71, 174–80, *see also* practical research
videographic essay   8, 9 n.21, 29, 103, 130, 141–3, 157–8, 164, 165, 167, 169–71, 175, 177–9
videographic film studies   9 n.21, 135, 141, 142, 144, 158, 159, 167 n.45
Videography 1978 (Álvarez López and Martin)   143

Waldenfels, Bernhard   135–6, 147
weird shapes   2–3, 5, 6, 9–10, 13–14, 17–18, 21–7, 29, 34, 35, 42, 49–52, 56–7, 63, 65, 68, 71, 79, 80, 86, 102, 109, 110, 116, 126, 133–5, 138–9, 144, 145, 150, 151, 153, 169, 173–4, 177–80
black wave   3, 13, 21, 24, 26, 27, 29, 83, 86–8, 96, 98, 100, 102, 109, 175, 177
color veil   2, 13, 15, 26, 27, 29, 31, 33–7, 39–42, 44, 45, 50–9, 108, 109, 144, 147, 149, 174
electric horses   2, 13, 14, 24, 26, 27, 59, 63, 68, 74–5, 77, 79, 80, 109, 127, 174–5
scratched kiss   3, 13, 26, 28, 105, 108, 110, 116, 120, 125–30, 175–6
stitched head   3, 17, 26, 28, 132, 134, 135, 138, 145, 149–53, 176 (*see also* Frankenstein's monster)
wind in the trees   11, 13, 14, 18, 112, *see also* detail
world-without-us   25, 50–3, 55, *see also* Thacker, Eugene
world-for-us   50, 54, 55
world-in-itself   50

yellowish-orange color   5, 16, 21, 26, 27, 32–4, 36, 40, 42–3, 51, 52, 54, 56, 59, 80, 109, 114, 144, 149, 157, 173, *see also* weird shapes, color veil

zoom   9, 20, 29, 54, 55, 103, 166, 168, 177

www.ingramcontent.com/pod-product-compliance
Lightning Source LLC
Chambersburg PA
CBHW052039300426
44117CB00012B/1892